0

About Cover: The "Angel" on the front cover has been with me since the first creation of a website for Soul Counseling. I always loved her and wondered where she came from. When in California for something else, for some strange reason I wanted to go to Cambria, a small town on the mostly empty coast south of Big Sur. There's an elephant seal colony there and Hearst's Castle. I kept feeling that I should visit the Castle. This is not something I would normally enjoy- I'd rather kayak on the coast and see the wildlife or go walking in the hills. But something inside kept suggesting I go. So I took the 'tourist tram' up there. While in the main hall of the 'castle' with the group of visitors to this extravagant anomaly on this lost coast of California, as I'm about to leave the main hall, something turns my head to the right and a voice inside me yells Stop! Look! ... And there she is! My Angel! ...in a 5 foot bronze statue. I'm dumbfounded. I just stop and stare.

The guide, watching my reaction, takes the time to share with me that she was created by Adolph A. Weinman in 1915 for the California Exposition in San Francisco. Later she was acquired by William Randolph Hearst for his Castle. She is called "Descending Night" and her brother statue is "The Rising Sun".

Here's a picture I took of her -

Awakening Souls

By Tobias Lars

"Angel Wings and Bestial Rage,
On a dare then turn the Page,
For time is Now,
To Dis-Solve the Sage."

Now It Begins

And Now I Begin,

To Live,
For Me,
A Deeper, Expanded
Life,

A Life of no
Explanation
of no Doubts
of no Second-Guessing,

Perhaps Alone,
But not Lonely.

I am Born
in-two
a bigger Space,

I cannot explain
Sense Me
And you will Know,
Measure Me
And I am
Not
With you,

I can take
No one
With me
On
This Walk
Over the Chasm
Will be
(w)On(e) by One,

With Love
Waiting
The Other Side
Is
Good
Bye
Inside of Time

Personal Love
Melts into
The Larger Water,

Now it Begins.

3

I'm Going to Appear*

I'm going to appear.

Childish,
Uncouth,
Vulgar,
Unstable,
Wise,
Insane,
Sacred,
Profane,
Uncontrolled.

I will appear
on the Verge
of breakdown
at the Gates of Madness,

Because
We have been programmed
To fear
the loosening
of our
Enslaving Lords'
Control.

A Message

A Message to those who'll wonder
After it's all over.

As I set out on this Journey
I may be greeted with
undue adulation,
misplaced fear,
irrational hate,
undeserved love,

I may be labeled
Both Messiah and Devil
And everything in between,

I don't know what Gateways I'll encounter,
That will be mine alone to pass through,

But I have nowhere else to go,
There is really nothing I want
in a world of quiet desperation,
Of fear filled servitude to the collective denial.

So I will upset the collective 'laws'
of morality,
of socialized rights and wrongs,
of civilizational unquestioned 'truths'...

Here I go...

*All Verse in this book is from the collection
"Shackled Gods Uni-Verse" by Tobias Lars
Available at www.SoulCounseling.com*

5

Author's Note: This is a holographically written book. 'Holos', (Greek) = complete, down, full. Each title is a whole subject by itself and also an integral piece of the whole that is this book. I would suggest looking at the titles and choosing ones that catch your interest in the moment. The book is not meant to be read through in order, or quickly, or just mentally. Allow yourself to relax, to just Be... aware. *Feel* what you are reading. Allow the swirling-whirling yakking mind talk to come to a still – point. Allow your Self to stop and just be with it. The times you stop and just imbibe-contemplate-absorb-sense-merge with what you are reading are the times your Soul can talk to you. This book has the power to activate your life towards Awakening if you let the in-form-ation in-form you into the birth of a new form of your Self.

By the way, notice there are several radical titles about *Sex*, (Oh goody, we all like that!) with ideas of how to finally heal ourselves from humanity's arrested development regarding sex.

A 2ⁿᵈ Note: We all have potential direct access to the Creative Force, Love, All That Is, God, Goddess, Creator, Source that created this whole Uni-Verse (Song of One). We are this Source at our center. We can't get away from It even if we try. Our hearts could not beat another single beat if the Life Force of God-Source was suddenly withdrawn. When we start being willing to hear from our Souls-our Hearts-God-the Source at the center of our Heart-septums, then the language that this information will come to us in is much bigger than our current human languages because God's language is much bigger than our languages. Written language is limiting when trying to express these energies of our Souls, our Spirits, Suns, Stars, Galactic Clouds, Creator, Source, God...so as I perceive-receive this energy-information I also give myself permission to play with our (not always so) current human language to try to give a better taste of what these God-energies feel like to me. At times I break the current rules of language that bind our ways of commune-icating. At times I push outside the rules of grammar and use words not sanctioned by the Dictionary. Language has always evolved, will always evolve, and soon perhaps language will evolve back beyond spoken language to felt-direct energy transmission-telepathic language. Today this evolving of Consciousness is accelerating in all arenas of our lives including language. As consciousness accelerates and evolves so will our exchanges of in-form-ation energy (energy coming into form) which language is one expression of. My style of writing and the wor(l)ds I invent are my ex-press-ion of this new energy consciousness evolving, moving, expanding into our human consciousness. Title number seven below speaks more about the New Language that is coming back to Earth... which is in fact our Original Language.

Tobias Lars- BS, MBA

Thank You's:

To those who have shared in Love with me-- I have seen you watching me in perplexity at times but somehow you have still surrendered to the Love having its way with us... Thank you for being willing to play and for having the courage to follow the Heart those times it has broken the rules.

To my non - physical helpers and friends who are-have been the in-spirit-ations that I consider my closest intimates...thank you...what can I say...except...feel my Heart.

And to Love-Source-God...I'm amazed continually that You are willing to play with me. That You are willing to keep hoping in me, encouraging me, that You are there when I ecstatically expend my self in You, that you don't take my moaning hopelessness seriously, that you find me interesting enough to spend time with is yes, amazing. My Heart's wish and my Intent is that I am able to be with You until The End.

Tobias Lars

Table of Contents

~Section One~

~Section Two~ 66

~Section Three~ 102

~Section One~

1.   Conclusions

'Categorizing Minds' want to know

Why is western society obsessed with reaching 'conclusions' and 'explanations' about everything? A kind of false 'understanding' of the world around us? (Under-Standing = 'standing under', i.e. seeing from a limited, clouded perspective.)

"What's the bottom line Bob?" What conclusions have you reached George?"

Why do we need to have everything fit into a neat category, a box, a pigeonhole?

Why do we want everything to have a slot, a place, a neat info byte to 'sum' up what it is?

Does this not limit things, crush them, squeeze them into boxes, prisons they don't fit into naturally?

Is it a false sense of security to think we 'know' about something if we can 'name' it?

What are we missing of the amazing explosion of Life-Light electromagnetic energy that is in each of us and all beings by 'Categorizing' everyone and everything into little mind-slots?

Is it that we are afraid of the unknown? Have we become so afraid and obsessed with naming things that something undefinable scares us so much that we develop extreme fanatic beliefs such as for example: "an unnamed baby that dies will go to hell"? Which many people still believe today.

"A Rose by any other Name (or No Name!) would still smell as sweet"

What kinds of feelings are triggered in you if you think of someone having a baby and not naming it, but just letting it BE? Just letting the baby be, pristine, pure, unadulterated, natural, the way Love-God intended it? Does it make you uncomfortable? What kind of beliefs do you have about it? Does everything have to be named or we believe it is sacrificed to some terrible Void and doomed to wander eternally in the darkness? What is it about the Void, the emptiness, the Nothing, the Womb of All that scares us? Scares us so much that everything has to be defined, categorized into little boxes? The animals don't name each other. They know each other by their essence, by their personal "vibrational fingerprints", because they live by feel, by intuition, by instinct, by still being in touch with the Source of all Life and don't need mental 'names' to feel falsely safe.

11

Scapegoat – ism & "Divided and Conquered"

The fact is that if something remains un-defined-no boundaries-no fences it then remains outside of our 'categorizing minds'. Then the only way we can know this thing is to 'feel' it with our solar plexus-emotional-intuitive sense and if we are so habituated to only knowing our world through our 'categorizing' minds and having lost our ability to sense or 'feel' something with our hearts or solar plexus it then scares us. It becomes a mirror for all the fears we've relegated to our subconscious and then we project these fears onto the 'unnameable'. This is how the 'Categorizing' Mind has taken over most of us and the world. The Mind 'divides and conquers' by categorizing everything, then pitting these different categories against each other--the Left-Right, Conservatives-Liberals, Gay-Straight, Muslims-Jews, Male-Female, Bloods-Crypts, Democrats-Republicans, your High School-the 'rival' High School, US - Russia or now upcoming US vs. China, Management-workers, etc. etc. And then mostly anything that is outside these mental categories is to be feared and gotten rid of, either imprisoned or outright killed. The sacrificial 'scapegoat' has arisen out of this, we think we can pour the fears and 'sins' in our own subconscious into this innocent creature and by sacrificing it we'll be rid of these 'sins'. Look into the eyes of a goat or sheep sometime, they are very empty and dependent on us humans, so we made them the receptacle of our 'sins' and we used to kill them and drain their blood in 'sacrifices' to 'god'. And so did the Greeks, the Romans, the Macedonians, the Norse, the Celts, the Aztecs etc. Notice how the 'devil' is often pictured as a He-goat. It wasn't that long ago that we actually killed animals in sacrifice. The Old Testament of the Bible is full of these animal sacrifices. Muslims still sacrifice millions of lambs on their once in a lifetime most holy journey to Mecca. We kill over 35 million cows every year in the US in our 'modern sacrifices' and then eat them.

We don't have a Roman Coliseum where we watch humans or animals tear each other apart to the physical death anymore. We don't actually watch the guillotine, or executioners behead, or draw and quarter, or stretch, or crucify our 'criminals'. But really we do, the 'Coliseum' is still there at our sports arenas with our 'side' our 'gladiator' team beating, 'killing' the 'other' team. We watch the news every night and hear about how we are being 'kept safe' from the 'dark', 'sinful', 'bad' guys. We hear about their executions on the TV news…and many of us like it, we actually get a blood thirst subconscious thrill from it if we could be honest about it. It's the same thrill we get from watching car accidents and our sports 'heroes' fight each other. At hockey matches the fans feel cheated unless there is a *'And the gloves come off!'* fist fight. Boxing is always hugely popular and now something called 'Ultimate Fighting', which is bare fist fighting in a cage with no rules, is becoming very popular. If it was legal and we televised fights *'to the death'* on pay per view TV it would be watched by millions of us. It would be a huge money maker and win the ratings numbers every time. If we televised executions of our criminals, millions of people would tune in to watch…and many would cheer.

So this fear of our own subconscious, the 'un-nameable', our own mysterious nature has caused us to perpetrate all manner of atrocities on each other. Once we have been brainwashed, mind controlled into accepting the practice of labeling-categorizing of each other, we are then easily 'divided and conquered' and pitted against each other like pit bull dogs made to fight to the death in the pit. We're almost there again with humans, the next step from the 'Ultimate Fighting' Rage in the Cage is bouts to the death between humans.

Imagine having No Name

Imagine if you met someone that refused to have a name, refused to give your mind a slot to put them in. They simply were-- a being just Being. No name needed, didn't have an 'occupation' i.e. wasn't possessed-occupied by anything. Your categorizing mind wouldn't be able to pigeonhole them. You wouldn't have a neat file in your mental computer to file them in. It would force you to turn to your Intuition, your Heart, to feel and sense who they were and if you're not in touch with your intuition-heart-soul-love then the 'unknown' would terrify you. If you are in touch with what the Buddhists call 'emptiness', or the Bible calls the *peace that passeth all under-standing*, then this open, empty, just radiating person would also trigger this peace-stillness in you and you would enjoy-love them. This is the fate of every Messiah-Teacher-Master. The Messiah-Awake-Enlightened person has connected to God, the *"I Am that I Am"* Beingness beyond time and space. They have become *'One with the Father'* as Jesus puts it, or *'One with All That Is'* as some Yogi's have said. And then every Teacher-Master-Messiah is loved-worshipped-made into a 'God' by those that recognize them and hated-feared-killed by those that fear what will happen to 'society' if the people wake up, and those that 'run the world' through money and control of the masses consciousness have most often killed the Messenger-Messiah. It's still where we are at today. If Jesus came back to earth today he would be killed as soon as he started to have an impact on the people again. If he started setting people free, having them think for themselves, start using their God given spiritual powers of real freedom, miracles, physical healings, not needing to work for a living, not caring about owning property, not obsessed with 'things', but wanting to love, to enjoy, celebrate and live as a human family, all Children of God---he would be assassinated by covert special forces directed by our shadow governments very quickly. Just like those forces assassinated Jesus, Gandhi, JFK, RFK, Martin Luther King, John Lennon, Osho, and many others most of us have never heard of.

Meeting someone without a name would scare most of us wouldn't it? At least make us uncomfortable. Our minds would immediately scan and try to find a 'category', a 'box' of 'eccentric, crazy, shocking, weird, bizarre' etc...to try to make us more comfortable. This is an example of how far from grace we've 'fallen' on Earth-- that the undefinable, unnamable, Source of All Things, God Him/Herself scares us so much that our minds that now rule us have come to label the undefinable, unnamable Creative Force 'evil' or the 'devil'.

When we are controlled-gripped by the categorizing Mind we can't let something be open ended, we need definitions, categories, a place, a slot in our computer files to put everything. We need to conclude (close off) things, to come to 'understandable' conclusions. How long do we want to

13

under-stand, stand-under our throne of divine inheritance?   When will we decide to come out from standing under our thrones of being pieces of God, All That Is, and reclaim our rightful inheritance?

When Prince, the performer, the singer-artist got rid of his name and wanted to be referred to as a symbol, we had to ridicule him or at least call him weird. And that was only moving from a normal name to a symbol. Imagine if someone refused to be named at all! We're terrified of the unknown inside our own selves...we have to make fun of it, ridicule it...and if it's too strong...we kill it.

"All truth passes through 3 stages.
First, it is ridiculed.
Second, it is violently opposed.
Third, it is accepted as being self-evident."

-- Arthur Schopenhauer-- Nobel Prize winning Physicist.

Wizards like Merlin (who was and is a real person) assumed a name only so we could interact with him without being too scared. But no defining facts of his birth or death are written in the history books. Just because something is not definable, not controllable, not able to be fenced in by the categorizing mind doesn't mean that it isn't real. In fact it's more real than this shadow, illusion world of Maya that is all around us. Having seen the coming conflict, there were whole tribes of Native Americans that left no trace of themselves to be found by the white settlers as they 'walked into' other dimensions before the Europeans came to the Americas. Because these 'Bird Tribes', as the other Indians called them, left no material traces, no tools, no **names**--- doesn't mean that they weren't real. In the Superstition Mountains here in Arizona, a friend and I have made contact with these Anazazi, or 'Ancient Ones', that 'walked through the stone' into the 'other worlds'.

Naming it doesn't mean you know it!

How many times on the 'investigative' news shows have you heard the person afflicted by some 'unexplainable' disease express overwhelming relief when they find there's a NAME! for their ailment? Just having a name for it! Somehow naming it makes us feel safe and comfortable. As if naming something makes us understand it or know what it really is. Naming something doesn't mean we know anything about it! It just means the doctors or scientists or professors or lawyers or government leaders invented a name to hypnotize us back into our numb sleepwalking state of unawareness. No one (at least in the scientific community) has any idea what magnetism or gravity or electricity for that matter are, but because we've named them and hear the words repeatedly growing up we think our 'expert' scientists understand them. Science has no clue what these things really are. The properties of magnetism, electricity and gravity can be described somewhat in how they manifest in our limited energy spectrum

14

most are calling 'reality', but how they operate, where they come from, what their real source is, the energy operations of the finer interactions of the subatomic ('sub consciousness' for the vast majority) worlds our 'scientists' have no clue.

"Oh, you have 'Chronic Fatigue Syndrome' ma'm." This is getting so obvious that the 'expert' medical doctors have no idea what this general malaise is. Calling something 'Chronic Fatigue Syndrome' is like calling something 'We have no clue what this is disease'. They have no way of measuring the soul, the essence of Life. The Soul Essence that is getting fed up and tired of having to live in these economic robot prisons we term 'existence'- 'civilization' today. Is it any wonder that the soul isn't all that enthusiastic about existence when there is no joy left, when free time-- our vacations are spent getting sedated with drink? When a 'good time' is when we go unconscious? We've come to prefer death (unconsciousness) to Life, we want to be sedated. America, One Nation under Sedation, Land of the Toxic Shame Children. Billions of dollars every year spent on synthetic psychoactive drugs that sedate our feelings out of existence.

"Genius is a mental illness!"

Life, feeling feelings is considered to be an illness now! The newspapers ran a front page story a while back that declared "Genius is a mental illness!" where the 'experts', those psychotherapists (psycho-the-rapists) explained that most creative people are mentally ill and suffer from manic depression! So now feeling anything outside of the narrow spectrum of sanctioned by the mental health experts acceptable feelings, whether its Joy or deep Sadness will now be considered a 'mental illness'! Pretty soon unless you're one of the robotic economically programmed, dead, shuffling masses of 'normal' people, they'll take you away and use drugs and behavior modification technology to 'fix' you, the same way we 'fix' our pets, de-soul them, castrate their aliveness out of them. This is how much we're killing our souls. I for one am not surprised that 'chronic fatigue' syndromes of the soul are starting to appear all over the place. Our Life Force-God-Love is leaving us. Erectile dysfunction is apparently such a big problem that you can't watch the evening news without being bombarded with advertising for several erectile dysfunction drugs. This means the Life Force, the place where new spirits are created from is dying out in men! Women are having their breasts and uterus's removed. The Uterus is the Source of all of us! It's where we are created, made, formed, and birthed from. The breasts are our sustenance, the 'manna' of god, the nurturing of the Mother of All. Our current society is killing the very places where Life-God seeds itself and grows.

Spirits with Life in them who want to experience, to feel, to be alive, are 'sick and tired' of being pigeon holed into demographic computer files, into categories of dead existences, prisons of predictable behavior, for the political anal-(c)ysts and advertisers to use to manipulate the sheeple.

Whew! I feel better now...good ranting is always healthy for the soul.

A Conversation with Spirit

The following is an excerpt from a Conversation with Spirit about the lack of need for names in other dimensions.

No Names

Tobias-Right now I feel the energy entering the top of my head. I feel it activating my forehead, the back of my skull and neck. I can also feel it in my creative chakra as a relaxation, a melting. I am interested in learning how to create by intention from inside this space of comfort, of "being taken care of" that I feel right now. That's really how I want to live. By the way, what shall I call you?

Guides-(they felt like beings that guide and assist us) *"It doesn't really matter if you call us anything, we don't use names in the space we exist-operate from or with each other. We know each other by the energy we are, by our vibrational "soulprints". We envelop you, lay onto you layers of activating energy, to encourage, to enlarge, activate the energy that you have inside you, that God energy that is in your core. We would really like to see it turn into a flame, the pillar of fire that Moses saw, and "consume" the old you and ascend, liberate all your energies that feel trapped inside this dimension you are in on earth.*

In a sense we are impersonal in that we go wherever there are openings to receive us.

No-name

I love you,
No-name,
I find in you
Yet
I know you
more than my
named (br)others.

2.   No One is Listening to the Sun

The Sun dangerous? !   Have we lost our minds!

I'm lying by the pool in Phoenix Arizona; it is June 22, 11 a.m. I do not have any SPF protection lotions on my skin. I am Swedish with skin that turns lily white in a few weeks if I stay out of the sun. I'm a **W**hite **A**nglo **S**axon **P**rotestant male, the WASP's that have stung the world with our technological wizardry. I am the demographic that all the advertising about the loss of our ozone layer and danger of the suns rays is aimed at. I am also the demographic that has caused it! It is my genetic colleagues (colleagues= in league w/ collusively) that have brought the industrial, then technological revolution to the planet. My father wrote the computer program back in the early sixties that is used all over the world today to control the cores of nuclear reactors so that we can walk that razors edge of getting maximum efficiency out of the nuclear power plants without melting the core down and irradiating the life out of the surrounding countryside! I almost became a scientist bent (that's apropos) on cracking the "genetic code" so we can manipulate nature from the DNA level. There but for the grace of God go I. Wow!

So I'm lying by the pool feeling the belief that is currently being pumped into my head by the media about the Sun. The Sun! Our creator, our life giver, our source of perfect packets of information that are given to us directly in the very light that streams forth from it, the very nurturer, life giver, pattern creator, inventor of all the myriad of life forms on the planet. Now we are being told that we must fear it! Why?

Because No One is listening to the Sun!

We have not listened to its plan, its blueprint for this planet. Each sun, each explosion of life-light, each star in the heavens has a unique makeup, a unique electro magnetic "fingerprint" if you will, in its composition of finer light and electromagnetic energies. This "fingerprint" is coded with information perfect to guide, in-form (help take form) the life forms and expressions that will be appropriate for each planet. There are planets with much stronger sunlight and ones with much less sunlight and they have life forms appropriate to their situation, i.e. where they are situated, how far or close to their sun, their surrounding matrix of electromagnetic fields, their particular gravity etc.

We have deviated from letting the sun in-form us of what will work, what will be harmonious, and fun! For Earth. The sun has the original and best plan for us to have a "blast" on this planet. To have your body on the verge of cosmic orgasm all the time, to be able to pop in and out of different bodies, of different forms. To be much more fluid, to melt and merge with each other on energy and physical levels, to have no need for "working for a living", as after our exile from the Garden of Eden. To receive the energy of sun-life directly and live off this "manna" from heaven. This is all possible if we listen to the Sun.

17

The old Sun worshiping cultures had this knowing at their source. But they were the tail end of Golden Age civilizations. The history of Earth that we are taught at present has been sanitized and cleaned up to fit the Darwinian model, man as beast, survival of the fittest, nature is something to fear, fight and conquer, might is right, the strong survive etc. That there were civilizations on Pan(gea), Lemuria, and Atlantis simply would blow away the limited scope of today's hysteric little historians. As you've heard from them they are (mostly unwittingly) engaged in promoting the patriarchal HIS-story. Pawns of the Big Daddy.

So I'm lying by the pool and feeling the information that the sun is giving me. It is saying (now you'll think me eligible for the asylum, talking to anthropomorphic entities, my oh my) that we have not listened to it in it's natural gentle state, when it is just enough information filtering through a perfectly designed atmosphere to give us the appropriate blueprint to create harmonious, joyous life for this particular planet. Again-

"Wake Up Humans, listen to the Plan for Earth"

So now that we are destroying the transducer (the atmosphere that translates and steps down the energy-information of the Sun to the appropriate levels for us so we can absorb it) we will be getting the sunlight in stronger doses, more insistent wake up calls. More direct light, unfiltered, Sun-Star light.

"Wake up humans, listen to the Plan for Earth" the Sun is saying. The stronger "dosage" of the Sun that we will be getting is like ingesting concentrated substances. This "poison" can also be a liberator, a "wake up call". The Taoist monks on Huashan Mountain in China took "poisons", heavy metals, strong herbs, stuff that would normally kill an ordinary human but they transmuted these substances into pure energy, life-essence, the source of forms. It was a way for them to kind of nudge themselves into their bigger natures, like the Toltec master Don Juan having his disciples jump off a cliff when they were ready to dissolve into light bodies. You fly or you die. These were the Alchemists in the Taoist tradition. We re-fine sugar and it becomes a poison to our bodies, cocoa leaves become cocaine; any extract is a concentration of the natural way the substance occurs and usually becomes a poison. But these "poisons" can also be wake-up calls for our bodies, for our souls, to heal when taken in the appropriate doses. If we open to them and heed the wake-up call, otherwise they will eventually kill us. Nature (in-spirit-ed by the Sun) creates perfect forms for us to eat and absorb energy if we leave Her alone.

So we're creating a more intense sunlight by having not listened to the Sun in its naturally occurring dosages. It is a self regulating system, we are unbalancing it and if we unbalance it enough by destroying our atmosphere the sun will turn us into "crispies", be rid of us and the problem (us humans that is) will be gone after a period of cleanup and rebalancing. And in the scope of creations of solar systems a few thousand years is a blink in the Cosmic Eye.

The Push-Pull Steal your Energy from you Game

The idiotic "experts" are telling you that you need sunlight for vitamin D, but also that sunlight will cause cancer. This is the normal method of the controllers, the energy vampires on the planet, to instill fear and need in us and keep us swinging back and forth between the "must have the cure" and the fear of death. The controllers of the earth's "sheeple" will get you to fear all sorts of things and then they will sell you the "cures" for these made up "dangers", take your money and energy and then think up new things for you to fear that they can manipulate you with and milk you further of your energy and money. Think how sad it is that we are now being mind-programmed to fear the Sun. Yet we are so well programmed that we swallow it unquestioningly when mouthed by the plastic robot reading the teleprompter on the evening news. Do you notice how the "news robots" are starting to look like androids even more now? So we become convinced that the life-light source, the bringer of life itself is dangerous and will cause cancer! We're pretty far gone when we're starting to believe that. And with enough of the mass consciousness believing that it will cause cancer, it will! So you have your evidence and can parade the victims of "solar skin cancer" on the TV with the expert doctors interpreting reality for you. What will it take for us to wake up? Ripping the atmosphere off our planet? Mass control by computer systems, silicon chips implanted in our brains to "keep us safe" from our "bad" emotions? Euthanizing the hopeless homeless, wipeout of total civilizations? Uncontrollable viruses? Mass consciousness thought control? Genetically breeding-cloning "perfect" soulless bodies? It's happened before....

It's happening now...more than we let ourselves know. Do you really think that our Governments haven't cloned humans when they have already cloned sheep and cows? Of course they have they're just not parading those clones out before the TV cameras...yet.

Is this the reflection we really need to finally begin to wake up and want our souls back? The Wake up Call that we need to listen again to the Sun, to our Hearts, to Father God and Mother God?

What are we going to do? Follow our "leaders", the pied pipers of Death like blind lemmings over the cliff (again)? What will it take for us to say enough is enough? When will we just quit the economic robot programmed lives we lead and sit down and *Be still and know that I Am God"?*...so that something new can begin to be born. Yes at times it's terrifying to face down your inner fears, yes it'll seem like you're going to die, but so what...if you keep going the way you are you are guaranteed a horrible physical death.

Do you want to know what and who Death really is?

That's the next title

3.   Death in its Original Role Makes an Appearance

Death shows up... At the Gang Banger gym!

I'm at the gym. I go to the gym that has all the gang members pumping up so they can rob, steal and beat you up better. They don't know what to make of me. I'm obviously not one of them, but I have enough of some kind of antisocial rebellion energy around me so that I'm allowed in. I have long hair. My energy is aware, I have the aura of a "brain-expert-intellectual" at times, that egghead Poindexter type they make fun of, but they can't dis-miss me totally because I feel real too. I do bench-press sets with 225 lbs so I'm not a total wimp. I look somewhat muscular, wear black muscle shirts. I look young, but I have some grey in my hair. I don't fit, mostly they avoid me. I'm the alien with-out categories, I'm the Chameleon. I admire their skull and demon tattoos and the easy tribal interaction they have here in their testosterone sanctum.

So, I'm at the gym. I've just finished with the free weights and I'm on one of the stair stepper machines and I'm 'daydreaming'. And after looking at a Grim Reaper tattoo on a muscled young animal, Death, the big guy, the Grim Reaper, the Harvester of Souls Himself, in his black empty hood, appears before my inner eye and gives me a packet of information, a grok, an instantaneous exchange communiqué, in the eternal Now. He tells me what and who he/it really is -- what the original role of "death" is. Not this to be feared twisted, grotesque thing we've turned him into. I'm putting it into words now but the experience took place in an instant in the Eternal Now, the timeless place, the point of joining of dimensions where Death 'hangs out' mostly. (I can't say spends most of his time because there is no time there.) Instantly I received the whole 'message', the meeting, the interaction. It's like energy information 'groks'. Words obviously can't do it justice since words are a de-evolution from direct communication of energy essences, an ability we had in the past but which we have lost (mostly) in our present state. But it felt something like this...

Death was sad, soul tired of the prison we have put him in, a prison that he can't choose out of. He is an Elemental, an Archetype, a stay, a stanchion in the creation of physical, in-form life here on Earth. He can't choose not to play his role. Humans have free will but these Elementals, of which Death is one, have 'assignments' that they can't choose out of because *they are their assignment. Without it they have no separate existence. They would cease to exist.* He conveyed to me his sadness at us fearing him, us having made him out to be a 'bad guy', something to be scared of. By the way I'm using 'him' because it feels the closest but 'he' is an energy that doesn't easily fit the limiting categories of male-female that we have sunk into classifying everything into. He was originally and still is OUR HELPER, not in a servile way but as a co-player who has a particular role that he enjoys playing and that we enjoy having him do. Here it is: This is what Death really is, are you ready?

Death's original role was as helper at the moment of form change.
Death's original role was as an elemental helper at the moment of form change.

If you take an Eternal Moment right now and feel that...

It could change on a deep level your experience of Life...

Don't process it with your mind...but feel it, sense it.

It was a moment of surrender-trust that death was an assistant at. Like a cosmic midwife between dimensional existences. He carries us like Mary is carrying Jesus in Michelangelo's famous statue, the Pieta, in the Vatican. He carries us in that moment, that instant of total surrender into our new existence.

Death helps us in "Popping" our Energy Form

I'm talking about that cosmic orgasmic moment when we we're "popping" our energy form, liberating the energy that has been coalesced into a physical form. This is not the role Death plays for the most part today. Now we 'escape' out and leave our bodies behind and abandon the energy used for physicalization, leave it trapped. No, I'm talking about when ALL our energy was still free, when we took it all with us. The closest well publicized example we have on the planet today is Jesus' ascendancy. Jesus sped up his energy to the point where it dissolved into finer energy and was able to move outside of form. He 'conquered Death' we are told by those who edit and interpret the 'sacred' texts. He didn't 'conquer' Death, he made up with Death, allowed Death to have His original role. It's not a lot of fun for Death when he only gets a handful of souls every thousand years that are awake enough for him to interact consciously with. Yes there have been other non publicized cases of 'ascension', 'conquering of death' but maybe they didn't want to start religions or have their life stories edited by the vampire pundits that alter the 'sacred texts' and use them for controlling the masses.

We all had this ability to speed up our physicalized energy (our bodies) before our 'fall', and we still have it in potential buried deep under fears and old beliefs. Those moments of speeding our vibration to the point of melting and dissolving our physical body into light, that is when Death would help us 'pop' the etheric blueprint of our physical bodies. Like a transparent soap bubble 'pops' out of existence. He was a helpful assistant, an ally at the last moment. It was fun, a game for us and Death that we played together. We didn't fear Death. If fact it wasn't 'death' it was no-name, assistant, friend, co-player, friend of transformation, just a thing, experience, part of our non-language pure experiencing of the new game of 'form', physical forms created on Earth.

There was a time...when Death had No Name

There's a band called Danzig, that has a song called 'When Death had no name' where they are feeling this concept of non-judgment of Death, just pure experiencing. Of course the band is mostly dismissed by the 'serious' students of spirituality as simply reactionary, angry, violent, antisocial young men etc., when really they are just reflecting the real death of losing soul essence permeating all of our society by their stark, 'heavy' imagery and music. And when someone reflects the lie, the hypocrisy, the real 'death' to us we want to as usual judge, dismiss, kill the messenger with the unpopular message. By the way, there is real death. Real death is when our energy vibrations slow down and we lose our soul energy-essence until we eventually can't speed it up again. We have then 'fallen' from Grace; we can't 'get our speed up' again to freely move our energy between dimensions. This is basically the current state for almost every soul on Earth -- real 'death' has invaded us so that we make our transitions between dimensions in unconscious states. Real death is when we give our life force away to an 'outer thing' (this is God's warning in the first commandment, *'no other gods before Me'*). For ex., we give our energy away in the form of attention, worship, belief in unloving individuals, belief systems, organizations, we feed our life force into these, we place them 'before' us, they become more important than hearing and following the voice of God in our own heart and eventually we are left drained and weak, they have sucked our soul essence, our energy out of us. But don't blame them solely, we are choosing to give our energy/attention/soul essence to these organizations, priests, leaders, beliefs, ideas in the hope that they will (ab)solve our 'sins', our fears, our problems for us. And then they move on to another planet when they've drained this one dry. This is not to be confused with the Death, the Elemental Helper I'm talking about now. But in this created universe He, Death has to perform his task. It is his 'job', he reflects our soul essence loss back to us, he wants us to wake back up, regain our energy. He would like to see us recover our energy and be conscious when we make these transitions between states of existence, dimensions.

Death's is a Gatekeeper...

Death is also a gatekeeper. He can't change this aspect of his assignment. He will not let any; get this, DEAD UNMOVING STATIC ENERGY PASS THROUGH the Gate into formlessness. You have to be 'clean' i.e. have all your energy, all parts of yourself 'up to speed', moving, free in order to pass fully free and conscious through the Gate. If you've left any energy behind, energy that you don't like because it doesn't feel good and you're using denial and saying 'that is not me, that is not part of me', then Death will point out that you must go back and retrieve this 'lost aspect' of yourself or you cannot pass through his Gate and remain conscious, or fully integrated. He automatically reflects this to you, it is his essence, his nature, his role in the Creation, his very being to be clean, pure and a reflecting mirror. He has no choice, it just happens automatically when you encounter him. So again we started blaming the Messenger. Death is the fine soul detector screen that helps point out to us if we left any parts of ourselves behind in our experiences and playing in form. We started saying to Death, 'No that is not part of me you must be mistaken.' And when He insisted, He doesn't even 'insist', He simply reflects, mirrors any denial since He has no other choice. So we started blaming raging against Death. We started saying that He was the problem not us, it couldn't have anything to do with us. Classic denial. And here we are still running from our selves' eons later.

...and He is Sad.

Well Death is sad because he has very few co-players, very little conscious interaction with his 'gods' (us). He has to do his job but all he gets to deal with are millions of beings that are terrified of him. Barely anyone arrives at the Gate conscious, awake. Most of us are drugged and arrive after having been sedated in some hospital bed hooked up to machines, or having some jarring accident that makes us go unconscious to deal with the shock. So mostly what He gets to deal with are unconscious half-beings thoroughly confused at being out of the body. This way Death's job has turned into him being 'the Bad Guy' and his role degenerated into bringing God more bad news that another lost and crippled soul is coming over and in need of healing and convalescence in the etheric Temples of Recovery.

Make a Friend of Death

Though we are all immortal souls, to regain being **conscious** of this immortality, you will need to make a friend of Death and allow Him to reflect your denials to you so you can heal yourself. I know that might sound impossible, but it isn't. You don't need any more priests, gurus, or experts to tell you what to do. God's voice in your own heart will guide you safely. You have the power to do this, most of everything else is just vested interests that don't want you to wake up and be the god you are because they are feeding off of you.

"Don't ye know, Ye are gods?" –Joshua Ben-Joseph (Jesus the Christ)

4.   The Reason Our Current Civilization will Pass Away, Why it is Corroding from Inside

A Civilization built on Denial

Almost all of the current Civilization on Earth is based on an inversion. And in this inversion it carries the seed of its own demise. Our Civilization is built on denial, on non-acceptance of the wild and free of the Natural Order of things. Therefore this 'civilization', this attempt to throttle, suppress, contain, alter, tame the wild and free nature of Humans cannot be 'sustainable', it can't go on indefinitely. It has the seeds of its own death built into it, in fact it is death! It is a static (static=nonmoving, frozen i.e. dead!) model, with unvarying 'laws' of behavior and final 'truths'. The very word 'law' implies that it is a static, unmoving, unchanging 'truth'. Anything labeled 'truth' has finality to it, is unmoving, unevolving, and therefore it is static-dead. A River that isn't moving is dead, stagnant. Mostly our current model of searching for and arriving at truths is to reduce and dissect whatever is being studied until it cannot be reduced anymore and then formulate 'truths' of what it is and how it operates. The Mind of beings afraid of change, afraid of flow, is what needs to 'know'. This (false most of the time) 'knowing' makes us feel (falsely) safe. The Mind categorizes, files everything, must have a slot for everything or it doesn't feel comfortable. The beings that have had most of the power on Earth for the last 300,000 years are Mind Beings that think the Mind can solve all problems, that Mind is God. Raw feeling, Nature, scares the Mind and in its view needs to be harnessed, controlled, and subdued. It's amazing how whole peoples in North America survived without destroying the land before our current civilization came. And the original people in the Americas had no concepts of ownership of the earth or needing to subdue, or more euphemistically, 'steward' her. They received the gifts from the earth with gratitude. We have been taught to view this as primitive -- but in the long run it will prove to be the only 'sustainable' way of living on the earth.

The Techno-Mind Scientism followers

Could it be that the Earth enjoys, yes I mean literally enjoys providing, giving to her children when there is interaction, respect, gratitude? 'Scientism' and mind control religion have almost wiped this Feeling Man out of existence and will most often laugh derisively if you suggest in 'serious circles' such a thing as the Earth being an alive, feeling, aware, awake sentient Being. Well where has our precious technology and 'better living through chemicals' brought us? To the killing of the Earth. To the killing of our emotional selves, to the killing of our hearts, and of course to all manner of invented designer diseases killing our bodies. This model of subjugating, controlling or 'stewarding' the Earth needs to have 'dominion' (i.e. domination) over the earth and all its creatures. The techno-mind-scientism followers' 'god' gives them license to kill animals, humans, and other living things indiscriminately. Their religion and science gives them license to genetically alter what nature and God have created, force animals to produce meat for them, and destroy the Earth for they are her 'stewards'. As if the Earth needs stewarding. It seems painfully obvious now that the Earth does much better if left alone. In places that are left alone, Nature-Mother Earth produces awe inspiring beauty and overflowing abundance. Instead of interacting energetically and freely with these wild places, we cordon them off, charge entrance fees to these 'national parks' and tell visitors to not walk out in nature but to 'Stay on Trail!' like so many cattle or sheep. We've truly become the 'sheeple' programmed to be afraid of our own mother Earth.

Why do we destroy what we Love?

If free wild Nature is what we long for then why are we destroying her? If our advertising encourages us to travel and 'get away from it all', 'take a break', 'recharge in Nature' and we use waterfalls, beautiful valleys, gorgeous big cats, wild free horses, soaring eagles etc. to sell our soap, deodorant, cars, phones, clothes, drugs….etc. etc. then why are we killing this wild free pristine Nature and the Natural part of ourselves? Again, it's becoming painfully obvious that Nature and the Natural part of ourselves when left alone does much much better than anything science has come up with. This Natural Life Force creates, maintains and cares for everything in the created Universe. For ex. no doctor, no drug, no medicine has ever healed anyone! Stop and think about it. The most a doctor can do is set up favorable conditions for the Life Force to heal their patient. It is the body (and the Life Force behind the body) that regrows cells, grows your nails, your hair, digests your food, enables you to see, hear, taste, feel, think. No human doctor can recreate these basic taken for granted natural abilities. The natural healing force, the Life Force of our bodies, psyches, emotions, spirits, is what heals us every time. Without this Life Force-Energy-God, Love-Life the body would never heal. I challenge any doctor anywhere anytime. I will bring them a lifeless body, a dead animal or person and let's see if they can bring them back to life. They can't- unless they are in personal touch with the Source, the Life Force, God, Creator by whatever name you call it. Science needs to admit its inability to fathom these basic energies of life or else it is an arrogant aberration that will never be allowed to see the finer mysteries of Life.

"The inability of science to solve Life is absolute. This fact would be truly frightening were it not for faith. The mystery of Life is certainly the most persistent problem ever placed before the thought of man."-- Marconi

Marconi was the modern discoverer of Radio waves, whose friends when he told them that he could send information through the air, the 'ether' by radio waves tried to have him locked up for psychiatric evaluation. It has always been this way. New ideas, new concepts are always violently opposed at first.

"True Innovation has always been violently opposed by mediocre minds." –Albert Einstein

By the way, our military-scientism-dominator model actually has park rangers dressing up in uniforms! Does Nature really need saving from itself? By Park Police? *'Please ranger Bob there's an unauthorized tree growing over here and there's a cloud out of place, could you have these boulders removed please, and these fields aren't growing in orderly rows...'* It's a joke, ludicrous when you see it.

So this process of 'civilizing' human beings becomes the killing of the spark of life in the Heart of Man, fencing in the freedom of the Life Force. It becomes a disconnection from Nature, from Love, from real God, from the very source of Life. And when you disconnect from the Source of Life-the Creator-your own Energy Source it is only a matter of time until you wind down, stop and die. It's like unplugging a fan; it slows down and eventually stops. It is dying before our eyes now. Our current civilization has as a cornerstone in its foundation the concept of draining the Life-force, draining energy from systems: 'Divide and conquer', split the atom, sift the slag from the 'precious' metal, 'refine' and 'purify'. Nature is not good enough just as it is, it must be whipped and beaten into shape to serve our acquired artificial needs and gluttonous appetites. The current 'civilized' model is to suck the very life out of the planet.

False Father Spirit Lucifer- Mars, Atlantis, Rome and our new Choice

These same beings, the 'Mind as God' followers of false Father Spirit energy (Lucifer) have (mis)led other civilizations on the planet. Atlantis and Rome fell through horrible destructions. We didn't learn then either and today we're headed down the same path. The same spirits that were incarnate in (Mars originally) Atlantis and Rome are back again to see if they can make a different choice this time. Last time these spirits were incarnate they were using Atlantean technology which consisted of an energy ray machine that could be directed at any point on the earth. This energy ray was pointed through the earth towards modern day Mongolia-China because the people there would not allow themselves to be ruled by the Atlanteans who wanted to 'unify' (actually of course control) the people of the earth. The 'death ray' was used and nuclear-radiation destroyed the civilization and lay waste the land that is now the desert north of Tibet and into Mongolia-China. Pointing this energy ray/death ray through the earth also had the effect of triggering the major land upheavals that became the final sinking of Atlantis. This occurred around 10,500 B.C. and is what is recorded as 'the Flood' in the Semitic texts (Torah, Bible). Those who don't learn from history are doomed to repeat it, on this we are right. The same spirits that were incarnate in Atlantis are now incarnated in the US and Europe primarily. Again the battle between the East and the West is coming to a head. China and the US as the new global superpowers are heading towards a global conflict that would be the prophesied Armageddon. Unless the Mind Followers, those denial dominator spirits that deny open hearts, deny open emotions, deny open feelings can admit that their model doesn't work, we will repeat the same pattern. It can't sustain itself; it carries within it the seeds of death. As things start to unravel and come apart, ("*...the center will not hold...*" W.B. Yeats). They dominator-denial spirits simply call for the old model to be followed more stringently. 'The collapse of morals and the nuclear family' will be the 'cause' of the down fall of this civilization according to them. People becoming free, free to feel, free to express themselves, and allowing Nature and other beings to be free looks like 'doom', Armageddon, the end of the world to those beings who have been controlling, enslaving, stealing energy from others and the earth. They will no longer be able to 'feed off' others energy...and this will be spell the end of the dominator, controlling, 'stewarding', suppressing, using, 'Mind as God' model of 'civilization'. And the more each of us invoke, pray, 'Imagine', meditate upon, ask for this real Freedom to return to Earth, the quicker it will come. *"Your will Loving God on Earth. Original Plan of Loving Source come to Earth....Now."*

I want an 'uncivilized' world. The ultimate Libertarianism, the ultimate Theocracy of each spirit being directed by their own personal direct contact with God-Source-Love-Higher Intelligence. I want a truly free world where the Law of Love has returned to the hearts of men and women. Like one of my favorite free thinkers, spiritually awake, radical freedom rebels said:

"The whole of the Law is Love" --Joshua Ben-Joseph (Jesus Christ)

Motivation by Fear has become an Art Form

The 'successful' humans in this current model of denial of feeling, denial of Nature, denial of Love, denial of the Life Force within, are the ones who can deny their true feelings and harden their hearts and work motivation by fear into an art form. And they then control others by fear. So this inverted model feeds on fear of loss, fear of 'losing face', losing our jobs, losing our lovers, etc. The False Father Image worshipers of the unattainable Image/Ideal can set themselves up to be worshiped as 'role models' as 'heroes' and thereby fed energy to in the form of attention through 'hero worship', through 'leader worship', through 'Father Figure worship'. The trick that is used is to get the masses of programmed people to send their attention and energy, (because attention is energy), the Life Force all things live off, to those select few set up as political leaders, experts, heroes, priests, doctors, and then these chosen ones feed, live off this attention-energy. I makes for most beings ending up drained and empty and hopeless and lost, capitulated economic robots. Think of all the millions of people now in the world who work jobs like robots and come home completely drained and take their alcohol and 'prescribed' (by the doctor-priests) drugs to help them forget how they've sold their hearts and souls to their leaders and 'heroes', then plop down in front of the TV and receive their nightly 'programming' on what to buy, how to feel, think and act. And the 'Chosen few' that talk endlessly about 'honor, duty, morals, God' party the night away in secret sex clubs with hookers and drugs, living off the energy drained from the masses. Most humans today will work themselves to death for recognition from their father figures, to get that approval from the father they never had. Then they project this father worship/approval seeking onto the president of their company, the leaders in their field, political leaders, actors and sports figures. But those unloving false 'fathers' never can or will give real, satisfying, heartfelt love back. It's very simple, you remove a loving father figure from people and they will spend their whole lives looking for that absentee father...in drugs, in workaholism, in 'proving themselves', in 'being good', in 'winning, in 'succeeding', in over sexing, in rebellion, in....(x).

Where's the Loving Father?

This lack of a real emotional, feeling, strong, loving Father Figure has now manifested in our "civilization" at the level where many kids are literally growing up without a physical father and those that do have a physical father most often those fathers are not able to be there for their kids emotionally or have time for them because the male is only valuable in our society as a 'wallet', a producer of money. Men are 'success objects' just like women are 'sex objects'. And men work themselves to death for money or prestige or fame or name. And we're all responsible for going along with this model....and the fruit of it is the death that is happening all around us. Death of the ability to feel in all of us, kids wanting to die, school shootings, war, drugs, diseases, hopelessness, pollution, terrorism etc. Do you women really want to kill your men by treating them as 'success objects'? Do you men really not want to listen and hear what the Woman has to share with you and just keep treating them as sex toys? Let's not let this false model of a 'civilization' pit us men and women against each other in a 'battle of the sexes' so we destroy each other. That's what the ultimate controllers want, they want to 'divide and conquer' us. Let us instead Love, listen to each other, and break the false ideals, false molds of what our relationships 'should' look like.

This model of draining the Life force and using fear as a manipulator to control the masses into economic robots and calling it 'civilization' is a dead end. It's beginning to crack seriously now if we're willing to see. Soon massive natural disasters and diseases will start 'cleaning up' the virus of humanity gone insane.

It's a Dying Race!

Who can race towards death the fastest, who can kill and deny their bodies and emotions the best and fastest? Who can sacrifice their emotions and physical health for the biggest pile of money? This is mostly 'the game' on Earth today. There's free will of course and there are many beings on the planet right now that **want** to give their personal god given power to leaders, they want to be sheep led to the slaughter. There's a deep death wish in our collective. They'll deny this fact and proudly point out that they live in a 'free' society but "*by their fruits ye shall know them*". Watch what people do and what it is that gets their eyes to light up. "For where their eyes light up there also is their 'heart'" i.e. what they're really interested in, and there also is their essential nature. This is how people will reveal themselves to you. Beings are free to choose how they want to exist and experience. There's nothing wrong with wanting to be followers and needing Big Daddy. But to give your power to unloving Big Daddies results in destruction. It's just that the Earth is a free will planet and will no longer play host to energy vampires, they'll have to go elsewhere and continue their energy stealing games. The tricky part is that many of the Free Will, the 'meek', innocent spirits of Earth have been infected and effectively programmed into believing that life is hard, you have to sacrifice, there's danger everywhere, and we need armies, police forces, weapons and the like. So in the coming years the trick is for God the Father and God the Mother to "*separate the wheat from the chaff*" as the Bible puts it, to get the Free Will spirits to wake up and let go of the vampirous energies. It's not an easy task; it involves that which we most avoid, claiming our power, going inside and being willing to look and see honestly where we give our power away, where we avoid feeling. Often we would rather die than be open and honest and admit to having certain feelings. Many men (maybe most still) today would rather fight and kill or be killed than have to feel their feelings, be open with their hearts, be emotionally vulnerable. All war is fear of feeling feelings turned outward into rage at the 'other' the imagined or created 'enemy', a scapegoat for our own internal self hatred or fear.

Just STOP and get Real!

If we want to reverse the death race that we are currently practically all engaged in on the planet we'll need first to simply STOP! Just stop and do nothing so that we can begin to hear the voice in our hearts. *"Be still and know that I Am God."* And then we'll have to choose to follow our own hearts voice. Often our Heart path will appear 'crazy' because God's will in our Heart is real Magic, the opposite of the current model of mind logic and being controlled by our need for 'security' that most of us are living our lives by on earth.

We'll also need to begin to be honest about our real emotions and feelings. This doesn't really work very well in the current model of being 'cool', macho, quiet, stoic, suppress emotions and you'll become a successful 'professional'. So be ready to be viewed as 'different'. It is helpful to often not tell too many people what you're up to unless they are also interested in waking up and healing themselves. The suppressor denial of life-feelings model which still runs most of the institutions on earth, may want to separate you from the rest of society if you start making too much noise. So until you are firmly established in your 'new being' it's good to play along and appear like a 'normal' suppressed spiritually castrated member of society. Mental institutions are full of beings whose 'dam burst too soon' and they started telling everyone about what they were hearing and seeing. Let God guide you in our unfolding process. If you lead with the Heart and heed your inner voice you'll always stay safe and grounded.

5.   **Programmed Love**

Through your li(f)e
You're dragged,

Programmed,

Feeling at most
A Pavlovian Love.

"Tainted Love"

Speaking about sexual love in regards to spiritual matters is akin to walking through a mine (mind) field. Actually speaking about spirituality in general is like walking through a mine field.

Most of us are so locked in, imprisoned, viewing the world through our prison bars that we can't imagine a world different than the one we "know" as "reality". What passes for "love" in most cases on this planet is energy addiction, energy games, trying to steal energy from one another. The basic problem is that we seldom experience divine, impersonal, melting, non ownership Love. Our love is so mixed with fear of loss, programmed 'shoulds' and ownership issues that we can seldom relax enough to just be with each other and let the energy of the Uni-Verse flow through our hearts for each other and through our bodies as we're making love.

When beings who are empty inside, addictively search 'out there' for something or someone to fill their empty heart void, they by definition cannot find someone to ful-fill them. And the kind of sex that accompanies this emptiness only magnifies the empty feeling. Sex is the energy source; it magnifies the vibrational state that it's done in. This is where all the spiritual prohibitions on sex have originated, because seers and masters have seen how empty sex only magnifies and allows entry for more empty heart energy beings onto the planet.

When Heart and Love are present with sex, with fucking, with sucking cock, with eating pussy in wild abandon, then also Love and Heart are magnified. Sex is like a magnifier, an energy adder (adder=snake, kundalini, dragon energy) to the blueprint or matrix being held in-form by your conscious intent, your consciousness during the sex energy exchange.

I purposely use "fucking" and "sucking" and "cock" and "cunt" to get us to feel where we still hold judgments on what is "spiritual" and what is "profane". There is nothing sacred and nothing profane except by us deciding them so, and one way to heal some of ourselves is to feel the feelings we've relegated to "hell" in the "dirty" words. These feelings need to be made OK in the eyes of God, brought back inside the Circle of Love. Otherwise we'll be forever haunted by these pesky "dirty" feelings wanting back into the Light. These "dirty" "wrong" feelings simply want back in the

31

circle of acceptance if they are loving, but we've arbitrarily decided to banish them because someone or something con-vinced us that they were "evil". We need to take sex back from the pornographers. We need to bring "fucking" back inside the "holies of holies" because that is what it is. Sex is the most high holy place. It is the Creator, the Creative Source represented in the physical. It is obviously how we are all born. Love "comes" through us and creates by miraculous growth a new body through the act of sex. It is the most powerful creative force in the UniVerse, we've polluted it, allowed non-love, non-God energies to mix with it and have created a world with "good" and "evil" energy mixed together.

The ET Zeta Reticuli phenomenon

The Mind-Lucifer- technology worshipers-blind adherents are now engaged in trying to create unloving ways to gain access to physical bodies through cloning and genetic manipulation. This will lead to a horrible loveless place in our future, a future that has already happened. All things are occurring simultaneously, there is no "time" in God. Time is a construct of consciousness therefore consciousness is outside of time. Time travel is real and happening right now for many on earth. The "Greys" the little ET's with large eyes, the stereotypical "aliens" that are abducting people and performing sexual genetic cloning experiments are from our own future, they are some of us who went all the way down the dead end of 'scientism', cutting our feelings, emotions, sex off and have ended up on the star system Zeta Reticuli and now have no feelings left, no emotional bodies, and their physical forms are dying out through cloning weakness. This is a billion year dead end that through our free will we are allowed to explore. God-Source-Love-Consciousness is giving those of The Zeta Reticuli who want it a chance to come back to the original plan of Love through creating hybrid "Grey" ET and human bodies and through soul agreements with their own souls and others in their soul group. They are doing this through time travel back to our time to undo the path they took down the dead end they find themselves in today. This is done through allowing the "abductions" to take place and creating this new hybrid body/race that will allow those Greys who want to try to wake up their emotional bodies and allow loving sex a way to come back to the Creators way of creating new bodies as vehicles for souls. In the big picture there is soul agreement for what is happening with the 'abductions', those 'abducted' (for the most part) have agreed on a soul level to help save their own future selves.

UnHoly Entry

They gain,
En-Trance
By Sex without Love,

They con-vince

32

The Mother
With their minds
To con-ju-gate
Then sub-ju-gate
Her truest feelings
and allow entry
for yet another
of their Minions.

And with their Religions
of Propagation,
"Be ye fruitful and multiply",
They feed themselves
on the terror of the meek.

Patriarchal lineage,
Children, family trees,
Tribes of meat
for Fodder.

They gain a claw hold
even
From beyond the grave
They maintain their grip
on their followers souls,

"Honor and Veneration"
Memorials, Services, Somber Rituals,

Feed your energy through
Your unholy prayers
to the "dearly departed",

For those that have hearts to feel, feel them.
Death is what they honor,
Memories in stone,
Graves of Grave faces,
Solemn rites,
Unholy Relics,
Dead bones enshrined.

And they have stolen
The Gentle Lord's Name,
They call on Jesus Christ
But mostly they just call
"Lord, Lord"
Lord and Master
feeding all their energy
Into the point of Death
They have gained
Through the ages

Unholy Entry
onto this
our planet
of Love and Innocence,
our planet
of tender Green
and Membranic Life,

Usurpers one and all
Unholy Entry's end,
The Gate is closing now,
You are losing
Your
Claw grip.

Sex is the Great Awakener

In the original plan, Love's Plan, God's plan, Higher Consciousness's plan, sex is an absolute miracle method in creating new physical bodies. When we are Awake, fully integrated, "enlightened", we have conscious sex. We can consciously choose to create a new body for a soul who wishes to come in. We can commune-icate with these souls, usually True Family members that are in the other dimensions and want to come in to experience having physical bodies. We have complete choice, no guilt, and there is no judgment. We can also choose to allow the sex to be for energy generating purposes, for just sharing love with each other, for expelling, exploding, expressing energy through our bodies, through our Chakras-Energy centers, sending the energy out to the creation around us. Sex is also meant to feed us, comfort us, rejuvenate, refresh, refill us.

Sex can be used now as the Great Awakener. Tantra, (a Sanskrit word meaning "weaving of energy") as a path to awakening is coming back into the collective consciousness now. Keeping Heart and God truly present will make this a safe path. And God is not namby pamby sweet sticky fake spiritual ness, He is wild, free, primal, 'no respecter of egos' and will melt you, merge you, consume you, resume you. Any attempt at control of the wild free energy of Life, of Love, of God does not work in the long run and will only hurt you. Tantra will deva-state (deva=god deva-state=god state) all of your clinging, your trying to control the energies or your partner. You will have to become the God and Goddess and allow the creative Source to pour through both of you to allow the energies that come through during real Tantric sexual union. During Celtic times, during Camelot and King Arthur they still had the Rites of Spring where one of the males would be chosen by spirit to represent the male aspect of God, and one of the priestesses from Avalon would represent the Goddess and they would mate, have sex, merge, melt, as they let the God and Goddess into their bodies. This was a ritual for the whole of the land, for all the people. This mating of the Creative Force as Male and Female pieces of Itself would bring Love into

34

the land; ensure good crops, harmony, bring God into the physical.   If we don't let God into the physical, of which the central act is making love, how can we expect Him-Her to be in our physical creation? We must let God and Goddess back into the physical act of Creation. The energies we generate during love-sex-fucking-union-godmerging affect the entire physical world around us because we are the "gods" as Jesus says *"Don't ye know, Ye are gods?"*

A Barrier

There's a Barrier
Between,
Sex and Love,
Guilt the Rebel King,

Time to Melt,

As Above
So Below.

6.   The Real Final Frontier

The Real Final Frontier is not outer space but Inner Space

The real final frontier is not outer physical space, is not decoding the human DNA, is not trying to find ever smaller particles at the center of atoms... No, the real final frontier is us reacquainting, refamiliarizing ourselves with our emotional and spiritual bodies. Not using our emotions for manipulating and stealing energy from others through guilt and image presentation, but learning again, allowing back in, letting the emotional body take its rightful integral, essential place at the "Round Table" of our Souls. And letting our Spiritual natures fully in-carne-ate, in-flesh-ate, come fully into the physical...which is the original experiment on Earth...to let spirit and material-physical-flesh freely exchange energy-information with each other, to actually merge and be of one Source.

You are a Star, a literal Star, you are a Sun of God

The emotional body is dormant or damaged in some way in practically everyone on the planet currently, or used in hidden ways for control and manipulation purposes. The emotional body is the power source of our beings and of all the powers we used to have. Powers like literal flight, physical transformation, telepathy, tele-vision, clairvoyance, clairaudience, communion with the Source, with God, are lost and held imprisoned behind the denial of our emotional bodies. This is a tremendous amount of power that we've given away, more than a hydrogen bomb. Your emotional body has more power in it than a hydrogen bomb. Your soul literally is a Star, a Sun with the power of a Sun. A freed being, with a freed emotional body is the most powerful and therefore most dangerous thing in the Uni-verse (Song of One) to those who want control over souls. Freed beings are very dangerous to those who want to mind control others for energy stealing, for enslavement. This is why those who come to set the masses free are killed by those who want to maintain control over the masses of beings. Stealing someone else's cattle is one of the highest transgressions in the dominator-ownership model. Jesus, his Apostles, Abraham Lincoln, JFK, RFK, Martin Luther King, Malcolm X, Nicolas Tesla, Socrates, Mahatma Gandhi, Osho, John Lennon, Jimi Hendrix, Jim Morrison, Mama Cass, Janis Joplin, Kurt Cobain etc...any spirit that starts to stir up the mass of people to question the "authorities" and get them hoping and feeling a real possibility out of the current mind control slavery is often eliminated, killed by the mass consciousness. Is it shocking that I included those musicians? Prominent artists that sacrifice themselves to the collective consciousness are powerful forces for seeding love and awakening into the masses and therefore become dangerous to the "moral fiber of society" i.e. the unquestioned mind control programming of what is and should remain "normal".

Artists get us to FEEL again, and when we start feeling we will start noticing that something is wrong. We'll start asking questions like -Why can't we be

36

free? Why can't I raise my kids the way I want? Why can't I make love with whom and however I want? Why can't we have extended families, several partners? Who says it's wrong? What is the church really teaching? Why? Do we really need war to settle things? Etc... these are dangerous questions to those who want to control the masses through mind control religions, "educational" systems, TV etc.

E-motion = Energy in Motion, our power source.

The emotional body inside us is the fuel for physical existence. It is the raw material, the power source, the stuff that allows us to embody, to fill out, to flesh out our dreams. The whole "outward" search, exploration, push for new frontiers has reached its limits because we will not be practically able to travel to other planets and other star systems without learning to wave skip through time and space. And these abilities to travel through time and space are only available to Masters who have integrated themselves, allowed their emotional bodies to become truly part of them and not suppressed into a "subconscious". Masters like Jesus, Babaji, Sai Baba, Krishna, Buddha, St. Germain, Emil, Merlin, Paramahansa Yogananda, and many less publicized masters have power over space and time and "death". They have freed their energy and exist in the "Eternal Now", the "*I Am that I Am*" that Moses encounters on Mt. Sinai. But these time traveling abilities are not available to beings that aren't willing to go inward and contact the Source of Life, to FEEL, to accept all of themselves. The whole "scientism" approach in its current form will not be able to create traveling to these more enlightened dimensions. A neat trick! We are effectively quarantined until we recover our emotional bodies, and rightly so since we're so unbalanced when we're not in contact with our Heart, our Feelings, Love, God that we would bring our spiritual "pollution" with us to these other "heavenly" realms. There are many races of beings watching the experiment on Earth currently.

Here come the Wake up Calls

The pain, the pollution, the survival fear, the mental and physical diseases that are now affecting-infecting Earth will force us to start looking inward to the Real Final Frontier. There is no other place to heal ourselves. Modern "medicine" is mostly "Denial Medicine" mechanisms. Simply put today's medicine is either surgery, i.e. "cut it out and 'out of sight out of mind'" (classic denial) or drugs which suppress the message the body is trying to give us (also denial).

In the US in particular we have been programmed to look outside of ourselves for "the next thing". It is even used blatantly in advertising slogans today to get us to look outwardly for the next titillation, stimulation, diversion, mindless "entertainment". "New and Improved" is so ingrained in our psyches it is assumed by the masses unquestioningly to be good. We are "cocooning" hiding in our houses and living through our TV's trying to escape from our selves. More and more "virtual reality" games are being created as escapes and diversions from the increasingly decaying real world around us. What will ultimately stop this are catastrophes like earth upheavals, volcanoes, earthquakes, the Sun sending massive ejections at the Earth, the pollution death of the planet, and the "unexplainable" viruses that will spell the end of our physical bodies. These are very harsh "wake up calls". We don't have to do it this way. We can choose to go inside and heal ourselves before we reap this outward manifestation of our denial.

Time to Get Real; You can't fool Mother Nature and *"God will not be mocked"*

Our healing lies in going inward and reconnecting with our emotions, our hearts and our spirits. By this I don't mean creating the fake, sweet, syrupy "presentation face" the masks we put on of "spiritually correct" emotions that we find in a lot of self-help seminars and workshops. Those fake happy, spaced out, unreal, make you want to say "It's been lovely but I have to scream now!" fake emotions is what creates cults in the mountains storing guns in the basement waiting for Armageddon. No, that doesn't work; we need to get in touch with how we really feel! **Get Real** with our emotions and heal the Blame Game, take responsibility for our personal emotional "pollution" and clean up our own backyards (bodies). The most denied emotions are severely damaged and it will have to be done with care, with Love, with asking God and Grace to help us in our healing.

If we **Get Real** about how we really feel we'll find that there is a lot of rage, hate, anger, deep sadness, seemingly bottomless hopelessness, confusion, wanting to kill, and feelings of betrayal at having lost our Paradise, having become disconnected from Love, from God. We will encounter basically all the emotions that we've run from our whole lives, the ones we've tried to avoid for thousands of lifetimes. These "abandoned" "orphaned" feelings are pieces of us, they follow us like shadows hoping we will turn around and acknowledge them. These are the feelings we need to go into and heal. Otherwise these "abandoned" emotions will kill the planet. It's already happening all around us. Actually our denial of them is what will kill *us* and remove *us* from this planet The planet will survive but as George Carlin says *"Pack your bags asshole you're going away, the planet isn't going anywhere."* That's basically it, either we begin to clean up our piles of denied emotions or they will start to show up in our outer reality more and more as what the "experts" call "unexplainable" diseases, or young kids being willing to die and kill each other, or mass wars, plagues, our plant life shutting down, epidemics, pollution, people dropping dead for 'no apparent reason', animals turning vicious, more intense weather, storms, hurricanes, floods, melting of the polar ice caps, extreme heat, cold etc. It's obviously happening already except for the most denied "holier than thou" people who see themselves as following the "light" while continuing to deny their emotions through any means possible; drugs, mental techniques, false "positive thinking", avoidance and denial. How long are we going to bemoan the fact that the "youth are out of control", "the world is going to hell", "I can't believe the corruption of the government, corporations…" etc. and continually see ourselves as blameless? Pretty good denial there! The world is a reflection of us. It is a direct reflection of our inner consciousness.

38

If something in the "outer world" triggers us, if it is occurring in our "reality" then a piece of it most likely is inside us. The Universe is a perfect reflector of our inner level of consciousness. There is no place to hide, there is nowhere to run. This is not to heap condemnation or blame on ourselves but to use the outer world as a mirrored reflection and "wake up call" calling us to our Awakening of our Souls, joining back with real God, accepting real Love back into our hearts, minds, bodies, beings and into everyday reality.

Tohono O'Odam depiction of 'Elder Brother' and the Maze of Life – when we reach the Center we become one with itoi – the Creator

7.   Lan-Guage as a Gauge of Intelligence?

I recently read an article on "Dolphin language" or "Dolphin intelligence". The researcher is quoted as he sums up what that article means for us (gotta have those sound byte conclusions!)

He says: *"We should never expect the dolphins to approach even the capabilities of young children in language performance."*

This sounds an awful lot like a human scientist trying to reassure himself and the population to stay calm and not have to entertain the idea that there are huge gaps in our knowledge of sentient life and how it communicates and expresses Itself.

Spoken language is not an indicator of intelligence

The idea that spoken language is somehow an indicator of intelligence is robotically implanted by our "schools" in basic biology/psychology classes. It is false. We supposedly "evolved" towards the spoken language and when this quantum leap occurred it was supposedly the "dawn of civilization". The truth is that when we devolved to spoken language it was more like the Fall from Grace.

A need for spoken language is more accurately an indicator of a "fallen" being. A being that is no longer in touch with their primal/divine nature, their essence, their very being. They can no longer feel Life directly; they have no direct linkup to the Source of all Life (that they are in active conscious communication with). But beings requiring spoken language, and spoken and written is what we mean today by the word "language". So beings requiring spoken language to commune-icate (be in common with) have lost their ability to commune-icate directly, instantly, co-incidingly with one another and the Life around them. Spoken and written language are an intermediary, a step in between, we take our feelings-thoughts and translate them into words and then write or speak them to another. This opens the door for untold possibilities for misinterpretations and misunderstandings. Which is exactly what's going on today. We have lost our ability to truly commune-icate, commune with each other. Come-union...come oneness.

For us to imagine that we can measure the "intelligence" of dolphins, elephants, dogs, cats, snakes by our spoken standards is just indicative of how locked inside our mental and spoken language prisons we are. Writing this is painful because it so slow and limited a way of communicating.

As I'm writing this I'm surrounded by three cats, and though it may "sound" crazy to some I do commune-icate with them.

The spoken-written language is a step backward

It is humanity in its "fallen" state. We fell out of direct communion with nature, with plants, with animals, with off planetary beings, with God, with Mother Earth. The only way these larger beings communicate with most humans today is by planting thoughts, in-spirit-ations in our minds and then we think they are our own ideas. It's time that we openly acknowledge direct commune-ication with these other kingdom entities. This is currently still considered "insanity" in most circles on the planet today. Our "scientists" our "experts" have implanted in their psyches (unbeknownst to them) automatic shutoffs if these "ethereal" things are talked about openly. Their eyes glaze over, they smile superior condescending smiles and retreat behind their walls of mental protection. This is quite the opposite of the "objectivity" they claim to have. Scientists have tended to be the most pre-judging, closed minded beings on the planet. Unless it fits their limited parameters of consciousness that is available to see their "cause and effect", double blind studies (apropos, they are double blind!) it isn't "real" in their world. But science has no clue about the fundamental energies of the universe. Science has no idea what gravity or magnetism or even electricity are. Just because we can harness the effect and have it light our homes doesn't mean we know what it is. And gravity is way beyond the scope of current science.

What's the real story behind the Tower of Babel?

The Tower of Babel is the metaphor in the Bible about this fall from direct communion with Life. This ability of Man to directly commune with all of Life threatened those "gods" interested in keeping man "down on the farm", docile, fearful, obedient. And yes there are "gods" who feed off controlling masses of consciousness, keeping the consciousness of individuals ignorant and predicting certain "static" mental vibrations of fear, survival, confusion, etc. So a huge control implant was put into mankind when we "tried to build a tower to heaven" and "god" punished us by convincing us that this attempt at becoming "gods" ourselves was bad, "sinful" and so this "god" got us to scatter our consciousness, slow our vibration down so we couldn't join readily with our minds and heart and souls (truly commune – icate). This way we couldn't threaten to end the domain of those controlling us and become "gods" ourselves. It kept us from seeing that "The Emperors (these false 'gods') have no clue!" It's a basic "divide and conquer" technique that has worked very well to keep humans in ignorance.

So with spoken-written language, divided fallen beings' language, mis-communication was born. Because when you don't send image, energy packets back and forth directly with one another but reduce the impulses, the heart, the soul energies down to a symbolic representation system (letters, writing, glyphs) you get subjective interpretations of the symbols being used to approximate the experience you are trying to communicate to another. A perfect device to keep mankind confused, not being able to join together but arguing, starting wars about interpretations of "sacred" texts! Instead of instant (co-incidingly, in two places at once) communication, with the birth of spoken and then written language needing symbols, we now have to send and receive communication between us with all manner of problems, translations and misinterpretations possible in between.

41

How Masters and Free Beings Commune-icate

Beings still in touch with their oneness with all Life, Masters, "gods", that communicate directly, instantly with feeling, imagery, essence grok packets, would wonder why we are using spoken, physicalized, slowed down language with symbolic representation instead of sending the real experience back and forth. Why go to the trouble of creating this extra step instead of just sending the energy telepathically directly to one another. It would be excruciatingly slow and painful for them to try to communicate by writing it down or having to speak it in long drawn out sentences. In fact it would be no commune-ication at all, it would be separate-ication. We would be separated, non-communing beings stuck in our individual prison-hells of aloneness, thinking that we are separate from others...which pretty much describes the current level of consciousness of most of mankind today. Original Separation and fear of Loss of Eden is motivating us as an underlying factor in craving, hunting security and Love but never finding it, being willing to kill and destroy to try to find security, acceptance, be in control, be home be in Original Joy. And that is the place sadly that we find most of humanity in today.

And we think ourselves "intelligent" and deem the still commune-ing creature of nature as "beasts" that could never be able to rise to our level of "intelligence", we say "...*never expect them to approach even the capabilities of even young children in language performance...*" Thank God for that, I hope the dolphins never sink to our level of fallen "spoken" language.

The "beasts" have no need or wish for our spoken inferior "language". Can you imagine the day we say goodbye to spoken language? When we retire all the separate languages? When we commune directly again with each other, *"No word passed between us, but universes were spoken."* Whenever someone communicates with the "other side" or has a near death experience (I would call it a "near Life experience"), when they "talk" to the beings or angels they always say that they didn't "speak" but communicated directly to them, right into their hearts or minds. Can you imagine returning to this instant knowing all things you wish to know, no need to try to "understand" anything, you get instantly all you and your soulmates-friends need and want to experience the Creation. You "hear" within you and without you all the direct commune-ication you wish for. No need for secrecy, hidden documents, paper shredders, secret surveillance, no FBI's, CIA's, all information available to all who wish it.

There is an automatic safeguard that cuts off "fallen" divided beings from this direct access to power and information. Not until we have become whole again, in touch with the Heart of Life will we be able to again commune-icate directly with Life and link back up directly with each other and this is another interpretation of the Tower of Babel story. Our heaven of oneness and instant communication with the Heart of Life is waiting for us.

It is time to graduate and remember our Original Language.

8.   Sex & Enlightenment

After Enlightenment Sex will still be there!

After "Enlightenment", waking up, becoming normal again, re-focusing our identity in our soul, returning to our original existence, becoming sane again, flipping back, collapsing back into oneness, returning home to God, rejoining all our soul fragments, merging all the different vibrations-dimensions that pieces of us are existing in, regaining direct experience of our real Selves, the drop merging with the ocean of Consciousness...etc.

After this, after we've woken up, after Enlightenment....

Sex will still be there!

There's a deep subconscious fear that if we get "enlightened" or "spiritual" that we'll no longer be able to have sex, or at least not the way we really want to do it. We fear that we'll have to give up sex if we become closer acquainted with God. No wonder most of us don't really make our search for Divine Consciousness, God, Enlightenment, a real priority in our lives! Who wants to give up the one thing that we all like the best?

"Of all the delights of this world man cares most for sexual intercourse. He will go any length for it-risk fortune, character, reputation, life itself, and what do you think he has done? He has left it out of his heaven! "
Mark Twain- Notebook, 1906

After you're enlightened you'll be able to have more sex than you have now if you want. You'll be able to have much more sex than you are able to without having God inside you. You'll have the energy to do it, and each time you do you'll have more energy. Partners will be everywhere. Others will be so attracted to your overflowing, "cup runneth over" energy that you will find lovers everywhere you go. You'll have to find polite ways of turning them away!

And "enlightened" sex will be better than ever!

And it will be better than ever! Nothing beats God-Sex. Having God "coming" through you when you come is the most amazing experience available in the creation. Do you want some of it? You can have it. It's how you were created. It's your birthright, just waiting for you to say yes to it.

Is that shocking to read? For most of us it is. We are so programmed by the collective soup of fallen consciousness on earth right now that it's shocking to us to read the words God-Sex, or God has sex, or God loves Sex, or God is Sex, Sex is God.

Once you are attuned to God, to Love, to Source, you will automatically know where and with whom to share your sexual energy. With whom God wants you to share sex with in a sense. Because engaging in this type of God-sex will promote love on the planet and in the universe. This type of loving aligned with Source-God sex will bring more energy of love into the whole creation. You will not want to, it won't feel right intuitively, your god-

43

connection will protect you from engaging in harmful, losing energy type sex. This kind of harmful sex, this kind of energy depleting sex is very real and used by beings who are interested in stealing energy from others. Because of this stealing of energy by non-god, non-love sex many spiritual teachers have taught abstinence or regulating sex until a strong connection with God is established and sometimes this is the right path for the moment. You cannot set hard and fast rules about specific conduct in a free will universe. The only "law" if you will, is Love. "*The whole of the Law is Love.*" Jesus says when asked by the Pharisees to comment on the Mosaic "laws" of scripture. The only way to know what is right for you is to contact God directly inside yourself and your inner connection will tell you what is right for you moment to moment. If you fool yourself into believing that you are engaging in "god sex" when you really aren't, the universe will lovingly automatically assist you in finding your way back onto the path of real Love. Sexual diseases are hints that something is off, there's not enough heart, soul respect, love present when making love for ex. The simple rule is if it doesn't feel right for you...you probably shouldn't be doing it. But you cannot judge what others are doing accurately until you are at a bigger level of consciousness than they are. And there will be times when your heart, love, God will ask you to step outside of your comfort zone of old boundaries, be willing to expand yourself into a new level of loving and sometimes that includes new experiences in sexuality. God Him/Herself is truly "Omnisexual"...loves all things and makes no distinction in what form that love expresses itself. Again the key is, does it feel loving for you. Is Love present while you engage in the sex. And it is high time that we take back sex from the pornographers, that we reclaim sex, bring it back inside the circle of Love. Make lust a holy part of the creation. If we judge lust it will turn into a deformed child acting out inappropriately. We will have the minister of the church trolling for underage girls on the internet, the superior court judge coming down hard on prostitution in his court room during the day and visiting the prostitutes himself at night. We get the whole Jekyll and Hyde (Hyde=hiding our dark-shadow self) schizoidness we have today around sexuality. But if we allow lust to take its rightful place inside of love in the creation then it will balance appropriately and be enjoyable, fun, and become a part of God-Love-Source again as it was meant to in the beginning.

"God Sex" will become our "Manna"

And this new "enlightened" sex will be free sex, conscious sex, complete merging in the moment sex, truly full body orgasmic sex. It will energize you, fill you, connect you to the Cosmos, and send you traveling on beams of light to other stars, other universes if you want. It will fill your body with a liquid golden "manna" of love-energy that will feed you, sustain you physically, emotionally, and mentally, and feed you totally. It will truly fully-fill you and your partner, it will move you into the timeless moments of Eternity, you will create more Being ness, Is-ness, God-ness, Love-ness, I am-ness. You will not be left wanting more, you will be completely satisfied. Your orgasm won't be limited to your second energy Chakra, to your genitals. Your orgasm will spread throughout your body, rebalance your

44

hormones, re energize your whole system, send energy traveling up your spine feeding your body all along the way, and enter your brain and wake up the 9/10's of your brain that isn't being used. The energy of your orgasm will re-awaken your "god-centers", your awareness as a piece of the large Creation, your "seat of the soul" in your pineal and pituitary glands... you won't have any more doctors bills! Your body will completely re energize and heal itself. You'll have a choice if you want to stay in the body or not.

Is Physical Immortality Possible?

You'll be able to retain your physical body as long as you want. There are people who are doing it now. They aren't reported by our media because of our collective denial. We don't want to hear about it, it would make us uncomfortable and shatter our collective consciousness bubbles about how long it is possible to live on Earth currently, it would challenge us to wake up to our bigger selves. In "Autobiography of a Yogi", Paramahansa Yogananda speaks of Babaji, the modern Yogi-Christ of India who has retained his physical body for over 9000 years. His immortal body has the appearance of a young man in his mid twenties. He can travel instantly from location to location by de-materializing his body at will. He materializes any physical objects needed at will. There is no biographical information available on his personal history since he moves with the Divine Impulse and not the misunderstanding glare of modern publicity.

Thoth, Melchizidek, Atlantis, Egypt and the Akashic Records

In Atlantis we knew this practice of Immortality. This practice was brought to Egypt by Thoth the Atlantean who founded the priesthood in Egypt. Thoth, according to some sources retained the same body for over 50,000 years. There are no mummies of priests or kings ever found in tombs of Old Kingdom Egypt. They "ascended", took their bodies with them. In fallen Egypt, the younger "New Kingdom" Egypt, which is the history mostly studied by modern day archeologists and historians, the "immortal" practice had degenerated into mummification. The art of immortality, the "food of the gods" that transmuted your physical body into light had been lost so the priests thought that by mummification the bodies would be able to be revived again when the lost art of immortality would be rediscovered. The remnant texts that the Semitic people collected (the old testament) speaks some of the "men of old" like Enoch, Methuselah, Abraham, Melchizidek who lived for a thousand years. These stories were on the tail end of the earlier civilizations of Atlantis and the ET influence in Sumeria. This history can all be read by learning to access the Akashic Records. The Akashic records are a Universal library that stores all events that have ever occurred in a consciousness-electromagnetic energy field which is accessible to anyone who "tunes in" to the right radio station. You have this ability by going inward, quieting your mind and tuning your attention to any time and location in the Universe. You have a permanent library card good at the Library of Universal History, the Book of Life, the Akashic Records and whatever other name it goes by. And in this library you don't have to use the deadeningly slow process of reading, no dusty book learning here, but the events are presented to you through your third eye in living, full dimensional, hypercolor, full senso-around, reliving the events as they really happened. No chance for ambiguity by misrepresentation or misinterpretation by limited consciousness scholars and historians. We are heading towards full conscious contact with this Universal Library. As you notice we are moving away from reading more and more and into video-film-television as a step, a hint towards full 3-D universal 360 degree full sensoround, panoramic experience sensing that we will eventually live in again. All our outward technologies are ex-press-ions, have been outed, put out, exited from our inner consciousness and manifested in our outer physical realities as a mirror, forcing us to acknowledge our abilities. The telephone represents clairaudience, the television is remote viewing, the computer and internet are a small terrible, prone to 'crashing' and 'viruses' limited, hint at the Universal Library of the Akashic records.

So back to what we all love the best...

This new, "awakened" sex will be sex that doesn't have to hide from the light of day, from your self, from God.

There won't be any ideas of it being "wrong", of it not being acceptable in God's eyes, in your eyes.

There has been and still is in our collective consciousness the idea that the goal is to evolve beyond sex. Most spiritual schools teach this. That sex is somehow "lower" "base", "animalistic", not spiritual. This is true if you're engaging in non-God sex, anti-God sex. If you're engaging in sex where you don't let Love, God be present with you. Sex is a magnifying glass, whatever you're holding in your consciousness will get bigger or more when you add the energy of sex to it. So if you think sex is wrong, not God, not spiritual Love, while you're having sex then you will be creating that reality. And you will be opening portals for souls-beings to be born onto the earth who don't want God or Love in their reality. This is an exact description of what has been happening on Earth.

This is the problem.

"Original Sin"

Original Sin is placing sex outside of Love, outside, away, or not part of God...

...and you as a soul endowed with powers of creating realities, if you decide, or let someone con-vince you to believe that sex is outside of God-Love, then so it becomes! For you in your reality. It's not **the** "truth" but it will be "true" for you in your personal world view. And if you get millions of souls believing in this same idea that sex is outside of God's Love then you create a collective reality reflecting this idea. This is the "fallen" state for most people on earth today. The reality "out there" is a direct reflection of all of ours collective consciousness. Often us "spiritual types" think that we're free and open minded, liberated about sex, god and love when in fact we're simply covering over the subconscious programming about Spirituality & Sex that we have with our new more "enlightened" beliefs. The way we can really help the Earth and the Collective Consciousness is by healing ourselves, by getting to the bottom of it, by cleaning out our own misconceptions of God & Sex.

So if we create a collective reality that is not directly linked up with God, Source, Love, like we have done on earth, it then becomes "Mortal", it has to die. This is as it should and needs to be. Any reality not infused with God-Love-Source energy has to pass away. God's, Love's, Awake Awareness's reality is "everlasting" eternal Life. We as little "creators" are free to explore with our free will endowed to us at our original creation day, anything we want. That's free will. We are free to explore "dead" ends. And we are on earth. What happens on earth currently? Every 100 years all the bodies are "dead", recycled, cremated or dissolved in the ground. Our current creation is a Mortal (will at some point die) "dead" end creation. I just wonder how long we're going to continue doing it. When are we going to get tired of it and want to wake back up to our reality of unlimited God-Love-Source energy? Wouldn't it be more fun? More exciting? ….and as I'm saying here…the sex would be a Heaven of a lot better!

Whole ancient cultures liberated themselves through enlightened "God Sex"

In India there are tantric temples with hundreds of beautiful statues of men and women having sex. The whole outside of the temples are full of statues depicting various embraces, kissing and sexual intercourse. Historians don't know who built these temples, or when. When the Muslims came and invaded India they destroyed most of these temples as sacrilegious. Every religion does this. If people become free by contacting God directly they don't need priests or religions anymore! It's job security for priests to keep people from finding God inside themselves! A few of these "tantric" temples survived because they were overgrown and hidden in the jungles. Whatever culture built these hundreds of temples thousands of years ago knew that awakening to our full self is intimately connected with sex, love and God. Thousands of men and women it is said realized God, became enlightened through a healthy inclusive approach to sex and God.

God Loves Sex!

(That would be a great bumper sticker!) I dare you ☺…

God created sex. Would She-He create something He didn't love? The Source of all created sex. Of course, it's so obvious if you think about it for a moment. The transcendent cosmic awareness created sex. It divided itself into Feminine and Masculine em-body-ments so that It could enjoy merging, melting, 'coming' back together. That's why it's so pleasurable, so much fun, why we think about it incessantly…because it is the royal highway back to Oneness…it's the one place where Love-God-Source still is able to "erupt", 'come', manifest into the physical world. And we're thinking of getting rid of sex too now! We are starting to create all kinds of sexual problems,

47

infertility, in vitro fertilization, sperm donors, and now the final step...cloning where we will eliminate the natural sex act all together.

Was God wrong in creating sex? Was it a mistake? Of course not. And being made in 'our image' (why does Genesis say *'Let us create man in **our** image'* implying several 'gods'? but that's another article), us being pieces of the Source that created us we can also create more pieces of God, of consciousness, by having sex! Pieces of consciousness enter this dimension by 'coming' into this dimension through sex. What a miracle! From a seed and egg a human being grows. Unbelievable, beyond fathoming for our minds, truly miraculous. Same with the seed of a tree, or a mustard seed. Just with sunlight the seed becomes a giant tree. Amazing. Truly divine intelligence.

Temple in Khajuraho, India depicting Tantric sexual acts

Practicing the Presence—

The No pain and All Gain method of Healing our Spirits

The Simplest way home to God.

Do you want to know the simplest way home to God, to wholeness, to healing, to fun, to play, to ecstasy, to love? The no pain and all gain, no stress, no worry, no pushing but just a relaxing, allowing, being carried, lifted, becoming lighter, simpler, more filled with the energy of ease method for complete out of this world ecstatic orgasms of exploding Love inside your body and very being? Do you really want to know? Are you really ready?

It's too simple for our minds to believe, "it has to be more complicated" the mind says. But truth is that if you practice this method of being in the Presence of God your life will completely change for the better very quickly. If you do this, in 6 months you will be a brand new being. Your life will simplify, become more and more effortless, you'll be able to attract more of what you want into your life. And for us spiritual types who feel like we've been on the journey for a long time...this helps bring us back to basics. *"The life of the Spirit is always at the beginning."*

One of the simplest ways to heal our spirits, our hearts, our minds, our bodies and the planet is...to simply call on the Presence of God everywhere at all times. You bringing in the Presence of God into the earth plane more fully is the most powerful thing you can do for healing- yourself, others, animals, the government, the wars, the diseases, the overpopulation, corruption, ignorance, fear, murder, poverty, pollution, the planet, all of Creation.. Action centered in the Presence is the only real action. All other activity is temporary and in the world of duality, karmic, doomed to birth and death. So wherever you are-on the bus, at work, in line at the bank, fixing dinner, making love, in nature, walking, exercising, having lunch, on the phone with clients, wherever you are in the moment- simply call on God to be with you. If you don't resonate with the word God use a word like Love, Awareness, Consciousness, or Presence. Here are some phrases you could say internally or out loud if appropriate: *God Be with Me, God is Here and Now, I Am a Piece of God, I Am the Presence of God, I Am a Christ of God.* The last one is hard for most people to say because of religious collective programming that says we are "sinners", not good enough, could never be a part of God etc. But remember, we are all Christs of God (though yes most of us right now as potential seeds). Christ is the Crux, the Cross-roads, the Crisis, the Cross-ing of God or Beingness into this dimension. And we are all this gateway, a "Cross-ing" of the Divine into this dimension. It's your divine birthright; it's who you are in your essence. Let it help you. Receive the gift of the Present now.

No Pain, All Gain

As you start calling on the Presence of God, do it when you can remember. It's ok that you forget, simply remind yourself *"oh that's right, I can call on the Presence of God at anytime."* As you do it more and more you will remember more and more and eventually you will be walking permanently in the Presence everywhere you go. You will be transforming yourself automatically moment by moment. It will be automatic, effortless. It will sneak up on you, imperceptibly at first and then one day you will realize that you are *"a brand new creature in Christ"*. There is no work involved with this method, no effort, no difficult concentration techniques, no complicated breath work to master, no mantras whose pronunciation you're uncertain about, no visualizations that you're not sure you're doing correctly...but simply calling on the Presence of God. *I am a Child of God; I am a Piece of God.*

The *Lords of Language* are real Angelic beings who have left hints in the language itself to help us on our way back to waking up. The word 'present' is one of their good ones. Source, God, has pre-sent the present as a present for you. God has sent out ahead of you into every atom of creation His Presence. It is there waiting for you as you arrive. You cannot go or be anywhere that God's Presence is not. The Presence is in you, is you, so wherever you go there the Presence is. It is a gift, a present, that is your advance team of personal assistants that are there waiting for you in every Present moment. But if we're not present in the moment we miss the gift, we miss the present.

It's time to open this gift, this present from the one Presence of the Present that is just for you. It was given to you on your original birthday. You forgot about it. You have thought you don't deserve it. But it has been kept for you all this time. And now your heavenly Father and Mother can't wait for you to open it so they can see the joy on your face and share their Love with you. They want to kiss you from the inside, fill you with their love, and give all they have to you.

Keep it child's play; light your birthday candles open your Present and keep it simple...God is Here and Now...Forever and Ever... AUM-EN.

An Experience in Cosmic Compassion

Every word has an energetic, vibrational origin and has been created by the Lords of Language. The Lords of Language are real beings, real Angels whose reason for being is to create and maintain languages and leave hints, footprints of the path home to God hidden within all languages.

Compassion: come-passion, come passion unto, into me...fill me with your vibrating pillar of fire...let me ex-press it...out of me and onto and into openings for your Love in the creation around me.

As I'm driving back from the "bad" part of town, with the junkyards, I drive through downtown Phoenix. I'm coming back from visiting my friend the biker, who lives on the street where you take a right at the "Nude Palace", my friend who flies the Skull and Bones flag on top of his house. My friend who I was a pirate with in another life. My hardcore biker friend, who when invited to join the Hells Angels asked them why they needed to join a group, what were they afraid of and told them he didn't want to belong to any organization that told him how to think...whereupon they promptly beat the living shit out of him...my friend who gave up and dealt drugs after his wife left with his son and broke his heart, my friend who's been in more fights than you could count, in and out of jail, who's killed people...my friend who let the five strippers live at his house in exchange for "favors", my friend who had his house that was almost paid off stolen by unscrupulous lawyers when he went to jail... my friend who sat on my back patio and...cried... when God touched him about re-uniting with his son...his son, who is... his own lost heart.

So, me, the omnisexual, kamikaze spiritual God-Mad devotee Man Child (if you try to define me I will promptly enjoy destroying your imprisoning definitions) I'm driving back from my friends house and my heart is feeling, is opening, is feeling love, feeling Come-Passion for all of Us no matter where we happen to find ourselves in our current incarnations... Something happens to me...my consciousness enlarges...I "see" into people. I see instantly into the persons on the side of the street...I "see" into their essences, like I'm feeling them from the inside, hearing their thoughts, actually being them...the happy black lovers just having met, the businesswoman walking briskly to her scheduled appointment, the co-workers waiting to cross the street after having lunch together, the homeless man feeling joy-full and laughing. "Co-incidences" occur...the exact same people, and I mean the exact same people, I was drawn to notice on my way through earlier are now returning and I'm led to notice them again. I feel a giant synchronicity...I feel part of everyone...I feel a plan behind it all...I am crying...I am sobbing...I feel oneness with everyone...I feel love for everyone. I don't want this to end...I want to remember this, I want more of it...God I want this to keep going, I want it to grow larger...

so I keep driving.

10.   Become More Disillusioned

The Maya-Mitote Dream Fog

Say Yes! To becoming more dis-illusioned. Do you want to continue living in your illusions? Do you want to be controlled, ruled by the collective illusions? Do you enjoy being stressed about money? Do you like having your stomach in knots when your partner "cheats" on you? Do you feel fed by the patterns of your family insanity? Do you enjoy taking artificial medications? Do you enjoy the compulsions inside yourself that run you? Do you like the Illusion of the Government, the IRS, the MVD, our political system?

The Hindu's call it "Maya" or Illusion. The Toltec's call it the "Mitote", or unconscious dream-fog.

If you're incarnated on earth you are most likely caught in the "Maya Mitote". Our minds, our egos, practically all our structures, social conventions, traditions, ways we're taught to behave etc. are designed to keep us caught in the web of the Illusion, the Maya, and the Mitote.

What are some examples of this Illusion that I'm talking about?

It's an Illusion that you are a separate ego fighting other egos for position, fighting for scarce resources–"Hurry, hurry, sale only lasts thru Sunday!" That's a lie, there is plenty of God Energy available to all living beings. Scarcity is an artificial creation of those who want to control others by controlling "scarce" resources.

It's an Illusion that you will die. The one thing that can't happen to us is the one thing we're all afraid of and avoid feeling, looking at, dealing with at all costs. We pay these "costs" by having the funeral industry rape us, take incredible advantage of us because we are in denial of dealing with death. We end up spending way too much money on some ridiculous casket all because the funeral director can play our guilt and denial against us.

It's an Illusion that you need to "work" for a "living". You have enough energy inside you and enough creativity that you can be amply rewarded and enjoy the physical world without having to slave for your sustenance. This is the truth...getting back to that truth takes faith, letting go, being willing to change, allow the transformation of your being, beliefs, ideas, consciousness.

"Work is for people who don't have any talent" –George Carlin

Those are just three basic Illusions. There are many others that have become so deeply ingrained in us that we think they are real. "That's just how things are." We say, "Death and Taxes"---neither one is real! This country was founded on the trigger of an unjust tax on tea! The Boston Tea party! And the income tax was sneaked in illegally during a Christmas holiday when most congressmen had gone home. Death is not real; we are all energy that lives forever. The whole world around us is this Illusion, this web, this fog, this false ego projection that we've ended up sleepwalking through. So...let's...

52

...Become More Dis-Illusioned!

Increase your dis-illusionment. Become more and more disillusioned with "the world." This will help you wake up from the fog of numb sleepwalking that has become existence for most of us. When you become disillusioned with life...Great! This is a wonderful opportunity to wake up! The more dis-illusioned you are the closer you are to God and you can be assured that God is right there next to you working in your life.

Ask for more dis-illusionment, pray for it, invoke it, and bring more of it into your life. Make a sign that says "Viva la dis-Illusionmente!" and parade around with it.

Ask God for your lover to "cheat" on you. That's a great source of dis-illusionment. Ask to come home and catch your lover in the act of having sex with the pool man. You'll feel all kinds of suppressed feelings rising up inside you giving you the opportunity for release and healing.

Pray for your boss to fire you. That will get you on your knees praying to God real quick. Ask to have the boss fire you in front of everyone so they can all partake in your enlightenment and liberation.

Beg for you to have the sublime, spirit quickening experience of bankruptcy. The impersonal cold legal system will snap you right out of your sleep walking through life.

And Divorce...wow, this one will clear your clogged kundalini pipes faster than anything. You'll be feeling rushes of divine energy up and down your spine in no time. The possibilities of clearing ancient primal hatred between the Male and Female principles of Divinity are practically limitless with this one.

Prostrate yourself in front of the Divine and ask for Cancer...preferably prostate cancer.

The Holy Trifecta of Divorce, Bankruptcy and Cancer!

Why not go for the Holy Trinity, the Trifecta of Divorce, Bankruptcy and Cancer. This trifecta is guaranteed to wake you up, snap you out of it. You will get really present, living in the moment...instant enlightenment. Yogi's search their whole lives for an opportunity for awakening like this. Revel in your good fortune if this should happen to you.

I myself went through a bankruptcy and divorce at the same time. I wasn't brave enough to ask for the divine perfection of the Holy Trinity, the Trifecta. I was overwhelmed with divine energy and love just with those two. I most likely could not have handled the avalanche of God Love I would have gotten from the trifecta; I probably would have ascended to Heaven instantly. As it was I got more creative than I ever had been in my life. I wrote 3 book manuscripts, I learned how to feel music and play it, I connected with my soul's inspiration...I got actual experiential proof of God being there and caring for me that was undeniable. When I ran out of money

God stepped right in and took care of me. I lived in the moment more than I ever had. I was willing to look at things I had always kept in denial. I highly recommend this to everyone.

Let's start World Dis-Illusionment Day, a day when we have parades and speeches calling for more disillusionment in the world.

We should have a song: *"What the world needs now is more disillusionment, it's the only thing, that's there's just too little of."*

National Freedom Day—Everybody quits!

I want the President to come on TV and say he's dis-illusioned with the whole thing...the thankless job of being president...the Congress always fighting him...the nasty backbiting...the sycophantic media, the stupidity of the masses... I want him to be so disillusioned that he quits! On national TV. I want to feel his heart and empathize with him as he announces it.

I want the Supreme Court to gather supreme courage and...give up. I want the chief justice to call a press conference and say "I can't do this anymore, I am completely dis-illusioned, it has become abundantly clear that you cannot legislate morality. Laws simply don't work. The more laws we pass the more people are filling up our prisons. The Roman Senator Tacitus was right 2000 years ago when he said *"The more numerous the laws, the more corrupt the state."* Therefore today I announce that I am resigning and I strongly urge all other judges to also resign and the whole legal system be disbanded."

I want police chiefs all across the world to become so dis-illusioned with fighting crime that they all walk away. They simply can't fight it anymore. "Crime is rising, people want to do drugs, to fight, to steal and there are more and more people everyday who seem to want this...we're giving up, our own officers are becoming corrupted by being around it everyday, it's not worth trying to fight it anymore. Let people do what they want." The budgets and properties of police forces are then turned into new Freedom from Illusions schools for souls to awaken.

I would love to see whole nations of people so dis-illusioned with their political systems that they simply don't vote at all. No one votes, not one ballot is cast in elections and therefore no one is elected. All government employees quit, they're so dis-illusioned with the backstabbing office politics, no clear goals and no rewards for good work that they all quit.

Medical doctors become so dis-illusioned with the fact that most people simply are unwilling to do even the most basic exercise or healthy diet to take care of themselves and only want "magic pill" pharmaceutical cures that they quit en masse and all walk out. Nurses, having been overworked and under appreciated for years speak up finally that the whole system needs to be overhauled. No one shows up at work at the hospitals.

Teachers all across the world become so dis-illusioned that they all go on strike, none show up at school and threaten to quit completely unless the whole system is revamped. They say that instead of teaching rote memorization of false history and useless facts that they will all quit unless a completely new system of teaching, a system that encourages each child to express their own divinity, creatively and imaginatively, is implemented.

Everyone working at jobs that don't feed their spirits, that don't give them enjoyment, finally get so dis-illusioned that they all call in 'sick of it all' until further notice. Everyone quits paying their mortgages and car payments and demand that some new system that feeds and cares for the individual human heart and soul has to be found.

All the priests, mullahs, religious leaders in the whole world become so dis-illusioned with people who don't want to hear or listen to God that they just all quit. No more religion...the people don't want it..."the people are just so inveterately stiff-necked and determined to do sin that we give up" they say and quit. The churches, the mosques, the temples are all disbanded and their doors are permanently thrown open to the wind and weather.

I pray, beg, hope, and invoke this Dis-Illusionment to come more fully on earth.

Pray that this dis-illusionment comes to you before it's too late.

11.   Exchange your Money with Love

Original Intention on Earth

Original Intention on Earth is for beings (humans and others) to interact with the medium of exchange being Love, by exchanging Love with one another.

We are meant to exchange energy with one another by means of Love. We're meant to interact, give back and forth, evaluate one another by, see the world through...Love.

How do we interact primarily with each other today? Through what? Money. We give back and forth, evaluate one another, see the world through...primarily Money.

Money has replaced Love as the primary medium of exchange on Earth.

This does not make money "evil", it's just a fact that we are now in a place where we've ended up replacing Love with money for the most part. Love is still the only real thing necessary to survive and thrive but energy in the form of Money has become more important than Love for most of us. We trust money more than Love at this point for survival. Having exchanged Love for money as the medium of exchange we've also opened Earth up to the reality of unloving ness. This occurs when money is being used as power without Love backing it up. Some people say our money needs to be "backed" by the gold standard again. That would be a good step in the right direction perhaps. I say it needs to be backed by Love again!

We've all heard it said that "*The love of money is the root of all evil*". This became dangerously twisted to "*Money is the root of all evil*" , which made us spiritual types avoid money all together, which only made us still disconnected from a full relationship with God and then poor on top of it! Not a good situation. But the love of money does create problems because it creates "feedback" in the energy system. We (as little gods) are the source of the energy of love inside the Creation. God/the Unnameable/ Source/ FatherMother is the source of Everything, the big Love. This Love has to come from the big Love-God first and then through us in order for the organism, system, earth, universe, to function "lovingly". When we put something else besides God-Love first the system starts feeding on itself and eventually drains itself of all energy and dies. This is like the "feedback" that occurs with electric amplifiers and is why musicians can toy with the feedback but they can't let it accelerate and feed as much as it wants because then the amplifier will blow up. This is as it should be. Inappropriate "feedback" in any system eventually kills it. Love of money is killing our hearts, (leading cause of death in the US is heart disease!) it's killing our souls and eventually will kill the whole system if we don't step in and interrupt the "feedback", feeding on itself that is occurring in our current model for civilization. This has happened in other civilizations, Atlantis, Greece, the Roman Empire and we are headed the same way. It has also happened on a larger scale where a whole planet has been destroyed. The Asteroid Belt in our solar system is the remnants of a planet named Maldek that literally blew itself up. Mars the god of War is in the collective consciousness right now (no surprise there). Many souls on earth today have had lives on Mars in the past. We lived there. We created a self contained system that protected itself by "star wars" type weaponry in space. Mars sealed itself off from the rest of the universe and after hundreds of thousands of years these weapons eventually turned on the planet itself and all biological life was wiped out on Mars. Some beings escaped through jumping forward in time and came to earth in the civilization that was Atlantis and there they started the pyramid building and energy weapon technology again, which eventually sank Atlantis as well. (This is the short version of the fascinating story). You can read all of this real history of life in our solar system yourself by tapping into the Akashic records, a sort of supercomputer that stores all information in the created universe. The point is systems destroy themselves by feeding on themselves when leaving Love out of the loop. Every teacher who's ever come has taught this. *"The whole of the Law is Love."* (Christ) Do we want to destroy another planet again with Earth?

Money becomes LOVE!

(When we mix our Love with it.)

Seers and saints through the ages that have seen the unloving use of money have tried to communicate this need for relying on Love primarily and not relying on money primarily. Their messages have been twisted and misunderstood that somehow it was spiritual to not be involved with money (at least not openly) and it's an old misunderstanding that God or real spirituality and money don't go together. This then means that we refuse the "frozen" love that has become money if we're "spiritual". How can we "unfreeze" the Love trapped in the money if we won't interact with it? Some spiritual traditions have become so fanatic that their leaders won't even touch money physically. And the law of Spiritual physics is: Anything you judge and have an unconscious emotional/mental reaction to ties up some of your energy until you forgive/allow/don't judge it. All you have to do is walk through the endless corridors of treasure in the Vatican to see how much wealth our religious leaders actually amassed in their denial of openly allowing money to be a piece of God, to be part of Love. And all that accumulated treasure is just what they show publicly!

Alchemical God-Money

So how do we change money back into Love? How do we re-infuse money with Love so that our money will do loving things for us and the earth?

Let's let the money come in as a gift from God and then let's perform alchemy and start transforming the money back into Love. Let's do loving things for our money, let's buy loving things with our money, and let's exchange it with Love with each other. Then money really can buy you Love!

I was struck by how when exchanging my money for products at the store with the "cash-ier" (love-ier ?) that we don't exchange love or energy between our hearts and souls. We keep ourselves separate mentally and emotionally and then we exchange money. The only exchange taking place is with the money.

So let us start exchanging money with each other with some love mixed in with it...and then add some more....and then some more love...and then some more love...and then some more...and then...one day there will be no need for money and only Love will be left.

As it was meant to be in the Beginning.

Walk in(g) Through my Walls

Walk in(g) through my walls,
into my life,
Melt my veils,
Merge the Worlds in me.

Near and Dear,
It becomes
A simple human process,
Easy as ABC,
The Child's Play.

Gone are the realms of "The Mysteries",
The "Sacred CereMon(e)y", the keys, the locks
and their gatekeeper priests.
My veil is torn asunder.

I meet You at the Pic-and-Save
as you smile
And give my Change.
I love you, want to tell you
everything will be alright,
Yes, you say, and love me back.

"Higher Vibration is not Necessarily Better or More Loving

&

How our Judgments have "Colored" our Experience."

There is an underlying assumption, a prejudice, especially in spiritual circles, that higher-faster vibration is automatically better, somehow closer to God, to Love.

This is a fundamental misunderstanding that has caused problems and ripple effects throughout the universe and for the manifested spirits (us).

Why has this happened? What is the original cause?

How has it manifested in Creation?

What patterns has it created on Earth?

How has it taken our Freedom away?

Who has been interested in promoting this idea?

How can we learn to intuitively feel the difference between Loving Light-Vibration and Unloving Light-Vibration?

And

How can we heal and set this right so as to let Love, ease, the Golden Age, Heaven, The Garden of Eden, fun, play, openness back onto Earth fully manifest (As Above, So Below)?

 Alacrity, speed, sharpness, intelligence, the lightning running across the sky, the quick wit, the quickness to anger, the blinding flash of rage, the intelligence that shames others...these are all of fast or "high" vibration. But they are clearly not all loving.

 Speed of Spirit, of Mind, Intelligence are exhilarating, like a roller coaster, like driving a car really fast, a speeding motorcycle, a space ship that travels through space and time, a mystic who can travel in his consciousness instantly to all parts of the universe. This is an exciting energy and can be really fun...but it is not always healthy or loving.

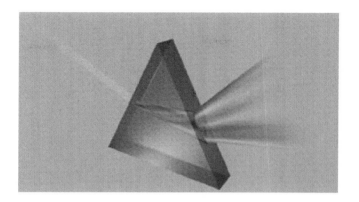

When you look at the visible light spectrum from black to white, R-O-Y-G-B-I-V, (Black)- Red- Orange- Yellow- Green- Blue- Indigo-Violet- (White) it goes from slower to faster vibration of electro-magnetic energy as you go up the spectrum from black to white.

Does this mean that we don't like red or orange? Just because they are "lower" and "slower"? If we're honest, the opposite is true on earth, many of us like red, orange and black better; they feel more powerful than the other colors. It's crazy to label any color "bad" or "wrong" because they have a lower frequency of light vibration. The whole spectrum is needed for light to function.

But that's what we do...we label the "lower" Chakras more "base" more animalistic than the "higher" Chakras, which are supposedly more "pure".

An Updated Description of the Colors of our Chakras (wheels of energy)

1st Chakra - Red is the color of our survival chakra, the perineum, our rectum, our asshole, which by our judging it harshly has been turned into our "kill or be killed" chakra. When someone feels their life threatened they often lose control of their bowels and bladder. The Red chakra in its natural state is passion, heat, incredible warming sustaining, nurturing energy, like the red molten core of the earth itself. We shame each other by calling each other "*assholes*". The words a culture uses for profanity-swear words, tells us what that culture has judged and we have judged our first chakra severely.

2nd Chakra – Orange is the color of your creative sexual energy chakra, your wanting to live, to create, to explore. We

61

have also heavily judged this chakra as wrong when spontaneously wanting to express. We feel we need to "civilize" it, shackle it, and only give it certain socially appropriate ways of expressing. Most spiritual traditions have made this chakra "wrong", or "base" and needing to be controlled. Western patriarchal religions like Christianity, Islam, Judaism have just avoided dealing with this chakra altogether and if anything only let it be understood that sex is basically animalistic and wrong in God's eyes. More sophisticated spiritual schools have said that *"desire is the cause of suffering"* and we must raise our energy into the higher chakras finally achieving liberation out through the crown chakra. In these spiritual schools there is most often also a judgment against the second chakra and an attempt to avoid having to deal with sex, lust, desire by focusing on the higher chakras.   This does not work and often spiritual schools, monasteries, retreats, churches have active sex lives going on but in denial with everyone pretending it is not happening.

3ʳᵈ Chakra – Yellow is the color of our Solar (sun = yellow) Plexus, our feeling, sensing, intuitive center. This chakra   has in the fallen creation made the decision of "flight or fight". This is where we feel our fear, our "butterflies" in our stomach is when this chakra is vibrating and sensing, trying to send us messages. We have judged this chakra heavily also. *"You yellow bellied...so and so..."* We have shamed each other into denying our fears. "Oh, no I'm not afraid. I'm willing to do the risky stupid thing so I don't look weak in front of the group". It has become easy to control others on earth by challenging their courage and calling them scared- "pussies"- wimps. 5000 wars have been fought on earth in recorded history by getting men to deny their fear and "Charge!" ahead to prove their courage and manhood mostly to their death. This has caused massive damage to the intuitive 3ʳᵈ – yellow – solar chakra and so most men have lost touch with their intuition and are therefore easily controllable and without real free wills.

4ᵗʰ Chakra – Green is the color of Heart and also, not surprisingly, the color of Love expressing on planet Earth in her mostly green life forms. When earth receives the Love of the Sun with what color does she exuberantly respond and overflow with? Green! All over the place!

Heart is the solution, the pivot point, the gateway between the "above" and "below" chakras.   Heart has been heavily denied, shamed, made fun of as impractical, naïve, too sweet, too childlike to function in our survival of the fittest, dog-eat-dog world.   Jesus of course was a large piece of the energy of Heart that incarnated and symbolically Heart is hung on the cross between heaven and earth and killed, sacrificed. Heart disease is the leading cause of death in all the western countries because those are the countries where we have most heavily denied our hearts in favor of technology-mechanism-intellect. Without opening this chakra there is no possibility of having real enjoyable Life on earth. Real Heart is not namby pamby, soft gooey, syrupy sweet being "nice" all the time. It is tender, gentle, loving, allowing, respectful and courageous, brave, firm, wise, strong and at times

62

righteously angry. We don't often show Jesus taking the whip to the greedy merchants selling birds & lambs (to be slaughtered to some bloodthirsty "god"), trinkets, religious idols, kicking their tables over and telling them to GET THE...OUT OF MY FATHER'S HOUSE! But he did and of course when you start to interfere with the money making machines it gets serious and that is when it was decided that something had to be done with him. It's time we allow the full spectrum of Heart energy into our selves.

5th Chakra_ – Blue is the color of our throat chakra and the one currently controlling the civilization on earth. These are the police forces "The thin Blue Line" protecting us from those horrible "lower" chakras. Blue is the Voice telling others what to do, how to live, and shaming us with words if we don't do what blue "knows best". This has become the dominator color on earth currently controlling people with words. Police and military "forces" are the Voice of Authority and final arbiter everywhere and do "force" people to go along with the "rules". Blue likes to mix itself with White which they think represents God, but remember White is also the color of blinding flashing rage erupting from Denial, Lucifer. Lucifer's name means the brightest whitest light in the Universe. There needs to be the feeling of Love in the white light or else it becomes domination of others which is what it has become today. Notice that the people in power today, our political leaders, our corporate directors most often wear the colors blue and white. There is a suspicion in the blue spirits of other colors as being too "passionate", too "emotional" to the point that even wearing a colorful tie is cause for suspicion in the board rooms that run the world. The signs are everywhere once we have eyes to see. Seeing what people are wearing is a direct indication of who and what they are. A "tie" for example "ties them up", controls the energy flow around the throat chakra like a collar and leash on a dog. Why do we need to wear a "noose" around our necks? To remind us that we are dogs on leashes? The "suits" that most men wear in power positions are nothing more than military uni-forms. Uni = one, one form, all the same, cookie cutter, no expression of individuality. Look down the street in any business district in the world and the uni-form, the all thinking alike, the mind control cult of money making has taken over. "Business is war" becomes the understanding.

6th Chakra_ – Indigo is the color of the spiritual seer, the visionary, the third eye in the center of our foreheads that can see the past and the future. Indigo has been caught in between the Purple and Blue chakra, between Spirit and Dominator. Indigo has had a hard time because neither Blue nor Purple has wanted to hear from each other or cooperate with each other and Indigo has been the go-between that has often been rejected by both sides. Indigo can see where we are heading and tries to warn those in control (blue and purple) but blue and purple have mostly been interested in keeping their control no matter what they need to do, who or how many have to be killed, even if the Earth itself needs to be blown up and sacrificed. Indigo has had a hard time on earth trying to share what it sees.

63

7th Chakra – Purple/Violet is the color of this "crown" chakra. Kings, royalty have used this color, "Royal Purple", to legitimize their "crowns", their ruling others, their claiming to hear directly from God above and disperse the white light down into the body. But the side of purple that hasn't let itself be seen very much is the control, the feeling "above it all", ruling with an iron hand the "lower" castes of people. Purple sometimes has a perspective of *the masses are asses* and need to be controlled. Purple hasn't wanted to incarnate fully, has wanted to remain above it all. Sexually this has often manifested in wanting to watch the "lower" ones have sex, instead of openly accepting it and having it themselves. They hire poor women to nurse their children, the aren't very present for their own children often letting nannies and boarding, "finishing" (finish their spirits off!) schools raise their own children.

Most spirits on earth have one dominant color, we are blue spirits, red spirits, yellow, green spirits etc. This is the color that we originally liked the best and were birthed out of by God-Goddess, Father-Mother or created out of in the electromagnetic spectrum of visible energy for Earth if you prefer a more scientific, non-theistic approach.

So in the current creation on earth, Purple and Blue spirits have ruled while fighting each other with games of power intrigue for control of the "masses" with Indigo spirits trying to share a vision of a better way but getting used by both sides for information while rejected and killed as well. Green spirits have tried to inject Love and pleaded for balance between the first three Chakras with the last three. But Heart- Love has been mostly rejected unless it is willing to fit into the boxes that purple and blue tell it is its right place. Jesus, as Heart, acted out how Heart has been sacrificed in favor of control and domination on earth. Yellow tries to warn us that something feels off, is wrong, but is told to shut up and is mostly avoided and shamed. Orange is used as a slave to get pleasure from but is considered "base" and not accepted openly into the halls of power, and Red is labeled unstable, too passionate, given to fits of temper, uncouth, backward and needing to be strongly controlled and also enslaved to do the undesirable grunt work of society like garbage collecting, eliminating, digging ditches, building etc., but given no real respect or acceptance at the "dinner table".

So instead of a Rainbow balanced in Love with the colors melding, sharing, co-operating like a chorus, like a symphony, to give color, flavor, fun and millions of possible combinations to explore in the creation, it has turned into a hell of fear, control, domination and war with blue and purple spirits hiding behind money and gated communities in the USA and Europe, using their police forces, technological weapons and armies to maintain control and "order", while green and yellow spirits plead and implore for more love and justice, and orange and red spirits are practically enslaved in low paying jobs, quarantined in jails, or fighting amongst themselves for whatever scraps of energy they can get. The mental-spiritual blue/white/purple spirits are dying from lack of vitality, lack of healthy sex, lack of being able to feel their emotions and the feeling yellow/orange/red spirits are dying from lack of loving direction and understanding of wise use of energy with heart and visionary green and indigo are not being listened to by either side. This has become a "standoff" that will surely bring the whole creation down into real death, cessation of energy unless we open our whole "pillar of fire" and let the whole spinal column and all the chakras communicate openly with each other. And so most of the different colored spirits end up living short fearful, stressed lives on earth while hoping and telling each other that "heaven" is where there will finally be justice, peace, love, everlasting life, etc.

But the truth is unless the balance is found on earth there is no real balance in the other dimensions either. *"What you bind on earth you bind in heaven, what you loose on earth you loose in heaven."* Why else would we continually come back and reincarnate by our free will choice? It is because when we go to the "other side" after death we see that we need to reincarnate to become free, to free up our energies, our crashed chakra systems. With renewed hope after having our "vacations" on the other side in the instantly able to manifest any desire dimensions, we choose to come back here. Usually when we return to earth we wonder what we are doing here, because we forget our intentions. And so it has gone for the last 5 million years with civilizations rising and falling with spirits trying to understand why there is the control and heartlessness here on earth and others on the side of control and domination of others.

This message is from an Indigo spirit seeing and wanting to share the vision in hope of assisting in others awakening.

Radical True Emotion feeling is a first step.

Radical Truthtelling is another step.

Nothing can stop you from your personal Awakening...

All you have to do is to say Yes! And all hell & heaven will start breaking loose!

~Section Two~

13.   Decide to Take Your Journey

Decide to take your soul's journey back to who you really are.

There is a unique, exhilarating, energizing, exciting, riotous, surprising, novel, engaging, fall on the floor laughing, enlightening, fun, full of ease, awakening, sexually fulfilling, see the world, meet old soul mates, journey waiting for you.

You have come into where you find yourself today in a unique way. No other soul has had the exact journey into creation that you have had. You've made decisions along the way, much like taking left and right turns on roads, which have led you to your current "position" in life, to where you find yourself, to what you believe, to how you experience your life right here and now. And yes, most of us find ourselves in situations that are less than what our ideal or original vision-dream-hope-idea was of how we would like to experience the creation.

The Ex-Per-Iment has gone Terribly Wrong

It's been an experiment. Ex (to exit, go outside, leave) Peri (the Perimeter), Ment (Mental-conscious awareness). An ex-per-ience occurs when we have exited the safe perimeter of a "heaven" where there are no choices to be made, a safe but predictable place. In this current creation we chose the ex-peri-ment of free will to decide for our selves. We've taken this journey into creation and most of us have gotten stuck behind the "veil" and we don't remember who we really are. We are confused, we've lost most of our god-given abilities, we're experiencing unwanted pain and don't know what to do. Or we are living in denial and pretending to ourselves that everything is "fine", or we're hiding behind simplistic religions, or we're hiding behind our money because we think it will keep us "safe", or we've given up on anything besides the "death and taxes" model and are "making the best of the situation" and putting on a brave face.

If you are tired of the "time out", the "martial law", the "fallen", "federal (planetary) emergency disaster area" situation on earth today you can…

…Decide to take your journey back home to awareness again. Awareness of where you really come from, who you really are, not just the name you have today, the "clothing" your soul has taken on in this particular ex-per-ience. Decide to re-awaken to the bigger you. The Source you are a piece of, God, Love, All that is…is waiting on you to decide to take this journey back home. Because of Free Will God says *"I stand at the door and knock…"* waiting for you to let Her-Him-It-Your Self back in.

What's your other choice? Another lifetime of slow dying? You make your pile of money and then you spend it trying to ward off your health problems? Aren't you really tired of this not so merry-go-round? Even if you "win" at this current game of money, control, power you still lose! You still die…you still won't be able to have open hearted, sincere, fully filling relationships with your God, your Self, your body, your spouse, your children, your fellow beings. It will all still turn into "dust".

If you feel you are already on this journey, decide to relax, allow, simplify, enjoy, and trust into a deeper level of surrendering to your real Journey.

You will Gain Energy on the Journey Home

All along the Return Journey of the Soul going Home you will experience energy gains. Every time you clear-heal-reawaken dormant parts of your self you will gain energy, your physical and psychic bodies will feel more awake and aware, your body will heal easier-sometimes spontaneously, you'll gain more in-sight into yourself and what's around you, you will become bigger, more of who you really are.

One way to check if you are on the return path back to your real self is that on the journey away from your heart your life becomes more and more complicated with each step...and on the journey home to your true self your life becomes simpler, easier, more enjoyable.

This Journey back to your self, to God, to your destiny, will be your personal, unique journey. No one has the experience, the expertise, the knowledge you have. No one has the ability to take this journey like you. And you taking your personal, unique journey back home to Love will be the biggest contribution you could ever make to others or "society", or "the world". This is because you becoming whole will reverberate and affect the world around you by the actual electromagnetic physical energy that will be emanating from you. Others will be encouraged automatically just by your presence, you will literally "sow peace" where you walk, whether it is in the grocery store, in traffic, cooking food, in company meetings, addressing the United Nations, doing healing work, sending email, or just sitting in your garden.

When we decide to live our life, to follow the inner promptings for what our soul really wants to do, what we really want to experience, to really be who we are, to look inside ourselves as the source of what we want to do...this is when the Return Journey of the Soul begins. We then give up looking to others for what we should be doing, to social norms, to TV, to "experts", to systems of thought, to old beliefs, to outside sources, and we decide to live our unique, sacred, sublime, outrageous, wonderful, guided, scary, protected, hesitant, loved for, cared for, safe Journey back to our real selves.

By the way, **you know** that nothing else, no matter how gilded the cage, will full-y-fill you except your journey back home to your true self.

Your Angels become Activated

It is a physical law as well as spiritual law that when we decide to take our journey back to Love, to God, to wholeness, that all sorts of help will come our way. You show up on God's radar screen, the message goes out; "A soul is moving" and your angels are activated. Your angels are called over the loudspeaker in the waiting lounge in heaven; *"The soul you are assigned to is moving, time to move into action, there's work for you to do"*. Your angels are bored watching TV (other's experiences) up in heaven and just waiting for you to decide to say "Yes" to your path and start taking steps on your Return Journey. Your angels live for this, it is their bliss.

God = Simple, Easy.

Deciding to take your journey home is not work. It is not struggle; it is not a big project that requires sacrifices, struggle, and pain on your part. It's the opposite, it simply requires you stopping, stopping all the unnecessary "doing-ness", the "busy-ness" of spinning our wheels and draining ourselves. It just asks you to say "Yes" to Love, to ease, to God, to simplifying, to gentleness, to fun, to peace, to comfort. It requires you to retire from pushing, struggling, efforting, fighting, stressing, obsessing, worrying, scheming, manipulating. It requires you to stop keeping a lid on your real self and "become like a little child", to be willing to speak how you feel, to listen to others hearts and true feelings, to be willing to appear as if you don't "have it all together" all the time, to be real, human, open... But what a relief it is to not have to hold that house of cards together anymore, all that pretending that things are "super fantastic-couldn't be better."

And now you can just be you...and that will be more than enough! You will in fact have more of you available than you ever did putting up a brave front. Your "Presentation Face" can be re-tired (our 'Presentation Faces' have been tired for a long time already!).

I encourage you to Decide to Take Your Journey.

14.

Multiple Bodies,
Multiple Realities,
Operating in Several Dimensions at Once

A while back my mother called me and reminded me that years ago when my sister had been hit by a car I had been present and assisted my sister until the paramedics and police arrived. I, on the other hand, have a distinct recollection of being at a friend's house and coming home to hear that my sister had been hit by a car. My mother and sister however were saying that I had been there to help right after the accident. I was equally sure that I had been nowhere near the accident. I didn't say this to my mother as she was telling me the story. I was interested in hearing her and my sister's side of the story. I've learned to not alert the collective Mind to these "discrepancies" in reality.

I was sharing this story with a friend, Mary, and it prompted her to tell me about a similar incident that happened for her.

In Mary's words,

The Magic Necklace

"I'd hadn't spent much time in recent years with my brother or his family. But recently my niece, Linda, got in touch with me because she wanted to invite me to her wedding and let me know she wanted me more fully in her life. At ages 29 and 49, we started a relationship.

In one of our early conversations, Linda shared a story with me. She recalled a stressful time period she had gone through when she was about 11 years old. She said that I telephoned her asking her if she was stressed about school. Linda said 'yes, how did you know that?' I said 'Can I come over to see you'? Linda said 'yes'.

According to Linda, I came right over and asked her to go out into the backyard with me to look at the moon. She told me we stood outside for half an hour, looking at the moon, with me giving her instructions on how to use a pink quartz necklace that I then gave her. Evidently I told her that when she felt stress, she should hold or wear the pink quartz necklace while staring at and becoming one with the moon, saying "Moon shadows, please take this stress from my body". I told her that the quartz necklace would absorb and pull the stress out of her body.

I questioned Linda over and over because I didn't recall any of this. I asked her 'I gave you a necklace?' 'Yes', she said, 'and you told me that the necklace would help relieve my stress and that I should go outside, look at the moon, say a little prayer and the stress would be pulled out of me.' 'Are you positive that this really happened' I asked her. 'Yes' she said. Then

70

while we were on the phone she went and got the necklace I had given her. 'I have the necklace you gave me right here' she said. I was baffled by it all. I thought about asking her if I could see the necklace hoping that it would help me remember something, but I didn't ask.

Three weeks later Linda came to my home and before I could say anything, she said, 'Here, I have something for you'. It was the pink quartz necklace that she spoke of. She said that when I had given it to her it was clear and that it had gotten progressively cloudy. She left the necklace with me. I asked her repeatedly about this and she is positive that it was me that came to her. I have no conscious recollection of doing this. Here is a photo of the actual crystal that Linda said I gave her."

Mary continued with another example of what she now calls her "twin" showing up.

"My friend Dan says that I show up for him a lot as well".
Sometimes he hears 'her' (as Mary refers to her double) talking to him. According to Dan "she" shows up anytime, anywhere, solid to translucent. "She's" shown up to Dan well over 80 times now.

Another appearance: A girlfriend of Mary's reported to her that she heard "her" (Mary's double) talk to her over a 10 day period while in Hawaii. The funny thing was the physical Mary was in Phoenix! This woman also said she saw glimpses of "her".

Mary says sometimes she is aware of being in two places at once. She feels herself in places like Hawaii, Beverly Hills, Carmel, Prescott, and Sedona while physically being in Phoenix. She says that when this happens, it feels very real. She says *"I'm literally in two places at once. It's so real that I don't have to go visit those places because I was just there. It's sort of like I know I'm there ... only It is about feeling like you've been there before. This is different in the respect that I am there now and here too."*

This is the actual crystal that my friend's 'double' gave to her niece.

Does the "Now" adjust our "realities" of Past and Future?

As we were talking about this concept of having multiple bodies, having our consciousness in different places at the same time, I started to recall being by my sister during her accident. I could recall watching from up in the air, sort of 10 ft above the ground and seeing the whole thing. And I also know that I was at my friend's house completely unaware that anything had happened.

Did some angel assume my personality to help my sister because that would be acceptable in the world's eyes, did I really manifest a second body but I wasn't ready to accept that consciously at that time? Are we larger souls with many simultaneous experiences going on in several dimensions? I'm not sure, but many people are starting to recall similar incidents and these stories are starting to be told. We are much larger beings and the energy of the created universe moves in much more mysterious ways than we've been socialized to believe.*

*After writing this I spoke to my mother again about what happened with this car accident, thereby alerting the "mind" to this discrepancy in "reality". She now says:

"No you weren't there but the day before you taught your sister how to fall like they train people for parachute landings. You taught her in detail the very day before and she feels this helped her when she was thrown from being hit by the car in landing so as not to sustain any more severe injuries."

Do we continually adjust our realities to fit our present? Is there really just a "Now" and that we are continually recreating the past according to the filters and beliefs we are currently operating with? Does this happen imperceptibly to our conscious mind until we are ready to start becoming conscious of this process? What is the clearer understanding of time-space what we call "reality"?

72

15.   Why Love?

What's in it for Me?

Why should you love? Why should you be open to love, why should you put forth my energy, my heart? Why should you love others? What will you get out of it? What's in it for you?

What's in it for you is your Health—

You will have a body you love and enjoy. The energy, the literal electromagnetic energy of love will heal your body, will make your immune system work at optimal strength, will make your vision stay clear, will enable you to feel shivers running through you when you receive a touch from those you love. It will keep your hair healthy and shiny. Love will make your feet move lightly as you walk. Why do we say that when people are in love that "their feet don't touch the ground"? We actually step lightly when the feeling of love is inside us. Gravity (seriousness) starts to lose its hold on us. It'll be easier to get out of bed in the morning, your food will taste better, and your lovemaking will be more outrageous. Love will make you stay young, literally. It will stimulate your pituitary gland to produce HGH (Human Growth Hormone) that will keep you from aging. It will keep your body beautiful, muscular, lithe, soft, masculine, feminine, sexy, aglow, alive, and sparkling.

What's in it for you is Laughter—

With love inside you will have the sense of the mischievous inside you. You will play, joke, cajole with others just because you can't hold it all inside. Love impels itself to share with others. You will be able to laugh at and help dissolve "serious" problems. You'll be able to see the humor, the absurdity, the cosmic joke in the world around you, the play of God.

What's in it for you is Romance—

With love inside you, it will fill your cup and after having filled you this love will automatically effervesce onto others and they will be magnetically drawn to you. You will find lovers wherever you walk. You'll be able to love others without fear. They will feel open, safe, and relaxed with you. Your love will activate the love within them and their love yours. You will not feel a need to cling or grip tightly, you will trust the process of personal-divine romantic love and this will open the flood gates of the bigger Love.

What's in it for you is Money—

Carrying the feeling of Love inside you will automatically move into practical manifestation in this world in loving ways. It will help, assist, care for others. Love will create elegant doings of participating in the world. The love given out will come back to you and some of this coming back will be in the form of money. This money will be Love's Money and this money is different than struggle's money, than conniving's money, than efforting's money, than manipulating's money, than fear's money. Love's money will feed you spiritually, emotionally, physically. It will give itself to you lovingly, it will support your awakening to who you really are. Love's money will care for you perfectly. It will know what you need, what you want, what will love you, what will excite you, what will make you feel good, before you do. Love's money will conspire to give to you what will create more love in you. Love's money will take no worry on your part, it will take care of itself.

What's in it for you is Power—

Those that have surrendered to "Not my will but Love's Will" are safe to carry power. Power to alter the physical, to manifest objects, to literally turn lead into gold, to lead others, to time travel, to dematerialize their bodies at will, to know all things, to read others thoughts, to fly through the air, to create multiple bodies, to heal others with a touch, to activate this same Love in others. Though some of these powers may be realized through wizardry and technique, Love lays these on your doorstep as an automatic gift when you go Love's way. These powers are self-sustaining and take none of your energy to maintain. All power is available to those who learn to walk in Innocent, Wise, Love.

What's in it for you is Wisdom—

Love is wiser than all the mind knowledge in the universe. Love enables you to access the skeins of time, to be able to view all things that have and will happen in the Creation. Mind cannot do this. Love has an all access pass and is free to travel anywhere and everywhere. You will wisely know when to assist others and when to let them learn by experience. You will know when to walk away, to not participate. You will know when to jump in, to follow Love's lead. You will know when to talk and when to be quiet. You will know where to go, who to be involved with, what to do to fulfill your Self.

What's in it for you is Peace—

You may not know exactly your fate, what awaits you down the road, what circum-stance you will encounter, fame, fortune or challenges. But with love you can remain in the place beyond the tumult of the world of opposites. You can accept what comes knowing that you are an eternal piece of the creator.

What's in it for you is Love—

The feeling, the energy of love itself. You can carry this feeling with you wherever you go. You can view your world through the lens of Love. It is indescribable, sublime, the poets muse, the mystic's goal, the song in the singer, the source of God, the dancing child's impetus, the flowers' reaching for the sun, the root of all that is. Love is the force that created and sustains the universe.

Some have said that every doing, every endeavor, every action that every being has ever and will ever do is in search of Love. And teachers and masters through time have shared with us that it can be a decision to simply be….in(side) Love.

Love is its own reward.

The Real Black Magic

As usual things are closer to the truth if you take the opposite of what is being said or presented as being the truth.

"Nothing is as it seems, skim milk masquerades as cream."

The real black magic is when there is a false front, when things are manipulated from a hidden place, when things aren't out in the open, when they remain hidden in the "black".

The "Presentation Face"

Real black magic is when there is a "presentation face" being used, a "front", "putting up a front", "Image is everything", etc. and using this front to divert attention from what is really going on behind the scenes. Overt lying-denial, *"I don't have any idea what you're talking about",* Public Relations firms twisting the truth for their clients to appear different than they really are", "Spin" i.e. massaging the truth to look better, "Plausible Denial" i.e. will this denial (lie) be believable, are all forms of schizoid, Jekyll and Hyde, false "black magic" being used to gain advantage, power over others.

Cleaning up the house for the neighbors for fear of "how it will look" is a small example of the "presentation face" we all put on. While that may be no big deal, it is a symptom of the collective consciousness that it's normal to be "two faced", to put on a "front", a "façade". It is so ingrained in us to want approval, live in fear of disapproval from the "neighbors" that this way of being is considered normal. Not being straightforward, not being able to express how we really feel, needing to temper the impulse, adjust, water down, "civilize" the real response we would like to give creates a "Gap" in what is being presented as reality and what really is going on in reality. This opens the space for hidden "Black" magic manipulation of others. This "Gap" allows unlovingness, lying, deception, manipulation to enter in and be exerted in "the black", i.e. hidden. The word occult means hidden, occluded, from sight or knowing.

Basically real black magic is putting up a front, a façade, a presentation face to pay homage to some "how it should look" programmed in ideal, "how will it play in mid-America", some imagined, idolatrous ideal/false god of "how it should be". And all the while the real power struggles go on in the "black" behind closed doors, in "closed chambers", "no access", "private party", "security clearance needed". That's where the real power games go on, where the deals are made, opponents snuffed out, "convinced" as to what's best for them to do. And then the results are sanitized, *"Mr. Harrison has decided to resign to spend more time with his family and is tendering his resignation at this time."* While they shake hands and smile for the cameras.

When there is no openness of motives, no laying the cards on the table, trusting that everyone will win, that there is plenty for everyone to go around, then there is no faith, no love, no allowing of the creative Source of the Universe to fill us and our cups till "they runneth over". Then there is true black magic in survival of the "fittest" i.e. the most brutal, heartless, ruthless, the "dog eat dog" world takes over. Pit-bull arenas everywhere vying for a feeding spot at the vein of Mother Earth. Vampires one and all. Basically this is a description of the "civilization" we have arrived at today. Current "civilization" is mostly the dog eat dog model. Our leader resort to war, to brutal killing of the "other" the "enemy". They may create a "World Court" in the Hague but when it comes down to it we use bombs, weapons, power, 'might is right' and violence. What is the motivator behind (in the black) all rules and laws? Violence! The implied or actual threat of physical violence! Get real! If you don't clean up your room you get hit. If you don't go to school you get sent to a special forced incarceration school. If you don't act according to the rules you are threatened with Violence to the point of the death penalty. If you don't follow the unspoken rules of this society you are threatened with violence. If you're gay you get beaten, if you look different, dress different, think different, act different you get psychically or physically beaten. If you speak your true heart and mind most often you get killed. Jesus Christ, Martin Luther King, Malcolm X, Gandhi, Osho, JFK, RFK, John Lennon etc. This is "civilized"? It truly is the "law of the jungle" that the people that promote this false civilization say we are getting away from! If this is the example the governments and leaders of the world set how can we expect our business leaders, our citizens, and our kids to behave differently?

Role Models?

Those who preach about "role models" the most often are the ones who set the worst examples. This makes sense since any psychologist worth his diploma will tell you that whatever we "crusade" against or for usually is the unbalanced part of our selves. We're fighting our own demons, our "shadow" that we can't accept as part of ourselves. So we then project it "out there" outside of ourselves. That's why you have the leading arson investigator in the whole country, the "expert", setting fires everywhere he travels to give his "expert" seminars. That's why often the moral crusader against "pornography" is found frequenting the prostitutes in his town. That's why the federal judge is caught red handed by the FBI mailing terrorist threats to his mistress so he can "save" her from the "bad guy" and win her back. That's why the minister of God actually hires a hit man to kill his rival minister, and a million other examples. The preceding are all true examples by the way taken directly from investigative TV shows like 60 Minutes, Dateline and 20/20.

So when government leaders pontificate about the need for setting good role models then go and start wars, refuse to negotiate with their "enemy" even though their self professed holy book, the Bible, says to go to your enemy 7x7x7 times and try to work it out before resorting to force, it makes sense. We can't see our own blind spots.

My Trial Lawyer is Bigger than yours!

So we get a schizoid population. We say "tell the truth" but we don't. Just look at the legal system. Power today in America translates to $ that can buy the best lawyers and "expert" witnesses that will lie for you for money. *"My trial lawyer is better than yours."* My war chest is bigger than yours. I have the $ to buy the consultants that will handpick a jury that will get me off. Where is *"equal justice under the law"* in this?

By the way, the feeders on this system will use the same "openness is the best policy", "we should trust one another", argument to get you to lay your cards on the table and then use that information to skewer you. The only safe place is for us to get back in touch with our Intuition which will protect us and instantly tell us people's hearts and help us see through the fancy words. The perfect bullshit detector is your heart. It will tell you when to stand up and walk out no matter what the "image" looks like or how right the words sound. *"Sounds right, feels wrong"* is often helpful advice. When we listen to our Intuition, our direct connect with God then also God-Love-Source-our own Higher Intelligence works in "mysterious ways" to assist us.

The Most Expensive Commodity in the Universe!

Do you want real power? Open up to your heart. There we will find an unlimited source of energy and power that no one can take away from us but that others that have not opened themselves to this Source of All will want and will tempt you in every conceivable way to give to them because this Heart Energy is the highest commodity in the universe. And you have direct access to this most valued commodity of Love, of Wise Innocence, of Power in your heart where you can commune directly with the Source of All. This direct communion with God, with the Source of All, short circuits all the "black magic" out there. It simply won't work on you. You won't have to know the details; it will simply not exist in your reality and "legions" of angels will come to your aid. This is absolutely true and no one can stop you from using this power.

It makes sense that the very thing that is the fastest road to liberation, freedom of the being, of the souls, would be the most shrouded, hidden and imprisoned in belief systems behind eons of guilt and confusions pounded into the emotional body.

The sexual energy is **The** Creative Energy. This is so obvious when you stop and feel it for a moment. Where does the elixir, the creative, loving light, the essence of Life "come" from? From our SEX. From our cocks and pussies. This is where we create babies from! New Life! It is Life, It is Go(o)d! The blueprint, the electric outline, the activation, the form shaper, "comes" from the male aspect of creation. The field, the matrix, the magnetic energy, the void, the womb, the space held open for creation "comes" from the female aspect of the Creator. The ulti-mate (ultimate mate) Source-Creator-God divided It-Self into two aspects to create the polar universe, Yin-Yang, negative-positive, male-female etc. And real magic happens when these two polarities mix and create something new. Wow!

So this "coming" into form, this last opening where the eruption of undivided essence can still enter the physical world is when we "come", when we have an orgasm. This is when the creative force reaches through all the filters and into the creation, unformed, raw, direct Life-essence, flows into the world of forms, fills them, designs them, mixes with the magnetic power to hold space open for their creation. Love moves into form. This is Real alchemy, the ultimate magic in the Uni-Verse, (the Song of One).

THIS "COMING" IS GOD! THIS "COMING" IS GOD! THIS "COMING" IS GOD! GOD IS "COMING", GOD IS "COMIING", GOD IS "COMING"!

I know it might seem preachy, the capitalization. I know. The truth is we all need to reread the preceding lines a thousand times, a million times, because a million times we've been programmed to think of sex as "not God". We have been programmed to think of sex as "evil", the "devil" or more sophisticated "private". They are "privates" after all. We have been taught for thousands of years to relegate lovemaking, fucking, coming, merging into the essence at the Source of the Universe, into the dark, behind closed doors, as something that is wrong, shouldn't be done out in the open, blah, blah, blah. Aren't we ready to grow up about this? Aren't you ready to have healthy, happy, enjoyable, life giving, nurturing God-Sex instead of repressed, guilty, uncomfortable, unhealthy, unfulfilling sexuality. It's high time don't you think? God gave us this "most high" gift, a piece of Him/Herself, made us in "our Image". Let's receive it, let's let our creative Life-Sex Force become a healthy integrated nurturing loving powerful force.

Those programming us have done a masterful job, but it's time to wake up from this stealing of our Life-Force that has been done to us. It is time that "all energy shall be free" on this planet. Those wishing to keep us controlled, weak, guilt ridden, dependent, don't want us to find out that our sexual energy, the energy of life that all of us have inside us is a ROYAL

HIGHWAY TO HEAVEN, THE "E" NERGY TICKET OUT OF FEAR, LACK, LOSS OF ENERGY, AND INTO GOD, HEAVEN.

We can do it and no one can stop us. God-Source-Love aligned sex is the fountain of youth. It is El Dorado, Shangri-La, Shamballa, Nirvana, Enlightenment, Satori, the Eternal Joy, Life Everlasting. We must contact our own life force within each of us and let it nourish us. This will literally keep us young forever if we would wish. It has been confusing to us in the past because one can open one's Life Force when it is not safe, when others will steal this energy. Having had this happen to us in the past we made judgments that sex is "dangerous", "evil", etc. Yes, sex can be misused for power purposes and control. **The safety lies in contacting our hearts first and letting them guide us.** Bring consciousness into our sex, be there, let's not go off into alternate realities while we are making love. Bring it out of the "dark", be honest with our fears, our inadequacies, and let's be willing to not have it "all together".

Follow your true impulse around sex

If we look around we'll see that most of us are very programmed into how sex "should" be done. We have been programmed to respond sexually to certain scenarios that keep the game of control and conformity going. And letting our sexual energy be turned on like we are Pavlov's dog feeds these preprogrammed collective scenarios. We feed our Life Force to these (idolatrous) Images. It's a neat trick, the imprisoned keep themselves imprisoned by feeding their energy to the thought patterns that are their "jailers".

Most of us feel that our impulses deep down inside our selves are wrong and we shouldn't share them with anyone, let alone act on them. Most of us don't even know who we are or what we really want. We've shut off the Impulse, God's Voice almost completely inside our selves. The Negating Voice, the "accuser" Jesus calls him, immediately shuts off any real impulse for exploring Life openly and freshly. God is the Impulse, trust it. It gets twisted when guilt and fear get in there and we're not open and up front about how we really feel. But we also shouldn't be open with beings that aren't interested in being open with you in return. This is the lesson that a lot of the Open Heart spirits on this planet are learning the hard way. One cannot, should not, be open with spirits who are not willing to be open themselves. Some of these "non-open" spirits will then try to feed off our openness, feed off our innocence, feed off our connection with the source of Life. Vampire spirits if you will. It might sound dramatic but nevertheless it is true and until we are willing to see this and not feed energy outside of God's plan this reality will continue to plague Earth. Look around you, don't you see husbands, wives, children, "friends", bosses, political leaders, feeding off "the meek" everywhere? Wake Up! It is not cruel, nor insensitive to stop giving your energy away to those who refuse to nourish themselves. This is guilt telling us to keep giving our essence to others. The truth is all Life loving spirits have a connection within themselves that is a direct link-up to the fountain of energy at the center of the universe. If they do not want to, or pretend they don't know how, to contact this Source of All Life themselves, that is their choice. No one "needs" another to help them with anything. We can share joy in experiencing together, but no one "needs" the other for their "salvation" or fulfillment. All these teaching can be twisted of course and misused by being made into "shoulds" and mixed with guilt. There is no formula for Awakening. The Intuition, God's voice inside you is the final Source of what to do in any given situation.

Don't push yourself, contact your heart first, let it guide you, listen to the impulse of Love, follow it as you feel ready and safe.

"Formula" Romance

Most women have been programmed to respond to "formula romance"- flowers, diamonds, remembered anniversaries, money, power, "respect". A lot of women are so programmed around this that they are easy prey for beings who mimic these "love triggers" and then use the women to feed off. And men are just as programmed to respond with their sexual impulse to certain triggers. I could dress up in a blond wig, short skirt, fake tits and I would trigger men's sexual response walking down the street. Our sexual nature has become predictable and uni-form having lost our individuality and real Impulse of Life in our sexuality. But this is where we're at. The good news is that the royal highway of heart, and true impulse directed sex- lovemaking-fucking will explode these prisons very quickly. But we have to choose to melt the old prisons and let the new God-Sex in. We have to be willing to let go of our old images, false idols, prisons that the programming has on the Life Force, Sex.

Sex is Love

Guilt the Rebel King,
Has us all,

Dimly remembered,
Times before the Fall.

Time to melt
the Barrier between
Sex and Love,
Then,
As Above
So Below.

And when that Great Power
Opens up from Below,
And
Inspires you
Your Seed to bestow,
Let your Heart
Be there
So(w)
That Central Love
You
Would Know.

80

More fun than the Stock Exchange! (Certainly more Secure.)

The Mastered Energy Exchange

There's an easy way to share expertise, to teach each other instantly, to exchange energy directly. It's called "Mastered Energy Exchange." A Shaman uses this all the time. The students of the shaman, the apprentices, learn the "hard way" at first, having to master the energy spaces themselves. This is partly to test their determination and see if they're worthy of learning the sacred techniques. Later they will learn the quicker and easier shamanic technique of "mastered energy exchange".

The Urban & Suburban Shaman

At this time on earth all the vaults are being opened by God and all spiritual techniques are being made available to all people who want to use them. You can be an "urban" or "suburban" Shaman. You do not need to apprentice with anyone but God, or your own Soul. No need to travel into the Amazon jungle, the Arizona desert, the Himalayan caves. You can learn this in your own quiet space anywhere. It is of course sometimes easier in pristine natural locations since Earth is the foundation of all harmonious energy.

Inner-gy Packets

What is "Mastered Energy Exchange?" It is the sharing of "inner-gy packets", inner energies. Each of us has mastered certain energies, certain talents that have become a vibrational part of us. For example, some of us know how to sit absolutely calmly, peacefully, in meditation, others know how to really enjoy dancing, exercising, being very active in their bodies. Some of us know how to tap into our intuition; some know how to incisively use their minds. Some of us know how to "get things done" by being leaders, others know how to organize very well. All these different "talents" are actually energy packets, vibrational frequencies. These frequencies are more intricate than just an electro-magnetic frequency. These mastered "Innergies" have the Creators Awareness, Consciousness in them, which we cannot measure with science yet.

How to do Mastered Energy Exchange with others:

1. Put on your "Intuition Ears".

First you are centered in your solar plexus, you are quiet inwardly, you have your "intuition ears" open, you are listening with your "third ear", you are sensing with your soul. You drop into your "quiet attention". You are in the space of "Be still and know that I am God".

2. Then when you meet other people you put your "quiet attention" on them.

Your intuition will tell you much about others, you will be able to see behind their "presentation faces" (what they are putting forward for others to see). This ability expands as you don't judge others. God judges no one and can therefore see everything about anyone. You will be able to avoid energies and people that are not healthy for you this way. You will also be able to avoid the unhealthy-clinging-unconscious parts of those you are close to, like family, lovers, husbands/wives. Being this aware with each other, prevents energy entanglement (codependence). We are all "mixed bags" of energies for the most part on earth. We are mixtures of awake/aware/conscious parts and asleep/programmed/unconscious parts. The game is to make all of your sub (merged) conscious, conscious again. By the way you will then lose the need for sleep. You will no longer need to go "unconscious" (asleep) to spend times in the deeper parts of your brain. This is why masters, awake beings lose their need for sleep.

3. Who and what part of their "mastered" energy is attracting you?

When someone is attractive to you, when you are attracted to their energy, there is usually something for you to exchange with each other. You can sit quietly across the room and simply "tune in" to that "mastered" part of the other person. A sense of appreciation for the quality you are admiring in the other person will guide you towards the energy you would like to acquire for yourself.   What is it you are admiring about them? What is your quiet attention drawn to, what is attracting your curiosity?

4. Would I like this quality for myself?

For example one time I sensed "a quiet-behind the scenes ability to go unnoticed yet be influencing the situation" ability in someone I met. I could feel my attention drawn to look into how he was doing that. I could feel how this ability would be helpful to have myself. Yes I wanted to acquire this "mastered energy".

5. In gratitude and appreciation you allow-intend this energy into your Self.

This is a letting in process. You simply appreciate the energy the other person has mastered and you "bask" in it. You infuse yourself with it, you merge with it. You sit inside this quality-vibration-energy and allow it to root in you. You thank the other soul for offering this for you. Sometimes people ask, *Don't I need permission from this other person?*" These "mastered" energy spaces are available to all, you are not stealing it from others, the Creator is the Source of it and S/He gives to all plentifully. Many times the other person won't know that they shared a mastered talent energy space with you. Those who are aware themselves will feel this and will gladly share with you consciously. Transferring these mastered energy spaces is like one candle lighting another, no energy is lost, only more light and warmth is created for all.

The Short Form:

When you meet someone you admire something about, simply take a quiet moment and make and inward decision to let in to you the mastered energy space of the other person that you admire.

Stealing Energy

Yes there is a "stealing" way to do this. And this is the way most of us have lost our God given talents. It has caused most of the loss of consciousness on earth. This way of stealing energy from others operates through shame, control and hatred. Does it feel loving? Or are you operating out of fear or shame? This is always a good way to check if you want to be involved with the energies.

Originally, when in our Innocence we used our powers of telepathy, healing, love generation, form change, clairvoyance-sentience-audience, bilocation etc. there were some beings that shamed these talents, denied them, put them down. These "denial spirits" did this partly because they do not want to be seen for what they are doing or who they are. They wanted their doings to remain secret. Whenever we agreed, made an "agreement" in our minds, when our thoughts accepted what we were being told by those denial spirits denying our powers, it became so! We lost those talents, those mastered energy spaces. You cannot lose energy or parts of your Self unless you agree to it in this free will universe.

Some of the statements these denial spirits used were:

"You can't do that...God doesn't talk to people like you, who do you think you are?"

"You think you are better than others? Why would God choose you...look at you, you are ugly, fat and stupid."

"C'mon prove it...read my mind... NO, that wasn't at all what I was thinking. You are crazy. You can't read people's minds."

"You are talking to devils, those voices you hear. If you don't stop doing it you are going to go to hell."

"Our way is the only right way, you have to do it this way or you won't go to heaven."

And a thousand other variations... It is easy to feel denial energies- denial spirits, they don't feel good. They don't feel loving, supportive, caring, encouraging. In your solar plexus you can feel immediately if they are of "love" or of "denial".

When shaming statements like this go into the innocent heart, they are like barbs, like implants that take root and the effect is to shut down these god-given talents. Also the energy is effectively stolen by the "denial spirit" that got you to agree with them. Sometimes the other spirit will take this talent from you as you give it up. This is what the real "black magic" on earth is. This does exist, does occur but you can easily recognize it. Just feel with your heart and solar plexus – does this person, this energy, this form *feel* loving to my intuition, heart. Not the words they use, not the right smile, but how do they feel underneath.

When you learn to feel with your intuition, you will be able to instantly recognize the methods of the denial energies and not be involved with them and you will start to free yourself from your old "agreements" that caused you to lose your energy and God given talents.

The good news is that nothing can stop you from regaining all your lost energies, talents and God-given abilities.

There truly is nothing to fear, not even fear itself. Fear is your servant, your guidepost, your helper.

God, Mother Earth, and all your angels are very much interested in helping you regain your full consciousness at this time. There is much help available. This is one of the methods to help us.

"I want all these marks on my body.

We are the real countries, not the boundaries drawn on maps with the names of powerful men.

I know you'll come and carry me out into the Palace of Winds.

That's what I wanted, to walk in such a place with you, with friends, an earth without maps.

The lamp's gone out and I'm writing in the darkness."

The character Katherine Clifton from the Movie "The English Patient".

Is Your Sex Free?

When you "make love" is your sex free? Is it allowed to go where it wants? Allowed to seek its own level? Or do you control it? Do you have "rules" about how it should be performed? How it should look? What is "loving" sex? What is "spiritual" sex? What is "sweet" sex vs. for example "animalistic" sex? Do you pressure your sex; push it in certain "directions"? I.e. make it "look" a certain way? Or do you hold back, using your partner for stimulation but you are somewhere else, imagining someone else, not showing your real face, who you really are? What really turns you on? Dare to say it! Be here now while fucking! If you've never thought of these questions, it may imply a severely denied sexuality. If sex is routine and just "banging" against old patterns, old images, scenarios that you keep acting out over and over again...then it's not moving, not evolving, not...Free. Because Life is meant to move ever onward towards new creations.

Humanity is stuck in Sex

Humanity is stuck in sex. We are like a CD, or record that keeps playing the same 2 second fragment over and over again....and over and over again...for the last 300,000 years. We have not evolved our sex; if anything we have "devolved" our sex. We've become more crazy, addicted, not able to enjoy it fully, obsessed with, denying it, craving it, not getting enough, creating sexual diseases like never before in history...generally all "fucked up" about it. Why do you think that FUCK is the most powerfully negated word in the language today, the "baddest" word? The pioneers in most of the programming for the Internet were pornographers! We spend untold billions and time on it, trying desperately to get "satisfied". But we "Can't get No Satisfaction", because we do it without allowing Love, God to be there fully and therefore it remains like the broken record, stuck in our energy fields. Our unexpressed sex is like a huge weight, huge balloon that runs us, and we aren't allowed to be open and honest about. *"You shall know the Truth and The Truth shall set you Free".* Are we ready to apply this powerful Truth by Joshua Ben Joseph (Jesus Christ) to our sexuality? How long are we going to wait? Do you know that if young men had real loving sex they would not go to war? They wouldn't be angry and frustrated enough to want to go kill. That is true no matter how your mind and mind control religion has twisted it and programmed you to believe otherwise.

Cut Your Penis off at the local Baptist Church

All pushing, adjusting, hiding our sexual impulses implies judgments we hold on our self and our expression of sex. We have been sold & told how to perform "loving" sex. Or we do sex in rebellion to the rules that society has tried to impose on us, for example, we do "dirty" sex. But this imprisons us just as much, because we are feeding our reaction against something and then this something is still controlling, running us. Reactionary sex, the classic example of the Preachers Kid acting out is just as imprisoned, not free, as the original denial-shame around sex itself. Or if we do it in an altered state, drunkenness, drugs, even fancy "romantic" environments implies that there is something wrong, unclean, not appropriate, dirty, etc. (we have thousands of judgments on raw-sex-love-energy-life) with sex in a natural pristine state. I'm not saying "romance" is wrong, of course not, just see if there are some underlying judgments on direct expression of sex that cause us to want to create these fantasy environments, turn the lights down, hide the light with the red handkerchief, put on mood altering music, make up etc....are we doing this because we don't like ourselves, our body is "ugly" in the light of day, in its pristine unadorned state?

I ask again, is our sex free? Do we feel free to express it how the Impulse of Life comes up? Can we allow it to express itself the way it wants? Or are we going to keep suppressing it and causing ourselves all kinds of problems? Recently a young man sat in his car in the parking lot of the largest Baptist Church here in Arizona and cut his penis off! What level of conflicted feelings between God and Sex cause such atrocities? We need to come out of denial and become healthy with our sex.

What Really turns you on?

This is not meant to make us feel more guilt and that now we aren't doing sex in the "correct" way. There is no correct or incorrect way, except that Love, God be allowed to be present. We are very different spirits. But often we aren't true to the way we really want to express our love, our (s)exploring the creation. One good gauge of where our energy really is, is what really turns us on, what sends sexual energy into us, what activates our energy. When we are on the internet alone in the wee hours of the morning what are the impulses, the scenarios we don't share with anyone and are afraid that God knows about? Of course He knows about it, and He doesn't judge it! We're the ones who judge it, who have bought into the right and wrong, the *"knowledge of good and evil"* of how to express sexually. We have been programmed to respond, like Pavlov's dog, to certain scenarios. I am only saying if we can allow, get in touch with what we really want to experience with our creative force –sex-love, and not feed these programmed pictures that those who practice consciousness control are interested in perpetuating, then we would start creating real freedom of expression, of individuality on the planet. We are meant to be widely different. We *are* widely different. This push by modern civilization for conformity into economically controllable robots is robbing us of joy, spontaneity and stealing our very beings.

Spiritual Machoism- *"I Can handle it."*

So let your sex become more free. But be honest about your fears, your self judgments about your impulses. Don't go past your fears, your doubts, your guilt. Don't fall prey to "spiritual machoism" where you act more evolved than you are. Remember "Humpty Dumpty had a great fall and all the Kings

86

men couldn't put him together again." Humpty didn't belong up on that wall, he wasn't ready. Be exactly where you are, allow it admit it, it is one of your greatest strengths and protections. If you push past your guilts/fears without clearing-healing them they will manifest in your outer world eventually as some form of repression, persecution, disease, or other "wake up call". It requires emotional honesty the real process of healing. Those of us who think we have no problem with sexual expression have usually put sex in an iron clad box and don't let it express outside of those sanctioned "OK" ways of doing it. For example, someone can seem very "open" and relaxed about sexual partners, does "it" in a "loving" way. But they may be really using sex to PREVENT feeling, PREVENT real intimacy and as soon as those feelings they don't want to feel start to surface they run to another partner. Your heart will guide you here. It is not easy, that's why we've avoided it for so long and have tried every conceivably (pun, pun) way around having to open our hearts, become vulnerable and allow in the emotional body in our fucking. And with good reason because when we've opened up our souls and hearts in the past it has SEEMED like it's given us a lot of trouble and heartache. It has! Romeo and Juliet, Oedipus etc. But these old patterns, programs need to be undone and now is the time, on the verge of the new world "coming".

A Truce in the Battle of the Sexes

Sometimes women will say *"Yeah, that's right, we want emotions with our lovemaking."* And they'll use this to point a finger at the man saying that he is not "doing it right". They'll make the man feel guilty. Making it a game of right and wrong, the "Blame Game" and this only keeps the battle going. But having a heart, love for each other and trying to share, "commune-icate" with your lover/partner is the only way to move on from the "War of the Sexes". Do you like having "War" with your lover? Well then why do you do it? No one is making you do it, you are choosing to do it. Someone has got to take the initiative and stop fighting. It "takes two to tango" and if one refuses to dance the "Dance of Anger, the Dance of Blame" then it will stop. *"I don't want to fight anymore, I want Love. I don't know how to do it, but I know that God, or larger consciousness knows how and I know that I can learn."* That's the starting point. And God, Life, Love, will always respond to your sincere wanting to know, to grow, to move more into real Love.

Romantic Programming = killing good sex and Love

These images of "how it should be done" are often just as much a prison for the energy of Life as having a hardened heart and not being open emotionally. There is so much pablumy "romantic" programming that's been implanted with sexual energy that needs to be undone now so that our sex can be free that it seems overwhelming at times. Holding on to our old ideas and pictures of how it "should be" will not be helpful to our evolving at this time. Finding our real self and how we'd really like to express is not an easy journey given the starting point of almost total mind control programming by "tradition", schools, parents, governments, religions that

87

we find ourselves in. But this Journey home to your real Self is the most real, joyous thing you can do. It is the only Journey there is, really. You will recover more and more of your lost energy until you'll have so much energy you will literally burst and ascend (if you so choose) or travel freely throughout all the dimensions. This is not metaphorical, it is for real. Someone needs to say it, and remind us that *"Ye are gods."* – Jesus Christ. You are meant to be free and your sex can be a royal highway back to freedom if you let it. Yes you will be "different" from others. But so what? Do you want to be one of the programmed economic robots that live out their lives inside their boxes, one of the lemmings going off the cliff here in a few years when the earth changes start happening? I thought not...

So "get (it) on with it!"

20.   You Can Never be Successful...at this Game

So what is the "Game" today?   What are we striving for, reaching for, working for, pushing towards? What are we getting up in the mo(u)rning and banging our heads against our hearts for? What do we want? What are we searching for?

Ok...so, Money, primarily, the *"In Go(l)d we Trust"* written on all our illusory, ephemeral paper pieces that we bow down to, worship, dream about, obsess about, stress about, worry about, are willing to cheat, steal, kill , betray our parents and children for.   That's what the "Game" is about....mainly. Let's be real, let's not lie to ourselves.

Let's say you make the $10-100 million dollars. You successfully sell a company that you built, or go public with a stock offering and become an instant mega millionaire. You can now live off the interest and never "work" again in your life...

Or can you?

The Sorcerer's Apprentice?

Are you going to be able to turn it off? Or will the years and energy that you spent pushing; stressing, "getting it" have invaded your mind, heart and body?   Will the monsters have gotten inside your mind and are now running you? Is your body already sacrificed by poisons and stress and beyond recovery? Are you going to be like the majority of people who die within 6 years of their re-tire-ment (re-tired=tired all over again)?   The people who are so addicted to "doing" that if they don't have anything to "do" they go stir crazy? Are you going to be like most of us who can never relax? Most of us can't go on a vacation and stop, simply *"Be still and know that I Am God."* We spend our vacations sedating ourselves with alcohol or being "active" with tours, sightseeing, draining our energy further. And then we have to get back to our hotel room and call in to check how things are going at the "office", the stock market, with our "doing ness", our "busyness-business".

Join the Club!--Prostate Cancer and Breast Cancer are Popular lately!

You're still going to die...probably a horrible death. Prostate cancer is popular lately for men. Breast cancer is a favorite for women. Which makes sense; we are not healthy with our sexuality so the "wake up call" of cancer manifests there.

With all your money you likely will still not know how to have a real exchange of love with those around you. You won't be able to share your love with your family. You won't be able to have real love with a romantic partner. You're still not going to be able to be real with expressing in the world all you are as a soul. You won't know what to do with the impulses that arise from the Natural part of your self inside you. You are still going to be caught in the Mind Swamp of the collective consciousness. What? Are you going to use your money as power over people? How long do you think that will be satisfying? To have "economic robots" doing your every bidding, do you really think you'll like that? Do you really think sex with robots will be satisfying? Ok, so you give up on that and now you travel everywhere hoping that will be a nice way to "see the world" but what you really see is that it's the same "Game" all over the globe, people using each other, hurting themselves and others for the pursuit of the false god, Money. How do you think you'll feel when your soul realizes this? Or will you sedate yourself with prescription drugs or alcohol to avoid these realizations? Would that be the "Glory of God" that Shakespeare wrote about? Or will you busy yourself with starting "The Foundation for Humanity" and travel around the world doing "good"? And then how will your heart feel when you realize you are having very little impact on the "poor" the "less fortunate" and that they go on betraying, hurting, stealing, dominating and killing each other no matter how many "good" projects you offer them? Or you 'liberate' and 'educate' countries and then when you leave, they go right back to corruption and killing each other. How will you feel?

You will most likely die a horrible death

And let me remind you again, your body will deteriorate and you will likely die a horrible physical death. Soon too. It's coming up quick; you only have 20-30 years left most likely. Where did the last 10 years go? Didn't they go amazingly fast? Can you see the end of your life? Every 90 years all the bodies on this planet are recycled. Dead, dust, bones...no one left alive. 90 years is nothing, it goes really fast.

Or do you think that the "game" is "living a good, godly life" or "going to heaven"? Are you "staying busy" being a good "citizen" following your leaders and doing what you're told? Or are you doing whatever your priest, church, minister, rabbi, mullah, therapist, psychiatrist, president, prime minister are telling you to do, thinking that this will lead you to some "heaven"? Are you sure? What if they're misguided and just feeding you the pabulum, the syrupy sweet lies that offer false "hope" out of this swamp of heartlessness all around you? What if it doesn't get any better on the "other side"? What if the energy that is in you goes with you to "heaven"? What if the energy that is attached to your soul becomes more powerful on the other side because you cannot pretend it isn't there any more? What if that is what people call 'hell'? What if Jesus is correct when he says *"What ye bind on Earth Ye bind in Heaven, What ye loose on Earth, Ye loose in Heaven."*?

You can't be successful at this Game

No matter what you do

Do you really think that raising "good" "successful" children is the "Game"? Think about it for a minute. Do you really think creating more slaves, more cattle, and more sheeple for the loveless machinery that passes for "civilization" is an honorable goal? Those children may end up hating that you brought them into this soul-slavery system. They may turn on you. That is already happening in increasing numbers today. Why? What's going on?

Or is the goal to find a "soul mate" to find "True Love"? Do you really think that you will find a psychologically healthy, "together", successful, loving, romantic, fun, partner that will love you "forever and ever"? In personals 85% of women are looking for a 'financially and emotionally stable' man. Do you think they exist out there as products of our current civilization? Would you get on an airline where 67% of the millions of flights that take off each year crash and burn? 7 out of 10 crash to the ground and burn. Would you get on this airline's planes? Then why do you go into a marriage thinking that it will be the exception and not "crash and burn" when it's a fact that 7 out of 10 marriages end in divorce. And divorce really is a "crash and burn" of your emotions and your heart. These are harsh wake up calls. But there is no other way when the people are "stiff necked", dogged, inveterate, determined, mad, insane, blind. This is how we create "pit bull marriages" where the wife and husband become like two poor dogs thrown into a pit in the ground to fight to the death. No one taught us how to communicate, how to open our heart, how to feel, how to love. How to resolve issues, how to work through what we see reflected back at us from the other person. Why did our schools not teach How to Open your Heart 101? Or How to deal with past issues and not project them on your partner 202? How to Honestly Communicate 303? How to Open to God-Spirit-Love 404?

The System is Irretrievably Broken!

Are we this blind that we stick our heads in the sand like the ostrich and don't want to see the facts? It is over, the horse is dead, it is not getting up, and it will take us no further. Trying to save this civilizational system, this current paradigm, our patriarchal family system really is like rearranging the deck chairs on the Titanic.

So, now do you think the answer lies in retreating from the world, joining some religious cult living in the mountains storing guns in the basement and waiting for Armageddon? Or in retreating inside your mind and meditating everyday, chanting ancient mantras, saying the "magic secret words" and this will somehow magically transform you? Or just toughing it out, "making the best of it" and plodding on with a plastic smile plastered on your face and avoiding looking at what really is going on? Or staying busy with your manic 'hobbies', or 'volunteering'. Or collecting 'memorabilia'-- all the Coke cans that ever were produced, all the Hummel figurines, the airplane models, the cars, the coins, the stamps, the....whatever. That's nothing more than Obsessive Compulsive Disorder of the Categorizing Mind desperately trying to keep you busy and not look inside yourself.

You Can't Bomb your Way back to the Garden of Eden

Or do you think that bombing the imagined "enemy" and obliterating "them" the "evil ones" will somehow bring Paradise back to earth? Do you think that suppressing how you really feel, becoming hard, emotionally cold, "tough" will somehow bring the Kingdom of God back on earth? Do you think that having more and more Police, Firefighters, Doctors, prescription drugs, Lawyers, CIA's, FBI's, DIA's, NSA's, NRO's, Tri- Lateral Commissions, United Nations, World Banks, World Courts, Offices of Homeland Security, Metal Detectors, Judges, Laws, regulations, controls everywhere etc. etc. will somehow bring the Garden of Eden back to earth?

Do you really think we can bomb our way back to the Garden of Eden?

Only the most blinded think this is the way.

And if you think you can, you are living in denial. There is no other way to say it. You are free to live in denial but you will most likely be creating some really hard, shocking 'wake up calls'. And I don't want to be standing close to you when you get those wake up calls from God.

Things like out of control viruses, all kinds of cancers and diseases, school shootings, earthquakes, disastrous weather, terrorist bombings, war, nuclear explosions, financial collapses of the world economic system etc.

Still...

There is a way to wake up.

Real God is waiting for you to ask how.

21.   "I Am not Opposed"

"I am not opposed", were the words I heard inside me this morning.

"I am not opposed...to anything." And in a flash I saw a whole scenario of how energy moves or how it gets stopped and dissipated. I saw how water is a perfect example of not opposing anything, of how not to be against anything, how not to fight anything, how not to struggle, work, effort...but to flow, to relax, to enjoy the movement itself, the changing scenery passing by.

What I resist Persists...

I saw how when I oppose something, when I fight something, that friction occurs. I set something up against whatever is presenting itself. Like two metal plates. Then the two sides rub against each other and "heat" occurs, and the energy is dissipated, lost. "Heat" of the Mind occurs. Heat of thinking, of strategy, of arguing, of trying to convince, of trying to change, trying to push. And if the other person has no intention of hearing, changing, being open, then the heat is wasted, the energy goes nowhere. It just wears both sides down and energy is lost.

...And What I Embrace I Erase.

I saw how water moves around the rocks, over the riverbed, around the bend. It is absolutely liquid, soft, silky, smooth. It doesn't stop and fight the rocks. It glides over and around them, it caresses them, leaves a gentle touch, and continues on its journey. Water is unstoppable. It will find its way back to the ocean. A dam just temporarily holds some of it back; there is still a constant flow of water out of the dam. Or if it is completely stopped it will flow over the top and continue on its way. Or evaporate, "ascend". The water "ascends" into the air, rises up, gets airborne, light, and moves on, collecting later to "fall" back to earth somewhere else on another journey. And it stays impenetrable and indestructible. You can't penetrate water. No matter how small you make it, it stays together. It still stays water. If you boil it, it just evaporates and actually gets purified in the process, and collects somewhere else. Boiling the water dissipates all the "impurities" that have gotten mixed in with the water. As I'm writing this, a rain has started. It doesn't rain that much here in Phoenix, but now there is a heavy downpour. I can feel shivers running up and down in my body; I can feel the cleansing the rain brings. I can feel years of resisting rain, when I lived in different climates where rain signified cold, dull, gray days. Wet, damp, something to fight against days. I don't feel that now. Here in Phoenix people fight the heat. I have found that when I relax into this "allowing" space of not fighting, not opposing anything that the physical heat here in Phoenix (110 degrees) is no problem. I actually feel a physical cooling coming from my center in my solar plexus and then the heat doesn't drain me or make me uncomfortable. And in the cold, this same center in my solar plexus warms me.

"I am not opposed...to anything", I heard Love tell me. And I saw how when not being opposed to anything, not fighting anything, that this Love is freed up to move everywhere and anywhere. It was free, it was liquid, like the water, and was unstoppable, could move everywhere and "dissolve", vaporize when it needed to get free of a situation. I saw how not opposing anything allows those things that present themselves in our lives to move, to not get stuck. We assist those things, or people, that set themselves against us, by being liquid and not opposing them back. They then have nothing to fight, no "heat" develops. People who want this "friction" in their lives will move on and find others engaged in the same game. You will not appear on their radar screen when you stop opposing them. You will be free to move on, move like the liquid water. The water does not curse the rocks in the stream bed and tell them to be different than they are or to *"get the hell out of the way buddy!"* No, the water simply glides around the rocks with a soft caress and leaves its soft imprint.

"I am not opposed". I also heard it as God/Love saying that S/He finds no-one, no-where, no-thing opposing Him-Her. Everywhere God goes S/He is not opposed because there is nothing in God that opposes the Creation. The creation simply Is, whatever it is. God simply says yes, simply embraces whatever presents itself. *"What you embrace you erase, what you resist persists"*.

My Yang Merges with your Yin!

Opposed...Oppo-sites...opposing creates the game of opposites. Without opposing you can play beyond the duality, beyond the yin and yang. This is the space of miracles, this is where you and your partner can't remember what you were fighting about and you fall on the floor laughing. This is where there is miraculously money showing up from "now-here", this is where you don't have gas in the car yet travel 200 miles somehow, this is where people who are suing you mysteriously fade away, this is where that leak from under your car stops, this is where people call you because they saw your website that you don't have, this is where your angels can give to you, this is where you feel safe to love others, this is where you walk in the worlds of big money and feel completely free, this is where you and God can start to play with each other again.

22.   "Appreciating" Nature
A Message from Mother Earth

After a day by Oak Creek in Sedona, Arizona sitting in a chair with my feet in the water, hopping on the rocks, sharing blackberries with a skunk, swimming, I received a message from what felt like Mother Earth herself about an easy way to heal ourselves and the planet.

The word Appreciate according to Webster's new universal unabridged dictionary means:

1. *to value, to esteem...*
2. *to recognize gratefully...*
3. *to increase the price...*
4. *to be fully or sensitively aware...*

Shamanic "Gazing"

Shamans use a technique called "gazing" to expand them and connect with deeper aspects of the world around us. This happens naturally whenever we slow down and enter the *"Be still and know that I am God"* space. Most of us naturally do this as kids, often while playing in nature, when we get absorbed in something that fully captures our attention and we become one with it, merge with it. Patanjali, the 11th century Indian mystic – saint in his sutras called this "making samyama" on an object , to become one – merged with something and yogic powers would then open up with this perfect attention – merging.

 As I sat and de-focused my attention while looking at the stream, I "saw" how when we love-"appreciate"-feel gratitude for Nature, we actually lift it up. Our love-gratitude-appreciation energy actually infuses the plants, rocks, water, the very air around us. We feed them with our Love (God's Love). We are the God seeds, we are the "made in God's image" creatures that can be the vehicles for Divine energy.

> *"The seed of God is in us...Pear seeds grow into pear trees,*
> *hazel seeds into hazel trees,*
> *and God seeds into God."*
> --Meister Eckhardt

The plants, rocks, water around us get "excited" by our love. The same way an electron gets excited by heat energy and speeds up. Love is the highest energy form in the created universe, it excites everything. The plants, rocks, water, the air – subtle ether feed off of our Love, they want to play with us, they want to share, dance, exchange energy with us. When we give them our attention they notice, when we give them our love they dance. And then they automatically want to give back to us in the form(s) of beauty they create.

Nature is the most chaotic, rambunctious, dis-organized system there is. Look at the fallen logs, the leaves, the "dirt", the plants trying to grow through rocks, the rains washing "away" the earth etc. Yet there is a perfect Order running through-out all of it. We instinctively are awed by Nature's grandeur and beauty. We feel the majesty of the creative force just behind the vista of Nature.

Mother Earth said to me:

"There is no 'work' involved with 'appreciating' Me. Just come out into my spaces and Love me, enjoy me, drink me, breathe me, sense me. It will fill you back up. And you will 'save' Me as well. Your Love for the trees, the streams, the rocks, the animals will feed them and keep them safe. Your appreciation of me will 'appreciate' me, will lift me up in vibratory rate, will strengthen me and I will be able to give you my beauty and love back."

Later I found a quote by Albert Einstein that seemed fitting.

"One feels as if one is dissolved, merged into Nature"

Albert Einstein

23.   "Refreshing" New Approach

"When one does the next and most necessary thing
without fuss and with conviction, one always does
what is meaningful and intended by fate."
--Carl Jung

When you are surfing the Internet do you use that "refresh" icon on the top of your computer ever? Some people don't. It "refreshes" a page, updates whatever you happen to be looking at, it brings in what is current in the moment, keeps you in the here and now, keeps you from making decisions on old information, let's you start afresh again.

You can do this at any time, anywhere, any moment with your own life. You can "refresh" all your mental constructs, all your memories, all your beliefs, all your ideas, all your identities, who you think you are.

You can enter the timeless Now, right here and now, every moment after every moment...it keeps coming. It is...always available...here and now...and again...and again.   This is a chance, a gift that is continually there...always...will never go away. You can choose to "clear the slate", "become like a little child", have a new, simple, "refreshed" approach to seeing – experiencing the creation around you and within you.

Moment by Moment

 Just feel that idea for a Moment (or two or three or...), that there is a limitless supply of Moments for you to "refresh" your self, to wake up more fully to all of You. There is no "hurry, hurry, hurry, while supplies last..." with this Gift from God – Universe – Your Self – Higher Intelligence – Love – Play – Fun. If you can let this idea into your self deeply, it will automatically start to dissolve many ideas and subconscious programs that make you stressed, worried, hurried, fearful, resentful, angry, unhappy, nervous etc. It is a seed that dissolves and clears the old fearful scarcity programming into a peaceful, faithful, confident, allowing, relaxed, joyful experiencing of the creation.

 Right Now just take a Moment and allow this idea of being able to "refresh" your Self at any moment into your self, into your belief structure. Sow this seed – idea deeply into your self and it will do its freeing work automatically, almost unseen. And you will find that over "time" you will live more refreshed in the Moment(s) that unfold for you.

 If you didn't do it...may I suggest that you go back and do it. It only takes a moment.

 Let the idea of being able to "refresh your self at any moment, instantly" into your deepest idea center, into your self.

The Seed of Awakening

Why not do it? It's free; you didn't have to pay anything. On second thought if you send me $100 it may work better for you, since many of us believe that things are more valuable if they cost something. I am totally OK with that idea. ('Twinkle' ☺) I give this to you however you would like to receive it.   It could be worth it for some of us to "sow the seed" with money, because then we will "get something for our money" and you will sow this Seed of Awakening more deeply into your self. It is completely up to you. It always is.

Let the idea that there is available an unending supply of Moments inside of the creation of "time" to help you back out of the idea of "time". You created time and it has always in it the seed of un-creating it, dissolving back into the Eternal Now, the "I am that I am." You can't get away from it, because you are it. If you didn't have "it" you wouldn't be here, you couldn't be here. Life only exists if it was created from the place of Eternity.

Many masters have talked about this "brand newing", being "born again", living without the past or future, right here in the Now. Some of us have "woken up" instantly in one moment of time. This of course is possible because once you enter the timeless space you have all the time in the world to wake up! So what appears as only a moment here inside of time could have been a 1000 years in the timeless space. Einstein pointed out that this relativity of time is real for us right here and now in the physical scientific model of creation.

"Refresh" your self...today. Now.

24. **Gods in Birth**

Our Upside Down World

A friend was just over using the computer to draft an invitation to spend a week with a woman who has melted back into the Oneness of All Life. This woman spent seven years in a black hole, the "dark night of the soul". Her family viewed her as insane, the clinical community (clinical, they don't want to get their emotional bodies dirty!) probably viewed her as manic-depressive, schizophrenic, etc. Well, after her puking up her repressed "dirty", "antisocial", "evil", "bad" etc. emotional shadow self, she is now healed. She stopped identifying with her old body, old identities, and old patterns. In fact all concepts, beliefs, patterns were wiped out. It took her years to re-program herself enough to be able to relate to our "upside down" world as she calls it. Now people gather around her and she tries to help them "wake up".

Healing the Eon Implants

Because of the heavy denial and repression of our emotional bodies, of any raw direct feelings, never mind the "dark" feelings being openly expressed, we never get to see a being in the process of cleansing, of waking up. It's too terrifying, unsettling, scary a sight/experience so that this process has had to have been done in private, behind closed doors, in caves, or the individual waking up usually ended up being killed, or incarcerated as insane. So we never get to see the process of a soul awakening to who they really are, the puking up the garbage, the emotional jerkiness as the emotional body vibrates out its literal demons, its old prison beliefs from its magnetic field. And we don't want to see it or be around for it because it "unsettles" us from our static behavior patterns. It terrifies us when someone is feeling anything real. We only get to see the enlightened "end product". And then we go sit with them because we enjoy the power, the clean energy, and the love that radiates from an awakened god-being. We think this "darshan" (Sanskrit for seeing-being in the presence of an enlightened person) will wake us up. Usually it doesn't, we turn on our masters, we drift away after we hit "the wall" and realize that to really wake up *We* will have to walk the walk through the Valley of the Shadow of Death, *We* will have to travel across the river Styx. *We* will have to go down inside our own psyches and heal the eon implants. It's too terrifying, some deep-seated avoidance program triggers us, possesses us and we're off on some manic creation for another thousand lifetimes. Sometimes it scares us so much that we label the awakened one "evil", "the devil" and occasionally we make it our mission to save others form this "evil" one, so we turn on them, the Judas Syndrome.

Get away from it All! The Ultimate Travel adventure!

Come visit the Abyss of Hopelessness & the Gates of Madness!

Show the pictures to all your friends when you get back!

It is time that this "waking up" process in all its glory and ugliness is seen so that we can see the "human" side as it is waking up and becoming the "endproduct"- a god. When we only see the finished "product", our minds will tell us things like—"they are different than me", "they're here on assignment from God", "they had better karma than me", etc. The Mind will have a thousand reasons why they could wake up and you can't. We are comparing ourselves with them as they are now, even if we're not doing it consciously, subconsciously our minds compare, store the information and use it to give us reasons why we cannot do what they did. Usually the reason is because somehow they were "different" in some way from us. We didn't see them when they wanted to kill themselves for months on end, when they were paranoid that the whole universe was out to get them, when they reached the Abyss of Hopelessness, when the Gates of Madness almost overtook them, when they laughed hysterically at the cosmic joke (they still do after they've woken up, they just keep a nice polite social profile so as not to scare us away). We weren't there when they talked to their cat, and the cat talked back! When the energies raced through their bodies, when they had physical "boiling out" of stuck energies. No, we are seeing the polished final end product. And the "endproduct" is seeing us in our pristine state and can't understand sometimes why we don't just all say "uncle, the emperor has no clothes!" just quit this absurd denial game we're all playing and all wake up. The awake one is guided by the Heart of Life to not threaten us, to not shake us up too much unless they have our permission. They walk tenderly around us because we are so emotionally scar(r)ed that they will send us into overwhelm with practically the slightest "truth telling", pointing out where our subconscious programming has us enslaved, which our egos will immediately use for fodder that we're being "attacked", or that this being is "evil", "in league with the devil" etc.

Moths around the Flame

So we hover around this "enlightened" one, (they're not "enlightened", they're just normal! the way we originally planned to be) but we're not ready to take the plunge, to go for total wake up. And that's good, because we must choose when to do it. We have free will, not even God Manifest knows when we'll decide to wake up. That keeps it interesting for Him too. God in the Absolute does know since it-her-him is outside of time-space-creation.

"Waking up" is the easiest thing we'll ever do...and the hardest. How many times have you heard that? It's still true. You know what's required—to simply open, hear, listen, follow, do, be in the moment, face the fears, allow Love in, hang in there, trust, and sooner than you think you're home, back with God, healthy, awake, enlightened again.

If a few of us could -would be willing to be seen doing this waking up process it wouldn't be this mysterious, (mystical) process anymore. It would be a homecoming to letting our emotional body take its rightful place as co-creator with our spiritual body, merged and guided by Heart-Love. But the emotional body needs to clear itself of all the repression, pain, shackles, rules, that it's been subjected to so that we can see what the emotional body really is in its Free state. It will turn out to be our savior, our power. As usual the opposite of what the programming mind has been telling us will turn out to be true; instead of having to "rise above it" it will be the merging back with our emotional body that will be our enlightenment.

~Section Three~

25.   **Rebels With a Cause**

We are rebels because we know there's something wrong and we can't stand for it. We will not succumb to the slavery of the soul that has been pushed on Earth for the last remembered history.

The Cause is to explode the stuck, imprisoned, drained, hopeless, confused, reality that is currently holding the Earth and its Free Will spirits in a straitjacket.

Look at what is acceptable behavior, acceptable emotional expression currently. Practically nothing compared to the unfolded, fully vibrating human being. The emotions that are socially acceptable to express are like the visible light spectrum on the electromagnetic spectrum, a small sliver of the whole, like a discordant bow dragged across a broken violin compared to a whole synergistic orchestra reaching a crescendo orgasm, exploding with free energy and joy. All this energy, this emotional energy expression that we don't have anymore has been siphoned off, "lost" somewhere. It needs to be recovered one by one. You need your energy back so you can participate in Life again. We are sleepwalking automatons, "the living dead", we are zombies compared to what we intended to be. Why? Because we have bought the lies about limitation, about right and wrong. We are straitjacketed, chained, throttled, muzzled, shackled Gods.

Rules, regulations, codes of "acceptable & unacceptable" behavior, the "knowledge of good and evil" i.e. judgments of what's OK and not, are the things that imprison human behavior.

There are no rules! You are the Law!

Except to stay in touch with your heart-God-Love and follow the inner impulses. Whatever you want to explore is OK.

An attuned Being, one who is in touch with their essence is the Law!

"The whole of the Law is Love" Jesus says. You are the "Law" when you've reconnected with Love in your heart. You won't need outer policemen when you're back in touch with the Source of Life. We have accepted, been talked into these imprisoning rules. Guilt has convinced us that we can't trust our inner voice, the Voice of God. Something con-vinced us a long time ago that the voice of the real God was our "sinful nature" and ever since it's been downhill. We have been losing essence and energy ever since we abdicated our throne in our hearts and quit listening and following the "inner voice". We have been listening instead to God – imitators, Guilt in particular, often called a "conscience", con-science, we are conned by science, conned by the logical mind. We started out as pretty aware and awake powerful beings. We could change forms at will, we had no need for language, we communicated directly with one another, we were in touch with the nature spirits, the Devic Kingdoms, we could see and hear several dimensions, we didn't have the need for "possessions", we didn't need to work for our living-surviving. We were children of God and received our sustenance directly

from the source of all Life. Look where we are now, where it has gotten us, this listening to the Mind, Guilt and Fear. We are burdened, stressed out, unhappy, psychotic, possessed, untrusting, manic, fear based, survival driven monsters! We fuck each other over at almost every chance, it's practically all constant strife with one another, if not all out physical warfare, at least with lawyers or mind games. We are always warring with each other, "I'm gonna win, win, win. I'm gonna beat you, get your $, your position, your man/woman, I will be better than you!" We "live" our lives without joy constantly being pressed for survival...and then we die! Wow, that's a lot of fun.

We've *"Paved Paradise and put up a Wal-Mart!"*

This is what we've created of the Garden of Eden. Pretty horrible don't you think? Do you think when God created the Earth S/He intended for us to take Prozac, Viagra, Lipitor, Halcyon, etc.., and stress about our 401K's? Do you think God said "Let there be Life Insurance, Let there be Alzheimer's, Let there be cubicles full of people in front of machines"...etc... It's ludicrous when you stop and think about it for a minute.

I Rebel! I call on Mother Earth and Father God to undo this choking web of death that has infested our planet. I will do my part to heal myself first. To undo-clear the guilt and fear in my own being. I will also be "wise as serpents and gentle as doves". I will not always let this be known when my heart tells me that it is not safe, when I'm faced with those that are bent on the destruction, draining of the Life Force from this planet. When I am faced with the ones promoting fear, guilt, control I will follow the still small voice of Love, and it will protect me. And when I need to I will trust the Impulse of Life when I need to reclaim my power to protect myself. I realize that guilt and fear have most of the power on Earth right now and shouting from the rooftops that you're going to undo the whole of "civilization" will probably attract some undue attention from vested interests. I am talking about an inner revolution first and then the outer changes automatically, easily, peacefully follow.

Do you want your planet back? Is that enough of a cause for you?

To be willing to rebel against this not feeling, this not expressing, this not living? Uncle, the Emperors have no Clue! I will listen to my own inner voice and yes I won't be "normal", I won't be one of the sleepwalking dead. It won't be easy always, but so what?

The Cults of the Funny Hats

You only need to start in your own heart. There is nothing to join, no organizations you need to be a member of, no funny hats to wear. Have

104

you ever noticed that most cults really are into wearing funny hats? Notice the military, the churches, the legions, etc. The bigger the funny hat the stronger the cult. You don't need to take up arms. You especially don't need to follow leaders any more; it's time for direct access to God in your heart. Get in touch with the Inner Voice and start following it as you're able. Start seeing where your energy is being drained off and start taking it back. Learn to say NO. Get a T-shirt that says "What part of NO don't you understand?" See where guilt and "shoulds" are making you do things you don't want to do. Anytime you do something you don't really want to do but think you must do you are feeding this false hypocritical reality on Earth. You starting to live as you really want will do more to undo the controllers of the earth at this time than all the "politically correct" or worse "spiritually correct" legislation you could ever get passed into laws. Because as we all know—laws don't work.

"The more numerous the laws the more corrupt the state" –Tacitus, c .AD 55-c.AD 117, Roman historian

And remember you are not alone, millions of us feel like this. Just because it's not the main model of what is talked about on TV yet doesn't mean that its not there. It's rising up everywhere. In fact we are becoming the majority. In recent studies "Cultural Creatives" those who don't buy into the old system, the programmed economic slavery robot system, are actually the majority! We are 65 million strong in the US alone. We just haven't learned to see through the outer yet and we still judge and categorize each other. Start talking to people and you'll realize that most people are sick of the old system and ready for this Awakening of their Souls.

"...And the Waters Shall Boil..."

Mama Earth will Shake, Rattle and Roll

The Earth is about to go through a major clearing, clean up, healing process. It is already beginning.

When the female aspect of the Creator wants to heal itself, it magnetically vibrates so that the poisons and unwanted energies She has absorbed, 'been willing to carry' rise to the surface, come out, bubble up.

The Earth's magnetic field has been poisoned, infused, injected with vibrational energies for a long time now. There has been a "toxic buildup" going on for hundreds of thousands of years, ever since "The Fall".

We've left our Ghost Bits behind

Just about every time the original "gods" of Earth (that is us) have been leaving our bodies we have been leaving essence, bits of our beings behind. These "bits" "lost energy fragments" are left behind as we ascend into our "heaven". Eventually the magnetic pull of these left behind pieces pulls us back into a new body. Some lifetimes we merge back, heal, re-integrate with some lost pieces of ourselves but generally it has been an overall loss of wholeness, a slowing down of energy, losing essence that has been going on for as long as we can remember.

The Earth has decided that She does not want to be the receptacle, holder of all this psychic "garbage". These pieces of lost essence, "garbage", rejected energies, oftentimes are called "ghosts" on earth. They are trapped emotional energies we re-fused to experience when they first happened so we left them trapped on earth. Now the planet does not want to continue to hold these energies, "their blood cries out from the very ground", these energies will seek their "home" i.e. go back to the beings who originated them. In other words all our "crap" that we've been avoiding and denying is going to come back to us to be healed, to be taken back in, the prodigal sons and daughters. And if we don't receive them we will not be able to stay in or on the Earth's magnetic field. The planet has willed to be healed, cleared, and cleansed of these discordant, abandoned soul energy fragments.

To do this the planet will vibrate its magnetic fields, shudder, shake, rock and roll, in order to vibrate out these stuck, static energies. These energies are going off the planet to other planets and magnetic matrixes in space that will allow them more time to heal themselves. But the "parents" of these denied energy essences will be going with them. We won't be able to "rise above" them anymore. The "Division Bell" has rung.

The Law of Karma has been repealed!

There is Grace, and God and Mother Earth will help all who are sincere in healing. It has more to do with intention, openness and sincere willingness than anything else. We are so far gone karmically that the "law of Karma" has basically been repealed for those sincere about healing. This is the Law of Forgiveness that Jesus talked about. We can't fake it this time; the intuitive Mother Earth and Father God know our hearts, not all our words, our manipulations, false presentations. They see our hearts. They would like us to make a choice for awakening, either now or for later. Either choice is fine. There is no judgment of us if we feel overwhelmed, not ready at this time to deal with all our lost energy fragments, our suppressed feelings, our accumulated "sins"-karma. That's OK. But a choice would help so we can get the show on the road. Father God and Mother Earth would like a conscious choice. Most of us haven't wanted to look at or think about what is happening on the planet yet. Not choosing is a choice, it is choosing avoidance and those of us who don't want to wake up, open up, feel again, get real, be honest, merge our polarities, will be "relocated".

In this "vibrating out" that Earth will be doing, *the seas will boil*, literally. When stuck psychic energies are let loose, when the "7 seals" the book of Revelation talks about are broken, these stuck emotional psychic fragments-ghosts will be reanimated. The reason we've called it "hell" is that we were so scared by, or have so judged these repressed experiences, emotional states of ourselves that we broke off from them. We said this couldn't possibly be part of me so I will send it "to the ends of the universe"; we cast these emotional "things" away from us into "hell". Well they need to be reclaimed and healed now. They will leave the magnetic field of this planet one way or another, through healing or violent upheaval, madness, plagues, pestilence, war, diseases, etc. Not a pretty picture. You may think me alarmist. I'm not. I'm offering a suggestion to consciously decide and get on with it.

Our animals will clear themselves

Many animals that have been abused by humans will seem to turn on their masters as this "boiling out" starts to happen. Seemingly docile and gentle domesticated animals will need to clear their energy bodies also. We have so poisoned the earth that large magnetic shudders will cause earthquakes, volcanoes and a general rearranging of the land masses. When you "clarify" butter, boil butter, the black impurities rise to the surface as it bubbles and boils.

The Energy Body Flu

We shall "boil" also. Our bodies will need to heal themselves. Modern "medicine" is almost completely about suppressing symptoms, not letting the body shudder and "boil" to clear out its impurities. We give our bodies anti-biotics (anti bio = anti life!) to make it "be quiet". We don't let the body express, don't let it be heard. So eventually we create cancers. Cancer is a vibrational misalignment, a "psychic sore" at points where the

107

energy body attaches to the physical. Modern medicine if it insists on its current approach will never find a cure for cancer until the medical doctors heal themselves first and let in and are able to work with the finer soul essence energies. Cancer is a desperate cry for help from our soul – emotional energy body to *"please listen, I am dying a spiritual death here."* You might have to go through some allowing the body to heal itself and not feel a 100% at times. Its been called the "kundalini flu" when your energy body starts coming back to life and starts boiling out all the impurities, psychic, emotional, physical. The best thing to do is to allow. Feel your feelings, allow the energy to move through you. Allow the body to tell you what an "asshole" you've been for not listening to it. Listen to your body; allow the space and time for it to tell you what it needs to. Allow real healing, real aligning back with yourself. The more you can let go into this healing the faster and less painful it will be. Don't push yourself either, let God, your Heart guide the process. Ask for guidance. Ask to be in the Presence, this is the greatest healing bath you can take... and let Love-God the Holy Presence "boil away your trouble."

"I'm dying here!" I screamed out spontaneously. All day this oppression and heat of "hell", these psychic pressures, feelings of oppression had been tormenting me. The feelings were feelings of being trapped, judged, cast out, no heart, no love to save me, cut off from God, no rescue in sight, no relief, no shade from the oppressive heat, I couldn't breathe, I couldn't receive nourishment from water to slake my burning thirst, my hunger had been a constant ache for so long I hardly noticed anymore. I felt like I was going crazy, like I was about to be ripped apart under the psychic pressure, torment afflicting me.

The Automatic Somatic

I'm driving a limo in Phoenix, Arizona, because I have been caught under the yoke of the Fallen Man, *"In toil shalt thou earn thy bread"*, a prisoner of this Soul Slavery that has been instituted on Earth for the last 300,000 years. I drive in a zombie like state by rote, with my dark sunglasses hiding my real being. I know all the questions that the programmed meat I haul around are going to ask, a thousand repeated earthling dead questions, automatic somatic inquiries into the level of my capitulation, the extent of my soul surrender to the economic and emotional slavery that rules the earth's in-habit-ants because knowing I'm also a capitulated slave makes them feel comfortable knowing I'm one of the dead just like them.

"So have you always lived here?"

(No, I'm from Arcturus and we're going to explode your sleepwalking reality here in a few years, how do you feel about that?)

"Wow, that's quite a difference from Connecticut."

(Look, it all feels the same to me wherever you are inside this dead collective consciousness.)

"You must like it here then."

(I can't fucking wait to have this "civilization" crumble and Innocence return to Earth so I can go home.)

"Is it always this hot here?"

(It's going to get so fucking hot here in a few years lady that you will wish you were dead, read your shrouded book the "Bible" Revelations in particular, and it will give you a hint.)

"How hot does it get in the summer? It's a very clean city Scottsdale."

(Yeah, earthlings have developed a program of keeping all the "dirt" on the other side of town, "out of sight out of mind", so you don't have to think about the 'dirt' as it represents the subconscious, repressed parts of your own consciousness.")

Blah, blah, blah.

These are the "successful" people in our society! From five star resorts, the leaders of the business community in the U.S., their endless drivel, their politicking about petty power/control within their company, "living to die, dying to live". Their "portfolios" of (in)security-ies. Keeping up with the latest corporate gossip.

Puke! Is this how predictable people are on this fucking planet? Have they all been programmed to ask the same idiotic questions? What happened to spontaneous heart? Does anyone think for themselves anymore? Is anyone not ruled by fear and economic programming?

Lost Pieces of our Souls

IT'S MY SOUL DYING HERE! Something inside me screams out after I've gotten the latest cattle out of the limo at the airport, ("leaders" of the western world, photobiology expert scientists killing the planet with their surgical laser death instruments) I can't contain it anymore, "I'M DYING HERE!" My soul screams out. Suddenly my consciousness is transported to the dying camps in Zaire, Africa! So this is what I've been feeling? These dying lost parts of ourselves. These are the lost parts of our souls that we don't feed, these are the magnetic feeling parts of our being that we have rejected and sent to the ends of the earth, to the darkest most far away place we can think of, and these are the "damned", the dying inner souls of our lost aliveness. Every goddamn "successful" white, mental, suppressed, heartless, denial of their emotions based asshole I drive around in my limo has sacrificed that part of themselves that is dying over there in Rwanda - Zaire!

Cleanliness becomes antiseptic Death

"I'M DYING HERE!" I can't help but feel thousands of lost bits of soul so far gone, so oppressed, not nourished, choking on the dust, dying in the filth, the "garbage" that we've rejected from our antiseptic, 99 44/100 % pure society, our obsession with cleanliness, our rejection of the body, of "unclean" feelings, our need for "perfect" bodies, souls. *"Oh, Lord antisepticise my soul, Oh give me the consecrated wafer of an antiseptic soul"* we cry out in America and our "dirty" "black" feelings are dying en masse over there on a distant continent. We don't want to know about it. Just send some "politically correct" money over there to get rid of the nagging guilt voices we hear. Or better yet, sanitize the CNN broadcasts and don't show this "ugliness" on TV, it will only stir up the population and depress us. Besides everyone "creates their own reality" don't they? And in the cosmic scope of things it's only "survival of the fittest" and cleansing of the weak, right? Just as it should be.

WE ARE ALL ONE! THOSE ARE PARTS OF OUR SELVES DYING OVER THERE! OUR ESSENTIAL SELVES, OUR SOULS! OUR FEELING BODIES!

Sending money and temporary relief is not helpful if we don't deal with the underlying problem. The relief organizations make money; we displace whole towns and villages and get them to move to the "handout" stations. We addict them to aid. And next time the catastrophe hits it's many times worse. And imposing our "solutions", our way of doing things in the West, our technology doesn't help, it hurts! WE need to feel exactly where they are at, not look at it through our perspective, and allow situation specific help. For example solar technology that pumps local water, not building huge dams and canals, hydroelectric power stations that upset the local ecology, diverting water and displacing people.

Most of all we need to FEEL

"Feeling is for(e)most

A Terrifying thing,

Yet it's the only Place

Where both God and Human can sing."

From Shackled Gods Uni-Verse by Tobias Lars

But most of all we need to FEEL, feel these beings, these parts of ourselves, of the Human Family, allow real interaction, so that real evolution, more power through hybridization, melding of energies can occur. We have to be willing to let go of our sanitized world view, thinking that our way of being is appropriate everywhere. The RonaLokan spirits incarnate in Africa also need to let go of old systems and allow, be honest with their fears of "the white devils" and then we need to communicate this to/with each other and allow the transformation, the paradigm shift and the stronger new model of Humanity will be able to emerge.

Feel in your emotional body your reaction to their situation, the poverty, the superstitions, the "baseness", whatever your judgments are. This allowing back into our soul these lost pieces now hungering for our attention is the quickest route to catalyzing real healing on the planet. Let them feed again at the Source of Life.

(A good rant always feels good.)

28.   Desire is G o(o)d

Desire is God

Desire is God. Desire itself is not the problem. Desire is God's impulse wanting to ex-press, push out, explore, experience. It is our attachments to specific forms, scenarios and trying to keep them static that causes the pain. Because Life, the Tao, the Flow of the Life Force of the Universe moves on, has a timing of its own and it is when we try to divert, contain, force, stop this flow of Life that we feel pain. The Essence of the form leaves, it moves on to its next place, like when B.B. King sings "The thrill is Gone". We are left with an empty husk, the empty robe of the master, if we cling to the specific form or expression it took. All is God. God expresses in every imaginable form.

The Old Teachings are over

The Indian and Buddhist spiritual traditions have often labeled "desire" the problem. Desire, meaning wanting things, wanting $, wanting sex, wanting to have power, craving, wanting, lusting, coveting. Yes, Desire when not in touch with Love, with Heart is unbalanced and never gets satisfied, never fully – fills the desire, *"I can't get no satisfaction"*. But these spiritual traditions often have thrown the baby out with the bathwater (as usual) and labeled all "desire" the problem. Desire is the Life Force! It is the wanting to experience, to explore part of God expressing through you. It is God that animates you; the energy of the Life Force is God, is you! And it wants to explore. It was this wish to experience, explore that called you forth from the belly of God and made you want to be born. God in you wants to feel, to touch, to experience, the Joy at the Dawn of Creation, the surge of new Life, of Spring, of yes, Desire. This is beautiful, this desire for experience is sacred, is God.

The old spiritual teaching says that desires cause suffering because they are endless, will never be fulfilled and thereby trap us in the material creation. The old spiritual teaching tells us in order to become free we must let go of our desires and reach the state of "desirelessness" at which point the Supreme Beloved can enter us and we go back to Oneness. Well this model obviously hasn't worked and millions of souls as usual have been deluded into feeding the priest system with money and energy and what they get in return is guilt that they aren't "spiritual" enough while the churches hoard the wealth of the world. The coffers of the Vatican are filled with unbelievable spoils from religious wars all around the world, more than any museum could ever hope to acquire. As usual a great con job, a give up your personal power for God and we'll manage your money safely so it doesn't tempt you. C'mon, it's time to wake up and go to God directly for ourselves.

A subtle Judgment against Life-Love-God's Plan

Underlying this model of needing to reach "desirelessness" is a real judgment against the Creation, that somehow there is something wrong with enjoying being in the material world. God is the one who had the original thought of wanting to incarnate, make flesh of the Divine and enjoy the physical. And we have the audacity to decide that that is wrong? We know better than the Original Impulse of Love for Creation? It is time to see that the physical is just as much a part of God as the spiritual. There have been problems because of fixation on the polarities—either wanting only physical and that the physical is all there is or disdaining the physical as the "problem" and trying to "ascend" above it and see it all as "Maya" or "illusion". We are both physical and spiritual beings and can't fight either part of ourselves inside the opposite polarity and ever reach some peace. It is now time for the Original Intent of Love to "come" fully into the physical, the Second Coming, the Full Incarnation, and balance the material with the spiritual. In fact melt and merge the whole thing so that there exists no distinction between the "physical" and the "spiritual". It all just becomes God-Energy, Love, Experience, Beingness.

This misunderstanding about physical vs. spiritual, misunderstanding about desire is a perfect example of how the Mind, the Ego, Lucifer uses a central truth and twists it just enough to taint the whole thing yet it retains the "ring of Truth" and whole religions are started to maintain these "truths".

Desire itself is not the problem

In fact it is the exploratory life juice creative force of God. It creates Life!

But it is desires run amok overrunning others free will that is not "right" in a free will universe. Desire not connected to the heart, to love creates discordant unhealthy energy.

Balanced desire is an essential part of the Creation. Without it the creation would cease to exist. There is nothing wrong with wanting to enjoy Life and its bounty. Enjoy bodies, enjoy food, enjoy bubble baths, music, nature, enjoy your emotions, enjoy exploring different ways of being. God delights in this exploration with the one caveat of not overrunning others free will.

So we've labeled our desires wrong. I shouldn't want that, that's not right to have, I should give it away to the church, remain humble. We feel guilt about having lots of wealth and on the other polarity we feel spiritually superior about not being involved in "the ways of the world". Neither is whole nor fulfilling but the balancing with heart, with Love, will heal this split in ourselves.

It's time-- we've had enough experience of separation.

29.   The False "Enlightenment"

Most of those who pass themselves off or let their followers pass them off as "enlightened" are really empty shells that have abandoned or as they like to say "let go", "risen above", "ascended", out of what they call the "lower" emotional body.

The Emotional Body has been labeled the Problem

From almost the very beginning of 'time' here on earth the Emotional Body has been labeled as the problem. We thought, or were convinced by the fallen Angels that the emotions held us back from experiencing the 'heaven' we had envisioned. She, the Mother, the female aspect of God, the emotions, feeling, intuition would nag us with some 'feeling' she had, keeping us from moving forward with out visions.

"There's something off with what you're creating" Mother God would tell Father God. (The Female aspect inside our selves would tell the Male aspect inside our selves is one way to experience it...**and** there is a real manifestation of Father God and Mother God as our parents 'out there' in the Uni-Verse – Song of One...both realities exist. Why not? Source-God creates all that is...not either or – both and more!)

"Well what is it?" He-God, our rational mind self would ask. And She would reply:

"I don't know, it just doesn't feel right."

This would irritate God the Father aspect, the Yang, the male, the outward 'doing' principle of God in the divided creation. And since She, God the Mother, the Yin, the female the magnetic receptive aspect of God in the divided creation didn't express in a 'rational' logical thought process what She felt was wrong, the Father decided that is must be 'all in her head' and 'we'll go ahead with our plans for Creation anyway.'

And here we are...

In a divided, schizoid, creation where the Male and the Female wage the 'war of the sexes' with each other...with the heart, caught in the middle, being hung on the cross to bleed, and in a very real danger of having the whole Earth experiment go down the drain.

Nymphs, Garden Devas, Rock Beings & Wind Dragons

Yes, so now here we are in a twisted creation of 'fallen' divided, schizoid, Jekyll & Hyde, un-wholy beings who are for the most part severely out of touch with their feelings, disconnected from their intuition, with not much joy or power left, addictively-obsessively trying to find nourishment in over eating, over thinking, over working, over exercising, over indulging in media etc. We can't even hear or see the Devic Kingdoms anymore, the Nature Spirits. Can you feel or see the water nymphs, the garden devas, the rock beings, the wind dragons? No, the vast majority of us can't and when our kids do we tell them they're 'imaginary' and that they'd better stop doing it or we'll give them Ritalin or Prozac. We're almost completely out of touch with our Selves and rapidly killing our selves, the animals, plants and Mother Earth.

From the original judgment against the Emotional Body came the model that to reach 'enlightenment' one must successfully 'kill' the 'lower' emotions that we've labeled hatred, envy, greed, lust, anger etc. Or more sophisticated: to 'rise above them', to 'let them go' through 'non attachment' to have 'no judgment' on them.

Ex-communicating parts of our Souls

How do you think a child feels when its parents 'lets it go', lets them loose as they are hanging from a ledge over the bottomless Abyss, we let our grip loose and let them fall into the Pit? *"Good bye sweetheart it is for your own good"* we say as they fall screaming in terror into the black, empty, cold, Void. How would they feel? This is 'loving'? That is what we have all done to those parts of ourselves that we've labeled 'wrong', 'base', 'lower'. We have literally abandoned parts, chunks, bits of our Souls because we labeled them 'bad', 'unspiritual', 'reactive', 'counterproductive', 'lower', etc. So we have 'let them go'. We have sent them to hell, banished them to the ends of the universe with our 'prayers' and 'exorcisms', and much of our spirituality. Is it any wonder that some of these 'orphans', these rejected aspects of our Larger Self are a bit pissed off!? And that they don't exactly trust us anymore because almost all our healing modalities have at their root still a wanting to get rid of these pesky, irritating, 'wrong', 'evil', or again more sophisticated, 'unproductive' feelings?

Every Emotion has its seat at your Round Table

Do you think God the Father and God the Mother or the Absolute Source made a mistake in creating the Emotional Body? Or that certain emotions, feelings like anger, fear, confusion, doubt, guilt have no purpose? Were these emotions created by something other than God? What? The "Devil" to torment us? How ludicrous. Of course ALL emotions have a role, have an important part to play, there was no mistake made as we were originally created. The Emotional Body part of each of us was made for a reason, made perfectly, to protect us, to warn us, to enable us to experience the Creation, to give us the Power to explore the creation. In our emotions lies our real power. For example, guilt and fear are meant to float around the creation so they tell us when we've reached the end of the creation. They're not meant to be inside us and certainly are not meant to run us as they do most beings on earth today. Fear has another role as well, to warn us of unexplored areas, experiential areas we have not yet mastered. It doesn't mean not to go there, but fear is a guidepost, our servant, a 'pay attention' bell. All the *"you have to choose either love or fear"* ultimatums are tricks of the Mind, of Lucifer, of false spirituality with the seed of denial in it, to get you to deny your real feelings. We don't ever have to choose either or --

115

choose both and more! You can always say 'I choose both' or 'I choose neither', '................' Or choose to simply not reply as Jesus did in front of Pontius Pilate.

The Dragon's Breath of Protection

Anger is our protection and having shut down our anger as 'non spiritual' has left us open to being invaded, controlled, soul implanted by those interested in controlling us for their own energy and power gain. Our **conscious** anger will spit out them and the control devices (social & religious programming, schools, TV, etc.) that are implanted in our minds and bodies. Our anger/rage will literally save our very beings. And we've been con-vinced to label our righteous anger/rage 'spiritually incorrect', 'evil', 'lower emotions' etc. We need to wake up and free the Emotional Body so it can merge with our spirits and then we can again function as the whole gods we were originally meant to be and safely explore the Creation without getting trapped in messes like the collective denial we've created on Earth today. I mean look around, is this the Original Intention of God, of Love, of Source, of Divine Intelligence, of Heart that we see around us? Of course not. God-Love-Source did not intend for diseases, killing each other, animals, plants, destruction, war, psychic torture, stress, etc....except as a 'remedial learning program' for us to wake back up. All those things are 'wake up calls' to get us to return to our Selves, to our Hearts, to Love, to God (ness).

"Spiritual Correctness" is worse than Political Correctness

Now it has become 'spiritually correct' to tell these lost parts of our selves that we want them back, now we want 'integration', 'wholeness', we've invited them to 'come out, come out, wherever you are', 'this time I promise I will take you back and we will live together again.' And every time we've promised these lost parts of ourselves that we'll be open and receptive to them, be willing to listen, hear, allow them their role in our Being, we've again betrayed, banished, punished them with 'white magic'. Today we use mental lasers, tronic mind wizardry, NLP programming, hypnosis, fancy mind techniques, visualizations, affirmations, 'prayers' to the 'Light' to try to ray gun them out of existence. These 'lost aspects' of our selves are terrified by now, are damaged in their receptive centers by our 'white light' and many of these 'lost pieces' have vowed not to trust their god (us) again. They are full of rage and rebellion. They are maimed, psychotic, demented, soul damaged bits of essence, because we've made them so! With our warfare with the power of 'light' that we've (m)aimed at them. And then we wonder when these lost, denied, cut off aspects of our self are so denied that they take separate bodies as our children and rage at the mind and soul control in our world by becoming heavy metal musicians, gang bangers, trying desperately to keep the soul control of the Mind machine at bay. We need to wake up and see, be willing to look, to end our denial, our fake glossed over society that is decaying, corroding from within at this very moment. Let's be willing to risk feeling again, get real, get honest, pray for guidance, for real healing, not to the 'Light' of Denial that will narcotize us into altered realities of spaced out, weak, etheric slow deaths. This is the false heaven, the heaven without the 'juice' of emotions.

It's going to take some time to convince these parts of our Self that we are sincere about really healing this time before they trust us again. But there is no way to have this Creation function according to Source's Original Plan without input from the **freed** emotional body, not the enslaved model where you make the emotions do what is 'spiritually correct'. ('Spiritual correctness' is the ultimate tyranny, much worse than political correctness and it is coming big time to earth) The Emotional Body is the power source, the magnetic energy that grounds the Creation, holds it in place. It can not be gone around. It must be brought 'up to speed', and really healed now if we want real healing. The Emotional Body is what gives the Spirit the power to operate in this level of physical density.

Masque-a-rading as Love

But back to 'enlightenment'. If you let yourself feel many of the people that call themselves or willingly let others call them 'enlightened', you'll feel nothing. They are an emptiness, a void ness that they pass off for 'peace'. And onto this 'blank slate' we've been programmed to project our **image**, our golden calf idolatrous **image** of what 'enlightenment' should look like, what our minds are telling us enlightenment should look like. And because most of us have lost touch with our feeling bodies and been programmed by parents-schools-society to not listen to them, we are at the mercy of these vampires of energy, we can't feel them and let our emotional body tell us that they are empty, soulless, dead, energy feeders. And then through their fancy light/intelligence words and using our hope for a lost Eden they in collusion with the Mind (and our minds) have convinced us that this emptiness is 'peace', is 'home' is 'enlightenment', is 'heaven'. It is not peace, it is emptiness at best and often heartlessness that hates the emotional body, hates the Mother of Creation, hates having to have a body and is masquerading as love. It is no feeling, empty eyes of death. Often these people are unaware that this 'enlightenment' that has happened to them is not real filled w Love, filled with Source, filled with Divine Play, filled with God(ness) enlightenment but instead being stripped of their feeling-emotional body, emptied of large parts of their own essence and replaced with a 'light' that is not loving light. They have decided to do this, they have opened themselves to this 'light' and been willing to trade their 'pesky' feelings for the false 'peace' of this enlightenment...just the way British Prime Minister Chamberlain was willing to go into a false agreement with Hitler and a false promise of 'peace' from the unloving light that possessed Hitler. Of course Hitler had no intention of delivering any real 'peace' to Britain. One reflects the other—our inner willingness not to feel, not to sense with our emotional body, in-tuition leaves us vulnerable and open to being 'tricked by the light'.

The Ultimate Bull-Smoke Detector—Your In-Tuition Feeling Emotional Body

117

Our feeling body, our intuition, if we are in touch with it will tell us immediately that they are empty shells that have abandoned their emotional bodies and are passing this off as being enlightened. Of course this isn't true for all teachers but you will need to learn for yourself how to feel them out. Most of them are fooled themselves and believe they have reached 'enlightenment'. Often this 'awakening' experience comes in some real from of 'letting go' and there is some draining of the old programming from the psyche. There may be a real experience of 'dying', of some form of 'light' entering their body...and the person's willingness to do anything to be rid of the emotional pain they are or have been feeling, opens the door to a wholesale 'letting go' of their emotional selves. *Please just take this pain away from me!! I'll do anything!'* a part of them is saying. This 'letting go' provides a 'relief' much the same way cutting off an arm or leg that is diseased will provide relief...but the person is not whole anymore, they can't walk or hug or function fully anymore. We cannot cut off energy parts of our Selves and remain whole beings as originally created.

And Loving Source, God, Divine Effulgence is a filling with Love...with Warmth...with Play...with Fun...with being tickled by Love – Daddy – Mommy... It is Wonder – Full, it is Full(y)-Filling, your Cup will Run Over...and over...and over. Of course...feel it for a moment...don't let the Mind trick you with its hall of mirrors of 'thinking'. Feel this with your 'gut' your intuition-your heart-your Soul, your sensing, your Inner Body.

Would a Source, A Divine Intelligence, God Him or Herself feel bad, painful, stressful, fearful, difficult to you as it was filling you up? Would you feel bad when the energy of Source, Love, God, Heart, Intelligence was reconnecting w/ you? Of course not.

The purging of the old, of the 'dis-ease' yes, as it's leaving doesn't look nice, or always feel nice. There's a 'draining out' of the old stuck energies. But I have even found personally for me and many people I've worked with for healing, that even the 'bad' the 'dis-ease' the old patterns, the fears, the energy of terror, or rage, or doubt, doesn't feel bad when it is being released-healed- re-capitulated-integrated when it is the loving Light of Love-God-Source assisting in the emptying and refilling. Then even the healing-purging-detoxing process feels fine, feels good and certainly when it's done...you feel wonderful, reborn, healed, light, open, clean, clear, happy...because the Source-God-Love that created us is effervescing, effulging, bursting, giving, overflowering, orgasming, feel good energy.

A Personal Note

I have had several lifetimes practicing yoga. I had a personal awakening in this lifetime when I spontaneously recalled the yoga Asanas (positions), stopping of the breath and heart and feeling the kundalini energies release in my body. It happened one night in my dorm room as a freshman at college. I had had no religion in my life, no family churchism, no organized programmed teachings on how to interpret life whatsoever in my life up to that point. I had felt drawn to read the Tao Te Ching and had started feeling God-the Tao-Essence behind Lao Tzu's timeless gateways of simple words. Then one night I came across a book with pictures of Yoga positions. As I

118

saw the positions my body wanted to do them. My body instantly 'knew' how to do the Asanas. As I did the yogic positions it was as if keys were being put into locks in my body and turned. Each position opened gateways- doorways of energy in my body. My body loved it- I felt rushes of energy course through my body, I saw and felt other lifetimes of doing this yoga in caves and with brother renunciants. My heart and breath stopped and I felt myself spin out of the top of my head. For the next 7 years I faithfully would do my yoga- the positions, the breathing, the energy work. This was an undeniable awakening for me as a 19 year old. I am very familiar with the Indian teachings, history, Sanskrit, the Vedas. Babaji, Paramahansa Yogananda, Sai Baba and have been a (several) lifetime student and practitioner of these traditions. 'Advaita' teachings are teachings of 'non duality', all is One, there is no 'other', no 'second'. It is an attempt to place the concept of Oneness before us. Like any other teaching, when the Mind gets a hold of it and uses half truths, then the essence of the teaching often becomes twisted. Because the Advaita concept is so close, the final 'concept' before merging back into Oneness-God-Source it is also particularly subject to false 'understandings' of it's idea. The Mind can never give us 'enlightenment'. The Mind can bring us to the 'end of under-standing' where we take the leap into heart-beingness-Source-God-the Unnameable. The Mind can follow and be part of the true awakening of the Soul, the Heart, the Source, the overflowing of God...but mind understanding is destined to 'stand under' (under- stand) the Heart as a trusted servant to assist in carrying out the Divine Inspirit-ations of Love, of the Heart, of God. The 'rebellion' of the Mind, having the Mind run the show, is the Luciferian rebellion of wanting to leave Love-Christ-Heart behind and create a universe without the 'pesky feeling of the heart' holding it back. It is an attempt at circumventing the Heart-Love-Feelings that is doomed to fail. It is a temporary mort-al non sustaining creation. Getting involved with this way of trying to live will only lead to dead ends, as it should! Thank you God, thank you Heart, for waking us up from false teaching!

'Waking up is Hard to do'?

Here's an excerpt from a self proclaimed 'enlightened' teacher promulgating the 'no pain – no gain' method of painful, stressful, excruciating pain process in order to wake up. These kind of teachings feed the 'no pain-no gain' belief system around enlightenment.

"Here's a simple test. If it's soothing or comforting, if it makes you feel warm and fuzzy; if it's about getting into pleasant emotional or mental states; if it's about peace, love, tranquility, silence or bliss; if it's about a brighter future or a better tomorrow; if it makes you feel good about yourself or boosts your self-esteem, tells you you're okay, tells you everything's just fine the way it is; if it offers to improve, benefit or elevate you, or if it suggests that someone else is better or above you; if it's about belief or faith or worship; if it raises or alters consciousness; if it combats stress or deepens relaxation, or if it's therapeutic or healing, or if it promises happiness or relief from unhappiness, if it's about any of these or similar things, then it's not about waking up. Then it's about living in the dream state, not smashing out of it.

119

On the other hand, if it feels like you're being skinned alive, if it feels like a prolonged evisceration, if you feel your identity unraveling, if it twists you up physically and drains your health and derails your life, if you feel love dying inside you, if it seems like death would be better, then it's probably the process of awakening. That, or a helluva case of gas."

It's so obvious when we see it. 'Love dying' is obviously not of Love-Source-God. This is where having your personal direct connection with your Emotional Body will save your Ass! If you can 'feel' beyond the fancy words-mind wizardry you will likely save yourself spending a lot of time (and money) with cults living in the mountains and storing guns in the basement!

"The Proof is in the Pudding!"

From one side of the dual coin of Awakening, yes it will feel painful, excruciating, de-toxing, like going through addiction withdrawal. Because we are addicted to our old mind programming. But if after your detoxing it does not feel freeing, fulfilling, open, looser, more clear...then it is not a real 'enlightenment' teaching. Re filling with Love, with God, with Source, with your Self will feel GO(O)D! The proof of awakening is in itself. Easy, simple. Stay in touch with how it is feeling for you. Be present. Stay in touch with your Inner Body of sensation-feeling-emotions and if it is feeling clearer, cleaner, more awake, more able to enjoy the world, less judgment, more love...that's the road to real en-Light-enment.

But if you believe that it would be painful, hurtful, excruciating, difficult to reconnect w/ your essence, Source, God, oneness, true enlightenment...then you believe that whatever created this Uni-Verse is at it's root painful, hurtful, excruciating, difficult... You are of course free to believe that...but the reflection you will be creating is not going to be a nice 'wake up call'. You will be fighting your Self, punching your self in the mirror. Of course you have the 'right' and power to do this...and ultimately yes it is a game...a play...of shadows...and you can play any game you want.

The false "Ascension" Schools

Emptiness-Heartlessness-Mind-Lucifer is working through many so called 'enlightened' teachers with his 'Light' and is giving them a false paradise for a season until he is finished with them at which point he takes his light back and they are abandoned like so much husk and they usually drop to earth back into the incarnational cycle they desperately had tried to escape from. The overriding escape wish that 'seekers of the light' often have, that wanting to 'go back home' to their remembered 'heavens', their astral worlds of no gravity, of beautiful instant thought manifestation, pastel colors, 'peace' etc. This escape wish, this wanting to step out of the reincarnational cycle and **being willing** to do anything, sell our soul to go back to our imagined heaven allows The Mind without Heart, i.e. Lucifer to use those of us who are desperate 'homeseekers' and to keep the lie of 'ascending', 'rising above the emotional body' spiritual teaching schools of 'enlightenment' going. These 'ascension schools' usually attract the intellectual, mental, blue and white light spirits, the ones of us that have never 'landed' on Earth, that avoid our emotions at every turn, that want formulas, techniques, methods for 'enlightenment'. We want a clinical, antiseptic, technological, Mind-thinking way of enlightenment. Anything to avoid having to go back in to our original terror imprints in our emotions, those Original Wails of Loss as we were separated from our Hearts, from our Selves, our God. We like to apply 'scientific' 'research' techniques to spirituality. We like the antiseptic, rational, mental approach to everything. In these rational-mental models of 'enlightenment' sex is usually 'base' or only meant for procreation or at least separated from God-Source, or just considered a body function and somehow subtly looked down upon or at least not held as the sacred Life Source energy gateway that it obviously is. It's where we create children, pure gateways of Beingness from! We sit and chant for hours, we use 'discipline' to control the physical and emotional bodies, the list is endless how we've subjugated and imprisoned the Body and our Emotions. One more dead end of fancy technique and manipulation of energies that give us occasional 'highs' to think we're on the right path. This is truly 'black' magic, using and imprisoning the emotional body and forcing it to give its energy up, without any gratitude or Love in order to send us back to our false heaven.

Real Ascension includes the Body and Emotions! $E=mc^2$!

The problem is we never achieve real ascension this way; we never liberate that part of ourselves that has congealed as a body and as emotions, so we never become really whole again. We simply leave our bodies behind when we die, 'ascend'. But that energy of the Body and Emotions is a part of us that we leave as ghosts, as lost energies forced to wander the Earth and we will eventually have to reclaim them if we want to be truly free. Jesus resurrected his body! He took it with him! So did Babaji, Sri Yukteswar, Patanjali, Krishna, Emil, St. Germaine and many others who are not known to the public. They sped the energy up to the point where they didn't need to leave their bodies behind at death. The physical matter of their bodies became pure energy again. Einstein with his simple equation $E=mc^2$ showed that matter and energy are interchangeable, that's what the equals = sign means, it can go back and forth from one side of the equation to the other, matter turns into energy and energy congeals into matter. So of course we can also do this because we are pieces of the Source that creates All That Is. We are pieces of God, pieces of Love, pieces of Source. We are made 'in the image' of this Source-God and we have the same creative magical abilities. I know that perhaps that sounds unbelievable but it is the truth no matter how much mind programming we've received that convinces us that we are just helpless pieces of flesh that live and die capriciously at the hands of some dominating 'god' or chaotic universe.

Real Masters are ever fresh 'babies'

And these masters that remembered how to set their souls and their energy free - they became free to choose when and how to incarnate again, to congeal another physical body whenever they want, not as a trap, not in a Karmic cycle, no veil of forgetfulness at birth, not a prison of body anymore.

121

And they told us how to do it. *"Become Ye as little Children." "God does not reveal Himself to the prudent and the wise...but to babes" Original Innocence*, openness of heart i.e. open up to our emotional bodies, allow them to heal, allow them to express freely, don't force or control them and they will heal themselves and supply the power on earth for magnetizing and grounding the spirit-god into full in-carne-ation (in-flesh-ation), which will be the real 'second coming'. Yes, it will seem painful, yes it requires you to listen, to follow, to choose to be aware in a world gone insane, but what else are you going to do? Put your head in the sand and hope it all changes magically without you having to become aware, awake, change your death creating habits? Those religions and their followers who believe they don't have to 'walk the walk' and actually re-spiritualize their emotional and physical bodies are infantile in their belief systems or spiritually lazy.

The Easy Way to tell a True Master

Do these 'enlightened' ones feel like they are the innocence of children, the *"Become Ye as Little Children"* that Jesus from his gentle heart talked about? Or do they feel above it all looking down in bemused, patriarchal (evaluating with the mind) 'love' on their 'wayward children', con-descending to come and teach us, themselves untouched by the 'lower' emotions? Do they become innocent themselves, can they let themselves go and be goofy, human, sad, not perfect all the time. Do they come off their throne and play like equals? Or do they need to remain up above and untouched by these human emotions? Are they afraid of 'descending' into humanness? Are these 'enlightened' 'gods' afraid of being human? Do they use all their fancy wizardry and words to keep talking so they won't have to feel, for 'feeling is weakness' the imprinted subconscious program says. The Impulse of God feels like Chaos to them, scares them, they must have their god 'Order'. They can't just truly surrender, which they talk about all the time, that we all need to 'surrender to the Lord' But they can't just surrender and be however the Impulse of God wishes in the moment themselves. They must keep themselves above and thereby put us down in the process however subtly and couched in the language of 'oneness' and 'love' they do it. 'Dear ones, we come to you in the Light...etc.'

"God does not reveal himself to the prudent and the wise...but to babes."

The acid test is do they allow their emotional body input into the Creation, i.e. their being. Or do they need to present an image of 'enlightenment', of never having these 'lower' feelings, always remaining calm, peaceful 'above it all'? If they are not allowing the Emotional Body to be part of the game of creation they still have learning to do, aren't fully healed themselves and most often create dead ends for themselves and their followers. They are not fully then of Love. They can easily falsely lead themselves and others into imprisoning Love, becoming controllers and usurpers of energy interested in power, not innocence and love. This is not helpful anymore to healing ourselves or the Creation. This way of being will not be able to remain on the planet earth as it returns to Love, Innocence, Free Will. Just as these deniers of the emotional body were kicked out of Tibet by the 'base', 'red' root chakra (anger) soldiers of the Chinese army, so will these false teachers be dethroned everywhere unless they choose to wake up.

(Wow, I bet I pushed some buttons in spiritual circles with that last one!)

Shiva – 'Lord of The Dance' – inside the 'Ring of Fire'

Including feelings, passion, power – yet unruled by them

30.   **Soul Anorexia**

Learning to Let In again.

Letting back in, letting ourselves be loved, believing that we are worthwhile, that we are love-able, allowing God and those around us to love us, is for many of us the hardest thing to let into our selves. To have the Creation work as originally intended, we as the beings in manifestation need to allow ourselves to be "fed" by the Manna of creative juices from the Source of All. The only reason we "die" a physical death is that we are 'soul anorexics', we all have defined boundaries, identities. We have become 'closed off systems' and all closed systems eventually run out of energy. The original model is for us to be open systems and be able to metamorphose, shift, change in and out of physical and spiritual bodies. There is not meant to be a solid veil between any of the worlds. The now separate dimensions are coming back together, the Nature Kingdom with its devas and spirits, the 'aliens' from other planets, the Angelic realms. There are many dimensions that have been 'divided and conquered' that will now merge and have free flow again now that there is healing coming to planet Earth. **You** are the Key to the unlocking of these dimensions, for parts of you actually live in all these dimensions. More and more people are having 'dreams', channelings of-from these other places where parts of their beings are existing. There is a moment coming on Earth that will melt all into One, where the now separated dimensions will merge. Your opening to and being willing to see your reasons for closing off, for walling in, separating parts of yourself into separate existences will help you experience this merging as a loving healing rather than a chaotic destruction of our civilization and social structure on Earth. In opening those places where we are not allowing ourselves to be fed by the Central Love we will heal this 'Soul Anorexia' that most people on the planet are currently experiencing.

***"There is no way around it, but there is a way through it"*—Me!**

Opening back up will be terrifying at times because in opening back up the reasons we closed down to begin with will come back up for review in our consciousness. We will have to face these reasons for shutting our selves off and heal them. There is no way around it... but there is a way through it.

Spiritual brutality has crushed our spirits

A while back I had a founder of a spiritual society call me just to talk. He and a partner had formed an organization that taught the ways of the Ascended Masters, the true Religion of Oneness with all Life. (Re-Ligio = re-connect, same root as Ligament, to connect, in this case re-connect with God.) Very beautiful, right on target, very loving, sweet, open, 'light' oriented, affirmations, visualization, the light of 'intelligence' (the Hindu 'chitti'). I had ordered some tapes from their organization a few years earlier, written them and generally related, tuned in to their energies. It felt like we were very similarly vibrating souls, the boyish Hermes, Apollo male energy of innocence, light, intelligence. Well he called and started by saying he didn't know why he was calling, he 'never calls people' usually but somehow he felt led to call me. As soon as he started talking I could feel intuitively that his partner had died of AIDS. He then mentioned it like a brother sharing his heartache and cried. I wasn't surprised. It is hard for sweet, spiritual souls to survive in the mental compression and spiritual brutality of the energy that has ruled consciousness on planet earth for the last known 'history'.

A long time ago this rawness of anger, control, heartlessness, fear turned violent, that rules the Earth ("*My kingdom is not of this world*" Jesus says) wounded, implanted, damaged, the sweet 'heart' spirits that came to earth. It so scar(r)ed us, put our tender emotional bodies literally into 'soul shock' that we went to sleep, amnesic, and dissociated out of the traumatized parts of the emotional body in order to deal with the overwhelming experience of landing in such a compressed consciousness environment. This dissociating from these 'evil', 'base' emotions has helped us to survive up to this point but now we need to go back in and recover these lost parts, these lost essences of our selves.

Finally…"Going Direct"

A lot of healing wholistic practices are essential aids, tools, to jump start us as we're starting to wake back up to who we really are. They make us feel safe so we can open our beings back up, they help activate our energies, travel back to other life times and remove implants, trauma, heal wounded spaces, get our body energies moving again, learn to sense with our Solar Plexus, become True Voices for Love etc. But at some point in our healing of our selves all these tools will become buffers, hindrances. Energy manipulation will become unsatisfying to us. We will want to **go direct** and live directly by intention, by allowing our divine Will to heal us. We will still use some methods; all methods have their place and time. But when our heart tells us that we're getting tired of the buffers between us and direct access to the energy source of all Life it will be time for us to graduate, to 'go direct'. It is time for us to commune directly with the "*holiest of holies*", time for our veil to be "rendered".

Free Energy for Everyone!

This Source of All, the cauldron of energy at the center of the universe, the 'throne of God', the Heart of Love, God, Father, Mother, is in all of us. It is our very life source. So we can all have direct access to it and live off of it. It is 'manna from heaven', 'man shall not live by bread alone'. We can literally live off this energy. Needing to derive energy from food means we have lost our choice to enjoy food for pleasures' sake only, to now needing it because we've lost touch with the Source of all Energy. Somehow something or someone convinced us that we don't deserve 'direct access', the 'all areas backstage pass'. But we do, because to Innocence all things are revealed. "*Become Ye as Little Children*". I mention this a lot because it is such a simple way Home, such a simple Truth. Innocence also angers the power seekers, the energy vampires who refuse to 'go directly to the well' themselves and instead feed off of others. This unlimited, free (no one can charge you money for this energy), lovingly given energy is your Emergence Right, your birth right. When you emerged from the orgasm of the Mother and Father on your Original Birthday one of your birthday Presents was unlimited energy forever! So all these games trying to steal energy from each other, trying to control the energy sources are lies. All games of 'lack' are lies, you are the child of the Source of All, you have **direct access** to the central core of All Energy. Become a real rebel; choose to go direct, to have radical freedom. *"Set the controls for the heart of the Sun."*

Cut the Ties that Bind

It will involve freeing your soul from all the places you've given your energy away. This is the part no one wants to do. You cannot be 'reborn' back into your original power as long as these belief patterns, implants, work as automaticities in your subconscious. If God was to restore all our power magically in our current state we'd most likely destroy ourselves or turn into monsters controlling others. We need to heal ourselves, clear up the guilt and fear patterns and take our power back from them. And as we're healing ourselves our power automatically returns to us as it is safe and appropriate. There is a plan. And there is no way around our "stuff", but there is a way through it, to transform it, to recover those lost pieces of ourselves.

Cleaning up the Energy Stealing Game

At this time on the planet one of the messes being cleared up is the energy stealing game. No one will be allowed to live off others energy anymore. All will have to go to their own source if they wish to stay with the Earth. So all energies are returning to their source. All the energies we've created will be returning to us. Some of us have trouble letting in our "glory" but this energy wants to go to its rightful home. Like Cinderella and the Ugly Duckling, a lot of us are "gods" and we've given our power away because we were convinced that being powerful, beautiful, strong, loved, was not spiritual somehow, that having power and beauty was putting ourselves above others and by accepting this twisted half-truth we were convinced to give our power away. We were also convinced that "serving" the ungrateful (the wicked stepsisters) would somehow "earn" us heaven. We've believed that expressing beauty, power, in the "world" would get us trapped here. So now "our fear has come upon us", we are trapped here because we are not allowing ourselves to use our Birthright of power and beauty.

Some beings have energy that is not rightfully theirs, they have stolen energy from Innocence-Love and they would like the civilization to continue the way it is, with control, fear motivation, a micro chipped trackable population and a coming one world government. You taking your energy back and simply becoming more of who you really are will automatically take the energy back from where it doesn't belong. The more of us do this the quicker "heaven on earth" will be restored. It is in our deepest emotions, our deepest scars of the emotional body, that most of our energy is being dissipated. And that is where it is waiting for us to reclaim it. We will need to walk our walk through our fear gateways and call out to our imprisoned parts of ourselves *"Rise Lazarus, and walk again"*. We will need to allow them to come back to life, and God will help us because this is a priority with Him and Mother Earth at this time. Again, it won't be easy. But it will be en-live-ening! Besides what other choice do you have? Are you going to die unfulfilled one more time? Put it off another thousand lifetimes? The tiredness we're feeling inside is that we are "soul tired" of this game of fear, lack, false presentation faces, lies, bullshit. We all want to feel again, something real, come back to life. It's OK to not do it now, there is no "time" no "urgency"...yet there is.

The "Spiritual Anorexia" is the Wake up Call!

The "spiritual anorexia" that healers, practitioners, seekers are experiencing is the wake up call. We need to go into our real emotions, get more real about our hatred, anger, rage, confusion, sadness, betrayal, hopelessness, rage at God. Rage at God when done with real feeling **and** a willingness for it to transform is one of the most powerful releases-healings we can have. It is not wrong, or unspiritual to feel hatred or anger. The red energy is in our survival charka. We are killing it by not letting it express. Goddamnit wake up and fucking scream! Scream at the walls of Jericho! The walls that have imprisoned us for eons. If we don't recover this energy in our first three chakras we will surely die. The "spiritual anorexia" comes from being imprisoned in "spiritual correctness". We have so many rules about what is "loving" and what is "not loving" that we start living in spiritual straitjackets. We don't allow the emotional body to express at all, never mind freely. So we start dying, because the emotional body is the magnetic spiritual power source. The vampires of our energy know this, that's why they like to trigger our emotions, make us feel things but then make it socially inappropriate to express them, because when we deny our feelings of the moment, when we suppress, push them down inside us, the energy goes somewhere and can be usurped, "fed off" by others. You may not want to believe that. But it's a fact and anyone who takes any time at all to look at it objectively with a honest mind will see it. This energy stealing game is why the Earth and its loving- gentle of heart spirits have been plagued by problems for so long. And this energy stealing game is the most hidden thing on the planet. What is the energy that doesn't want to hear-see that this is going on? Feel it. Why are authorities, the dominant paradigm afraid of openly looking at this? How does it feel when people make fun of a concept of energy stealing, when they deride it, call it silly-stupid-namby pamby B.S.? Who has an interest in keeping this energy stealing game going? In a supposedly "free" society why are we making fun of, putting down, laughing derisively at any point of view that is not part of the subconsciously programmed accepted dominant paradigm?

I say look around and Wake Up! See how the controllers of minds and souls live off our emotional energy. We are the Source! It's time we took it back.

127

Find a safe place to express (ex-press= press out) consciously your real feelings. In expressing with intention to heal you will transform your "dead spaces", bring them back to life. The word Sin means empty, without, without God, Love, Life.

The following verse is an expression of when I first realized that in my "spiritual" persona I was unknowingly keeping parts of my emotional body imprisoned.

I'm In Hate

I'm in Hate,
For the first time.

Finally,
I let myself FEEL
It's OK to BE REAL,
And part of me Hates,
Vitriolic, Soul Annihilation Hate.

You fucking Ignorant pabulum puking,
Spiritual regurgitating,
Sleepwalking fear mongers,

Wake the Fuck Up!
Oh, Liberation,

If you could but let your soul
SCREAM...SCREEEAAAM, again...
The Original Loss, hurt anger, sadness, fear,
Scream it out,
A fucking banshee, all you can,
Storm the gates of Heaven,
The Walls of Je(e)richo,
Scream,
the vibration of your separated Heart,
will annihilate, vaporize the
Mother fuckin' walls keeping you
outside of your Heaven,
Your Power, your Home.

Take it,
Goddamnit, I will have it,
Fuck all of you willowy, wispy,
souls who talk about it endlessly,
Analyze (anal eyes), explain,

"KNOWING" IS DEATH,
Don't you understand!

Please don't.

Don't you see,
That most insidious of prisons
is called "good".
You politeness,
Your sweet false Presentation Face
wishing "light for all beings"
is the very thing that imprisons you,
from being real,
Connected to the Heart of Life.
FEEL!
Pour out WHATEVER it is,
it is All
Just energy.

Get the fuck out of your minds,
Fuck each others "brains" out!
Come all Ye Faithfull!
Fuck all Ye Faithfull!
Hate all Ye Faithfull!
Kill all Ye Faithfull!

Then,
you will un-cover
The Heart of Love.

31. The Sacred Dance of the Vacuum Cleaner

I wake up late, noon. A sliver of guilt tries to tell me "You should...?" It doesn't work on me much anymore, but it still tries. I should...nothing. I want to just be...in the flow...trust it...to provide for me. I have more fun alone nowadays since the aloneness is fullness compared to the emptiness of filling with uncentered busy ness. I like Nothing, it allows fullness of emptiness. I love having my cup filled with-in my heart. No need...for words. Every moment...brand new...surprise...I know you...anew...my cat...I forgot about her...I forgot about "me"...wiped clean...not scared anymore...of being "nothing".

In-Spirit-ations

As I recognize the guilt voice, "you should be doing something, God wants you to start your 'work' now, you should be doing the ads, be promoting yourself, this is sacred work you know, it is time to create in the world again, you know you have no money in the bank, what about the bills etc...." I say instead, I will just do whatever in-spirit-ations come. OK, my heart is sincere, I want to listen and hear and follow the in-spirit-ations. Read this they say, the "Green Man", in touch with simple, with mother Earth, with doing, everything sacred, nothing better or worse, no *"knowledge of good and evil"* all just god stuff. OK I like, they say vacuum now. I start vacuuming, no rush, no "job to finish", just being with it in the moment, enjoy each stroke, back and forth, being completely with the task in hand, doing-being, no doing this to get that, just doing, being. My spirit is in the rug, in the vacuum, also in the cosmos, seeing all oneness, seeing feeling heart centeredness, I am god-being, no-place to go, sensing merging, other dimensions, other "me's". "Sacred" symbols, ancient geometric, merkabah, Kaballah, geo-metre, building blocks of life, of forms, basic units, sacred circles, triune-one, life symbols, earth sacred symbols in the "field" of my carpet, no aliens here except me, mother earth doing sacred magnetic humming vibrating building blocks of Life, designs of the vacuum cleaner on the rug, this is fun! No "work" just doing-being, it is doing me! It does take care of me, support me! I just have the intention and then listen for the "when" It wants to do through me.

"...your whole life can be like this...easy, do the moment-let the Moment do you, nothing else matters...the spirit of love-life takes care of you, under girds you, lifts you, no effort just be with-in it..." Spirit tells me.

I start laughing...out loud...and then tears... *"happy vacuuming"* it says. Da, Da, Do,Do, De...I am the Sacred Wise Infant.

The Sacred Golden Bough

There's a woman I've noticed before walking by my window. The tree, the sacred Golden Bough outside my patio fell down in the last storm that I reveled in. This tree has protected me, shielded me with its medicine (it is eucalyptus), kept me safe in my womb. Yes but the season is changing, I'm being pulled out into the world again, there is a time for every thing under heaven, and the wheel is turning, me out, after my wholing.

I see her cutting some branches from the Holy Tree of Medicine, inspiration, me too! I go outside and we talk of healing tree medicine, easily with nothing to prove, nothing to fight against...yes, eucalyptus is very powerful, olive trees also...what's the best branch to take...oh the mature ones...how do you hang them...cleansing...beautiful...my sacred protector tree...is finished...and gives me in its "fall"...a remnant...it's all right...nothing "died"...season-cycle-change...show me, my medicine tree, how to flow like you into my next doing. Thank you, you'll be with me forever.

Back inside, hang the Golden Boughs of Three in easy triangle around my home. I continue vacuuming, more sacred ritual symbols. I finish...sit and feel...and then I write...these words...now finished.

32.   A Message for the Mess-Age

I have a message for this mess-age, for those who want to hear, for those who want to heal. For those who want to take advantage of this polar merging occurring on the Earth, for those who want to allow the help from Father God and Mother Earth to make them whole beings again.

The Message is as it has always been

The Message is as it always has been—it is that the Seeds of Innocence, the Seeds of Love, the Re-Birth, the Heart, the Balancer, will see you through the coming social, personal, planetary upheavals. And if we are not in touch with our heart no place will be "safe" in the coming years. For this is the time of "ruthless" healing. The Earth and the Sun have decided to merge their energies on Earth, to balance the feminine and masculine. All the polarities of "good and evil" are-will be meeting and merging more and more rapidly. It looks like Chaos to those addicted to the god of Mechanized Order, to thinking, to static structures in their minds, to the status quo, to things remaining the same. The old concretized (all mixed up and permanently set like concrete) ways of holding the control reigns (yes I meant reign) will try to keep the lid on this rising tide of freewill, the bubbling up of open emotions, but the tender green shoot of rebirth will break through the "concrete" thought-belief patterns that are holding the (c)old polar world in place. It will be painful if we try to hold on to the places where we currently place our security, our blood families, money, laws, militaries, police forces, governments, pharmaceutical drugs, medical doctors, lawyers etc. The more we can become fluid, flow with the river that finds its way over, around, through, not by violence, but by silken water flow that leaves love-life wherever it touches, the more we can become like this, without locks, gates, barriers, the easier this meta(big)-morphosis(change) into this new world will be for us. All the old will be swept away by the stream, a wonderful renewal to those who welcome the birth of real freedom, a destruction to those who want the river bank to remain in the same place. *"...And I beheld a new heaven and a new earth..."*

Up-Heavals! = Up-Heavening!

All security systems will pass away. The coming "up-heavals"(up-heavening, bringing heaven up!) will be forcing (if we resist) us to find our security within, *"thou shalt have no other gods before Me"* is this meaning, no placing security in anything except our Hearts, God, Love, the Source of All. All this tinsel shall be swept away. The money system will be wiped out, all artifice (artificial edifices) swept away and boy have we edified the artificial! The Real will come and clean up the mess of this age. A very popular and often used Hindu prayer is:

Lord lead me from the unreal to the Real,

From the darkness to the Light.

Pandora's Box – Pan's Door is A'Opening!

132

One of the fastest growing industries in the U.S. is security systems! Everyone is feeling this rising of the Wild, the Free, the Chaotic, yet most of us are still resisting it. We use more and more drugs to keep the nagging feelings away from us. We are terrified of "losing it", letting our suppressed anger, disappointment, fear, loose. Pan-Door-as Box, we are terrified of Pan's Door, the wild flow of Nature. Yet it is our liberation, our only real survival tool. As usual it's backwards, the more we avoid our *inner* feelings of survival fear and the more we use outward security mechanisms then the more unavoidable the collapse of all our outer security structures. The more we run from our feelings of insecurity the more they will get us in the end. The more we face head on our inner fears, the safer we'll be in the outer world.

The Safest Place

That which seems most vulnerable, the newborn child, is the safest thing to be because the child has the least fears of survival. Because the soul has newly arrived from the heavenly realms it is vibrating-effulging-radiating safety, security, being cared for and therefore the baby elicits, draws out from the creation around it the impulse to take care of it. We can live like this little child and nature itself will feed and clothe us. That which seems the most protected, the strongest, hardest, most cynical, seasoned veteran of the psychic wars, leaders of nations, are in reality the weakest, most unprotected. They have built trust funds, guard gates, private security forces, body guards, armies, mental wizardry, fancy walls of separation everywhere trying to be "safe" and yet they are terrified to go to sleep for the monsters in their heads.

Your heart, that place where the Father God and Mother God meet with you is and will be more and more the only safe place in this Mess-Age.

Being Born(e)

Carried away
To the River,
Set adrift,
Trusting, Lisping,
Mother Find me,
Enfold me,

Gentle swirling
Time and Space's
Soft Curling,

Swaddling clothes,
This time
Brings the Age
To a Close,

A Childs' trust
Will carry you.

133

33.   Why Technological Scientism is in Power Now

...and the Pendulum Swings between the Ages

Those who feel Mother Nature and her Devic spirits often wonder why the 'Scientism' priests and the Warriors (the "something must be fought all the time" lovers of battle and conflict) are in charge of the current civilization on Earth. It feels cruel, as if the gentle spirits are being punished by God, which is their fear no matter how much they like to deny it by anger and defiance. Or that God is an impotent God that can't keep charge of the Creation.

No matter how much we don't want to hear it (and that is why the problem is there to begin with) Technological Scientism being in charge on Earth is part of the pendulum swinging back and forth in the Polar Yin-Yang Creation trying to balance itself. Admittedly on a large scale, practically the whole planet it being seduced into material worship with hardly any one listening or interacting with a personal loving organic Nature God. But there is a seed of truth in both sides of the technological-organic, scientism-spirit, rational mind-intuitive heart polarity split. Both sides are right! Balancing, huge corrections don't occur randomly in the Creation. There is purpose behind it.

Incan human blood sacrifices & "Smart Bomb" Warfare.

The danger with Nature based religions is that they often degenerate into ancestor worship & elemental spirit worship. Ritual becomes elevated to appease the "gods", the people live in fear of the "gods". Natural disasters come to equal punishment from "Baal" or some other power hungry elemental spirit that is masquerading as a "god". And then we are putting "gods" before us, before out direct connection to real God inside us. This causes "feedback" in the creation since the aligned, awakened god-human is meant to be in a leading position in the creation. We in human form are meant to incarnate the "second coming" into flesh, bring into third dimensional form the Divine. We are the divine, or rather we were meant to be, but we are not balanced anymore because Heart/Love the balancer does not guide us primarily. But rather power games and control of energy i.e. Lucifer-Heartlessness controls most of the human "civilization" on Earth now.

Either side, the mental-rational-scientific blue indigo purple top three chakras, or the feeling-intuitive-earth based red orange yellow first three chakras, when not balanced with Heart/Love green central chakra as the guiding force becomes unbalanced. The Incas sacrificing thousands of human beings and taking out their still beating hearts, with rivers of blood flowing off the pyramids is just as unbalanced as totally rejecting nature spirits, Mother Earth and relying on chemicals, metal, computers, Scientism, war and punishment to control, subdue and rape the earth without letting the Earth itself have any input.

134

The Balanced God-Human Bridges Heaven and Earth.

The key point is that the Balanced God-Human with Heart-Love leading the way is meant to bridge Heaven and Earth. And until we open to love and dialogue between the two polarities of "above" and "below" the creation will just continue to flip-flop, alternating who's in power. Even to the point of it becoming whole planets ruled by "techno-father" worship civilizations or planets ruled by "organo-mother" worship civilizations. Then these planets will try to conquer and resist each other in ways of trying to balance. Heart-Love can make the process happen without the pain, suffering, fear and violence. And we will never be whole until we do this opening to Heart-Love within our selves, balancing the male/female, the rational/intuitive, the outward/inward. All the polarities have a role in the Polar Creation (obviously) so none of them are "evil". It's only when Heart/Love is absent that it degenerates into fear based control organizations and inability to understand- relate to other polarities.

These polarities of the rational/scientism/techno and the intuitive/earth ritual/organic are still opposing each other on Earth today. And if it's not to degenerate into death, punishment, increasing paranoia, "camps" barricading themselves behind their physical and ideological walls and eventually (maybe soon) a collapse of the "civilization", then we need to one by one open to the polarities being healed within us with Heart-Love guiding us. The most powerful thing we can do to heal the Earth is to heal ourselves now at this important moment in cosmic history coming to Earth. All it takes is 100 fully Awake, fully vibrating, God-Humans to change the whole planet.

Really.

And you can be One of Them if you want.

34. Light Your Fire

The Fire has almost gone out!

There is a fire in the center of all beings of Life that has almost gone out in many beings on Earth right now. This Fire burns away all the dross, the death, the confusion, the not-Life-ness that has infested the energy bodies of most of us. Once this Fire is re-lit it automatically cleanses, burns away the creeping death and fullness of the Flame of Life is restored. You need only surrender to it. I know it might sound like platitudes but it is still true so go ahead and scream at God or me, or throw the book against the wall if it makes you angry. (God likes that by the way, if you do it sincerely and are willing to open a two way conversation).

It is easy, this surrender to the Flame of Truth, of Love, of Life, of Purity. But as the old "shit", the stuckness, the guilt, the stuck belief patterns, our old chains are leaving it will be painful at times. Afterward you'll wonder what all the fuss was about, you'll laugh in cosmic laughter at the "perfection" of your individual journey back Home to Love, to God, to your self. True, but in the middle of the storm you'll want to give up and kill yourself, forget the whole thing, curse God, annihilate the whole creation. This is understandable; it's the creeping 'death urge' being vibrated out of your emotional body. Better that you vibrate this out of your spiritual, emotional and physical bodies than you keep it suppressed and it manifests as wars, plagues, nuclear weapons, earthquakes etc. Could you imagine if we had 'Emotional Healing/Clearing Centers' instead of schools? How fast we could change and lift the collective consciousness' energy on earth.

"Ashes to Ashes" --The Fire of Shiva

This Fire is the Fire of Shiva. The fire that "destroys" everything, that reduces every Thing to ashes, it is the final state, where all things end up. It is the Cosmic Cleanser, the ultimate cleaning product. In "destroying" every thing it makes all things brand new. The Cleansing Fire makes you a brand new person. You are "brand new in Christ", you are reborn like the Phoenix after you've been reduced to ashes. You just have to make it through the "smelter".

So Light Your Fire! Set it ablaze, burn of the dross, let the "Destroyer" into your Life!

Destroyer of Forms

Be born in me,
The Destroyer longs to be,
...Our Friend,
...Our Lover,
We run for cover.

The Fire of Purity.

This is the fire I'm interested in reawakening in people. My bliss is to start the fire and move on. The Fire of Purity will automatically cleanse beings once it is started. I will wheedle my way into your hearts and leave a seed to grow, a seed of Fire of Love. It's what we all want, if we want Life. It is what scares all of us, because we know it will change our little boxed in lives, it is *"no respecter of persons"* i.e. egos, it is big, it moves, it changes, it is Life, it is unpredictable, it follows the Love Path that *"no man knows except the Father in heaven"*. We can know this Path of Love if we re-identify our selves with our larger Self. We are then one with God and our Will is His-Her Will.

The Direct (ed) Fire.

This Fire is the Fire of self-direction. We will hear directly from the Source of All things. In our hearts we have a direct linkup to the heart of God. Better and more reliable than the best satellite linkup available today. Radical trust. Following our hearts. It takes some time to trust it. We doubt it seemingly forever, our trapped programmed egoic minds tell us it's "wrong", "dangerous", "evil", "not working", and a thousand other reasons why we can't and shouldn't be listening to our hearts. Be allowing with your self, allow the process to reach towards trust again, be patient with yourself. And one day you will "give up" and "surrender" to your own heart, to Love, to God the Father, to God the Mother and you will still be scared but you will be on the road back to your fullness. You'll stop listening to the voice of Guilt. You will still hear it but you'll know it takes you only to dead ends. Because once the fire is started in you you can't turn back. You can put it on hold, for lifetimes sometimes, that's OK. The Father God and Mother God don't judge you for taking a break. You have total choice. Whatever you decide is OK. There is no push or pressure on you...but there is a choice to be made. There is a cleansing happening on Earth now and Father God and Mother Earth want to help you wake up if that's what you want in your heart. They want to help you regain your individuality, your power, your glory, your joy. They want you to be unencumbered by guilt, by doubt, by all the discordant energy that has crept in and prevented the Original Intention for Creation. When you let your Fire be lighted and start following your directions from It, you can't go wrong. There is no "wrong" place to go! Yes, things will change in your life. But your clinging to security models and stuck patterns is already death so what's the difference? What do you have to lose?

Call on The Fire--Bring it Down.

I call on the Fire of Love to burn away all the false, dead structures on the Earth and let radical Love and aliveness back into the heart of every spirit of Life. Let it blaze forth.

Open Sesame! (Says Me).

35.

Hurrying to Our Deaths

(another good bumper sticker!)

A National Day of doing Nothing

One of the hardest things for people today is simply to do nothing. Simply be, to be simply, in the space of emptiness. Even Zen retreats are assertions, they are trying to do, to make happen, the state of being still, empty. It is still doing. It is non-doing, doing nothing that we most need to learn, which is really to un-learn, to **allow** this space of non-doing, empty nothingness to simply come and infuse our beings. To sit-be in the Stillness.

Gotta be "Somebody"

We in the West and increasingly everywhere our "cult-ure" is taking over have been programmed since birth, and are continually being programmed every day that we must do something, must be somebody, or we're a "nothing", and being nothing, a "nobody", a "loser" is the most terrifying thing for almost everyone in the West. Can you see how this fear of being "nothing" makes us slaves to continually trying to assert that we are somebody? This terror of being a nobody, a loser, rules us, manically possesses us, makes us get up everyday with possessed eyes, pits us all against each other like pit bulls in the pit-arena. And we do this day after torturous day, our life force slowly ebbing until we die and reach "peace". Except it isn't peace we reach because we refused (re-fused, once again didn't open) to open to the Nothing-Everything beyond all opposites and allow the Source of Life to nourish us. We still think mistakenly that we must "work for our Living", when actually God the Father, God the Mother long to give to us the Horn of Plenty, all that Life has to offer, unlimited energy, unlimited pleasure, play, love, experience. But we are not open to receiving any of this even though it passes right before our eyes everyday most often we can't see it because...

...we are busy, hurrying to our deaths...

The Paradox is that in the Nothing, Everything is born. The Nothing can contain Everything, can give us everything. Once we're a "Nobody" we're Everybody. This is a real experience that we can have. It doesn't have to take lifetimes anymore of sitting in caves or monasteries. The time for mysteries and hidden knowledge is over.

Just Say No!

A few years ago I simply gave up and sat down in my room. I wasn't willing to assert anymore, to try to create through will power. I didn't want to "make things happen" anymore. If Life is meant to be easy, flowing, Tao, effortless creation then I didn't want to live the old way of "shoulds", and "have to do this in order to get that". The world of cause and effect was over for me, I was tired of it, ready to learn, to wake up to something new, a different way of existing. I "Just Said No" to the old drug of addiction to mind thinking (thank you Nancy Reagan), no more old world models of expending my soul energy as a sacrifice, no more feeding death. It has been the most terrifying thing I've ever done and the most cosmic orgasm thing I've ever done. I ran out of money, felt my fears about that, I felt like

138

a veteran of the psychic wars, paranoid, I felt omnipotent, I felt impotent, I talked to spirits, I felt crazy, I cried, I slept, my body felt like lead, my body felt like air, my emotions, my hopelessness, my rage at God seemed like bottomless pits.

Somehow I survived even though I stopped doing, I stopped doing all the things that were "laws" about surviving in the western world. Now it does feel like God, the Nothing, the Everything, Mother, is taking care of me.

I'm not saying that everyone should stop "doing" permanently. There is a right time for everything, for every mode of being. Doing and being active, consumed by a goal is as much God as not doing. But I am saying to first get in touch with the flow, our heart, the Voice of God and then do and not do as the Impulse of Love-God wants to.

The "Comforter" from Inside

Now I do more and more only what and when I really want to. I still do some programmed in things, but I catch myself and I'm patient with myself, I don't beat myself up that I'm still run by some automatic programs. I allow the mind programs to play out and then they leave when they are finished, and I'm finished with them. More and more I do nothing. I simply sit and feel. My whole body fills up with energy, it starts in my solar plexus, my belly, and it feels like molten metal, as if my bones and flesh are turning into liquid light. I like it. It is "the comforter" that Jesus spoke about, the real Holy Spirit. Usually I can't wait to get away from doingness to come home and sit and be filled up again. I'm not able to allow this state to be with me all the time "out there" in the world yet so I'm a bit protective of my new found Cauldron of Love in my belly. And eventually I'll be able to move around in the world and not lose touch with my Heart Fire.

"Be still and know that I Am God". Just stop, Just say No, no more manic running around while your Life, your Love is passing you by. What have you got to lose? Is your life "happy" and fulfilling the way it is going now?

I had a cat come into my life while I was sitting in my chair for 3 years trying to allow doing nothing into me. I saw her with my spiritual sight before she arrived in the flesh. She has taught me a lot about doing simply what she feels like doing, and doing nothing for long stretches. She survives, she is filled with the energy of the Universe and she has no "shoulds" no, "have to's", no guilt about relaxing and receiving.

Doing Nothing

Going NowHere
Doing NoThing
Being NoBody,

Oh, What Joy
I find
In This
NoThingness

36

To Programmed Beings a
Free Being Appears Insane

The "Gods" (us) have become demographically predictable economic slave robots!

Practically everyone on Earth currently is mostly run by subconscious programming, Freud was right about that. We are so run by unconscious motivators and fears that we are almost completely predictable. I used to think that advertising couldn't possibly work on people, surely it's such a blatant manipulation attempt that everyone must see through it. But the fact is it does work, it reaches our subconscious fear of death and our wanting approval, wanting love, programs in our minds. The "gods" (us) have become demographically predictable economic robots! That's the horrible truth and if we insist that it isn't so we aren't getting real and are probably hoping for some savior big daddy to come and fix it all with a magic wand.

In a world of almost complete programming of the masses most of us follow blindly the prescribed behaviors. *"But this is **supposed to be** the happiest day of my life"* says the bride to be in the aspirin commercial, having been thoroughly programmed that she has to get married and how she is "supposed to feel" when she does. And the fact that the ad agency uses this theme in a commercial means they've done their demographic research and know that it will work on the collective masses. *"I walked away from the confrontation **like a lady is supposed to do**"* says the young girl on the afternoon talk show trying to get approval from the audience and her own subconscious programming, while all the while seething with righteous vicious anger towards her perceived 'enemy'.

The Real Truth--Following the man invented "rules" & "being good" does not get you into Heaven!

It gets you into an astral Hell also full of "rules" and people exactly like you!

Our straitjackets of how we're "supposed to act" start forming in infancy and by the time we start school we are for the most part completely lost to the implanted "rules" in our minds. The rest of our lives we try to "be good" and do what we're "supposed to do". And we actually believe that this will get us in to some imagined heaven. I got news: following programmed "rules" of behavior doesn't get you into heaven, it gets you into astral worlds straitjacketed by rules of behavior as well! And this 'heaven' will still have other beings controlling you, i.e. it's really 'hell', unless you like being controlled by others. The energetic imprints you generate or believe in here on earth go with you in the spiritual worlds too. The way Jesus says this is *"What ye bind on earth ye bind in heaven and what ye loose on earth ye loose in heaven also."*

We're fascinated and intrigued by a free being...and they terrify us on a deep level.

Why? Because our ego, our programming, our subconscious implants, our mind control mechanisms, our demons, know that if we spend time with this Master, Enlightened-Awake person that the Mind-Ego will lose its control over us. The 'mind parasite' as the Toltec's call it can feel that its days are numbered if it hangs around this Awake Being. So the programming, the beliefs, the 'truths', social conditioning, 'rights & wrongs' i.e. the 'knowledge of good and evil' will start to come unraveled. This terrifies the Mind-the Ego-the Parasite because it will be thrown out and no longer able to feed off us. And when we are identified with our mind programming, our 'personal history', who we **think** we are, our name & place, our family, our country, our money, our degrees, our social standing etc...it terrifies us that Life-Love-Real God is no 'respecter of persons' i.e. our egos and that the Angel of Death (I love him! The ultimate Liberator) will "void" all our 'stuff', all our accumulated thoughts-ideas-personality. Since most of us humans today are almost completely identified with our 'stuff', our name, identity, history, money, family, country, thought patterns and have no real conscious connection to the eternal timeless Source we feel as if we're dying when the Angel of Death starts erasing our 'stuff', us , our history. A few of us, through deva-station, crisis, emergencies (emerge-and-see's), and near death experiences are starting to wake up now.

If people that are so thoroughly programmed as to 'what will the neighbors think', (we actually check up on each other to make sure that no one acts freely), encounter a free being they will think this free being is insane. The free being is in touch with the Impulse of Life and will allow Love-God to act through them. This is not predictable by any temporarily invented 'rules' of behavior. It is fascinating to the programmed beings to watch the free being, and that part of the programmed, enslaved being that still is alive will be attracted to this awake being. They will also be afraid because it is 'foreign' to them. The 'Free Energy' of the awake being will start activating the core, the kundalini, the life force energy in the body of whoever comes in contact with them. The Free Being-Awake Person-Natural Human will automatically start stirring up the soul energy of whoever they touch, look at, talk to. Can you explain why Jesus, a manifestation of God's Love, cursed and withered the fig tree? The Impulse of Life knows why. Source- Real God knows why. And the fishermen disciples were semi-awake enough to say 'Yes' and to be willing to follow their hearts when Jesus said 'follow me', they trusted the Impulse of Life that arose in them.

Programmed slow death is the experience of most souls on the planet today. Few are the ones sick and tired enough to say 'forget it, I can't pretend anymore' and start living for themselves and not to please some imagined false Father figure mimicking 'god' , or to assuage their need for approval from others.

141

Normal = Insane in our world today!

The real insanity is what passes for 'normal' in our current 'civilization' that we've created. It is insane that we have lost our souls, that we have lost touch with the spontaneity of the Heart of Love. The real insanity is that very few are saying 'Uncle! The emperors have no clue!' that we're sheep being led to the slaughter by our 'leaders', truly the 'blind following the blind.'

If you start living consciously, start trying to wake up, your friends and family likely won't understand you, you won't fit in any "category" of sanctioned behavior, you may scare people, you will feel alone if you look to the 'insane – programmed' world to understand you. They'll want to put you back in your-their box to 'keep you safe'.

But you will also start hearing from God directly, and you'll start feeling truly free again. It isn't always 'easy', you'll get to face your personal fears, the reasons you shut down to begin with. But with each fear you heal, that space is filled with that part of yourself that you rejected long ago. That 'sin' (sin = an empty space i.e. a place without God) becomes filled with Love and you'll start becoming a whole being again. You'll start feeling the stars in your body again, your skin will look younger, your heart will feel again, you'll laugh for "no reason", you'll feel whole and complete within yourself, and you'll start remembering why you wanted to be part of Life to begin with.

So go ahead....go "crazy".

~Section Four~

Innocence not "believable" anymore?

I just finished watching an interview of the director of the movie "Forrest Gump".

Since "Forrest Gump" was a hugely popular movie and the biggest movie of the director's career the interviewer, trying to analyze (we must analyze, 'anal-eyes' it of course, we can't just feel it) asks the question "is the movie saying that one has to be mentally challenged in some way in order to be 'believable' as being as innocent as Forrest Gump is in the movie." And the director answers of course not and those who see it that way are taking it too seriously and looking for messages too obsessively. But he continues that in order to have a character that will be "believable" as being so innocent and guileless, a character that actually "means exactly what he says", you'd either have to have a four year old or a "idiot savant type" character like Forrest because *"no one will believe that an adult will not have some hidden agenda"*.

In other words, Innocence, saying what you mean, meaning what you say, feeling openly and honestly, and not having hidden agendas **is not believable as adults in today's world!**--That's the level of tainted hearts and use/be used by power hungry games that have come to rule the planet currently! Sadly…it is how it appears. And the more of us believe that we need to live that way in order to protect ourselves and our hearts, the more of us add our belief energy to it, the more "true" it becomes.

I choose Innocence, not naiveté but *Conscious Innocence*.
I make a decision for Innocence!

Innocence is what makes life worth living. Why do you think we "light up" when we see babies, or puppies, or kittens? Why we enjoy playing with young children? It is their honesty, their no hidden agendas, their openhearted trust, their openness to Life that we long for. We have been con-vinced that this doesn't work in the world of business and other "adult games". The truth is it works elegantly, efficiently, powerfully and protects us from being drained, used up and slowly killed by our Minds, our fallen selves. Any master knows this.

Jesus said. *"Unless ye convert and become as little children, you will not enter the Kingdom of Heaven."* And *"Suffer the little children to come unto me, for such is the Kingdom of Heaven."* That's pretty clear. Was He lying?

My decision for Innocence does not mean that I don't know the machinations of the Mind of Fallen Man: survival fear, fear of disapproval, money hunger, fear of being a "nobody", greed, vicious revenge hatred, blood lust, power games and how these things do run the world for the most part currently and inspire the incredible atrocities and betrayals that go on between humans. I see these clearly, but I will choose Innocence because that is where God talks to me, it is where I can talk to animals, it is where I can hear the Elementals of the Earth speak to me. This is where I find Joy, where I find sustenance, where I find Love. Yes, I will be different, "weird" according to the shut down, programmed, economic robot humans. I will not be a "believable" character in the current mass consciousness projected movie called "Life on Earth". People will think they see and will actually find hidden agendas in what I do but I will simply do what my heart wants to do. But no longer with blinders on. I no longer will assume that others are open-hearted and that they will want openness "if only they can be shown the light". No, I know now that many souls on this planet currently choose hiddenness, betrayal, games of power, using of the innocent, feeding on the meek. Against these beings if need be I will set hard against hard. Actually for the most part I will let Love, God, Innocence protect me automatically, literally like a "reflector shield" of protective energy. Wise Awake Innocence will protect me from all these "tangled webs we weave".

Do you want to play?

An Innocent Savvy

Knowing the ways,
Vagaries of the Mind,
Its dead ends,
Universes of separation,
Alone spaces,
Fearful places...

The Lover chooses Innocence,
A pact with the Heart.

Safely now he travels through out,
Within,
Every space
open to him,
Who has unlocked the door.

He is a Visitor,
drawn to friends
caught in spaces,
Golden Cages.

Teasingly,
He'll move in and out
of Gates,
Prisons
Gently nudging
old playmates to See.

I have traveled here before,

145

He says,
The road is shrouded
From views of understanding,
Love dis-spells the Mist,
He seduces us,
We tag along,
"Follow the dancing lights"
cry the Elves.

The Under-Standing world
looks on in perplexity,
How, Why,
Where is your category,
He is,
Different,
To All,
Nothing,
and Absolute
A Heart Chameleon
Changing hue.
We marvel, delight,
Look, but not too close,
He's not of this world.
Inside he travels,
into the darkness,
Unnoticed,
Leaves a Seed of Loving Light,
The Beginning of the End.

Original Innocence

Innocence
In No Cence
In No Sense
Are we Born(e)
Then from this we're torn,
And so begins the Earthly Sojourn.

From "*Shackled Gods*" © 2004 Tobias Lars

"In our preoccupation with Original Sin we have lost sight of what will really save our souls, Original Innocence"—The Pope speaking to St. Francis in the movie "Brother Sun, Sister Moon" by director Franco Zeffirelli.

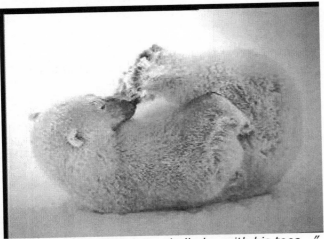

"...and the ferocious bear shall play with his toes..."

Jesus for President?

Being Innocent is not really a sought after quality in current human civilization, except in the sense of getting off in a criminal case. We're not so concerned with actual innocence or guilt but whether we 'got off', got acquitted and often, if we 'got away with it'. There from the phrase "plausible denial" i.e. believable lying, will the jury/court buy it.
Being innocent of motive, of manipulation, of calculation of trying to look good, of trying to get one over on others, is mostly considered naive in today's world. A politician that would actually tell the "whole truth and nothing but the truth" would never get elected most pundits agree. They would be considered too naive to be able to be the leader of a country. Our collective consciousness thinks that a leader needs to be tough, savvy, able to be a tough negotiator, "*speak softly and carry a big stick*".

Can you imagine the President of the U.S. breaking down and crying during a press conference? Speaking from his open heart about our need to soften our own hearts and return to Love, to God? Very likely that would scare most of us and we would probably think that he's not strong enough/"tough" enough for the job. That's how deep the collective programming against innocence/open emotions has penetrated all of us. We are so addicted to stoic, emotionless Father Figures; we are barely able to begin to imagine a woman president. Could you imagine a president with long hair, with a gentle demeanor, with soft loving eternally wondrous eyes? Wearing comfortable loose garments instead of suits and ties? Wearing open toed shoes? Walking amongst the people and talking to them about how to connect with God inside their own beings? Can you imagine a President like that?

No...probably not. He wouldn't be 'tough' enough, he wouldn't be willing to send young boys 18 years old to be killed or permanently emotionally destroyed in wars manipulated by the global power elites. He wouldn't be controllable by special interests.

What I just described was Jesus Christ as President.

And let's be honest, most of those who profess to be 'Christians' would never let Jesus be president if he returned to earth.

Be honest with your responses inside yourself and see how deep the collective programming is. It's just shows us how deep the programming about forms is, how things "should" look. Yet if we ask each other most of us agree that "it's what's on the inside that counts". This is the Gap between what our Hearts know is real, or should be real and what is really happening. Closing this Gap will heal us and the earth.
Being emotionally open and honest is most often considered to be a weakness. Strategy and "getting one over" on the other country/person/ business is honored in our current collective consciousness, the collective consciousness of war/competition/control/ domination/ winning. Openness of heart, absence of motive to control or win over others is simply considered naive.
But what about Jesus' saying *"Unless you convert and become as little children you will not enter the Kingdom of Heaven."*. How can the quality of Innocence of children's hearts be like the kingdom of Heaven? As Jesus says: the entry key to Heaven?

A Gift for Every Child

Many of us have had instances where we know divine intervention saved-helped-assisted our children and us. Car accidents we walked away from, near misses, falls, etc. I remember falling out of a tree as a six year old in the park behind where we lived. On the way down a thick branch hit me under the chin and flipped me over backwards before I landed on the ground. My friend came over and I got up laughing, completely unscathed! We thought the fall was "cool", like the comic book characters we loved imagining being. Interestingly there were no adults around to see my fall.

Their thought patterns and beliefs very likely could have projected onto me and created all kinds of broken bones for me. As an adult this would probably have snapped my neck or at least broken my jaw because that's "reality".

Another instance as kids we would ride our bikes down a hill by our summer house and then we would be "shot" by one of us and we would stretch our arms out and let the bicycle drive off into the ditch and we would fall with complete abandon wherever we and the bicycle would land. We never got hurt. The handlebars never hurt us, the pedals never jabbed our ribs, our hands were never caught in the spokes. At one point one of the neighbors came rushing out, because part of the game was of course to play dead, and he saw one of us lying still in the ditch. He was sure we were seriously hurt and   was about to call for an ambulance. We laughed and thought it was wonderful that we were creating such realistic falls.

The Safety Zone of Vibrational Innocence

There are Angels whose bliss, whose raison d'etre, reason for being, is to assist us humans. They are automatically called in to action and able to reach us when we are in the space of Innocence. The space of innocence is the magnetic pull, the activator blip on the angels messaging board that instantly attracts them to the place/person that is in the innocent space. The space of innocence, the vibration of innocence allows in the miraculous, because in innocence the "miraculous" is totally believable. When children play, the wicked queen imprisons the princess in chains in a dungeon that's impossible to escape, but then the magic flying dragon breathes the fire breath that melts the stones and chains and doesn't hurt the princess and takes her away to the castle in the sky with her prince waiting for her. Absolutely impossible by the "laws" of physics, by "rational" thought, it's fairy land, imaginary friends, naive, unrealistic etc.

When I owned a video company some years ago I filmed a baptism for a young couple. Later at the house they had a small celebration in honor of the event. One of the gifts to the newly baptized baby was a book full of nursery rhymes and children's stories. The five year old daughter of one of the couple's friends excitedly started telling the gathered parents about how she and her friends did the "Ring around the Rosie" rhyme. She got in the center of the room; got everyone's attention and started excitedly sharing this creative adaptation of the rhyme her and her friends had come up with and had lots of fun with. She beamed innocence, play and creative sharing as she shared with us adults, "We say it:

*Ring around the Rosie, ring around the Rosie, **Aw Shit, Aw Shit,** we all fall down*." (Of course it's supposed to be *"ashes, ashes, we all fall down"*.)

She was completely innocent, sharing joy, play, fun. But at the moment of saying that "bad" word the adults judged it as wrong and she was shut off. "Well, we don't need to hear that now" said one woman. Her mother embarrassed, quickly explained to the other adults that she had never heard her daughter say that before and couldn't imagine where she would have heard that. In the little girls world this was innocent play. She was in the space before the "knowledge of good and evil". But now the adults would teach her what was "right and wrong" and her education into the world of adulthood would begin.

"Wise" Innocence

A few years ago Jesus came in spirit and explained to a friend of mine and me about Wise Innocence, about Mature Innocence. Yes, he actually visited us in a spirit form. I'm telling my personal experiences. It's time to come out of the "spiritual closet". We can all have this experience. He talked about how when we are children we are given a "freebie", an automatic start in innocence in each new lifetime. Then this is lost mostly as we join the adult world of hard work, serious problems, money, survival, right and wrong etc. He talked about how after seeing the "evil" in the world, seeing the betrayal, the manipulation, the fear, the struggle for survival, the heartlessness, to then still choose to open our hearts back up to being innocent, but wise innocence this time. The difference between this reawakened savvy-wise innocence and the child's naiveté` is that in this reborn "second" innocence we are listening with our intuition and know when to share, when to open our hearts with others and the world and when not to. We know that we may be made fun of, may be considered "naive", but we are "crazy like a fox", or "wise as serpents and gentle as doves". In the example of the little girl sharing her nursery rhyme, we now know when we can safely open our hearts without being shut down in a way that will damage/hurt us. We may still be judged but not in a situation where we can't handle it. He said also that this Wise Innocence will make our lives worth living again, will have us open back up to Joy, to Fun, to being able to play with each other as adults. This Innocence will literally bring back in the life force and keep us physically young by being "young at heart".

Innocence as Protection

Innocence literally magnetizes angels to surround us. To walk before us, behind us, above us, and below us. It is spiritual physics. When you enter the space of innocence, the forces of the Universe click in and support you. The vibratory rate of Innocence unlocks the keys to dimensions. This is why children still see the other dimensions, the devic kingdom, the fairies, gnomes, Pan, departed Grandma etc. If you insist on explaining this space to the Mind, the rational, logical, then it can lock you into its rules of logic, cause and effect. This is why you can't tell others sometimes what you're experiencing; it simply makes "no sense" to the world of cause and effect. One of the traps of spiritual teachers and helpers is to try to explain this Grace-Space, Innocence, Love continually to logical minds that have no real intention of trying to wake up to it. This has been one of my personal Achilles heels.

Invisibility

You can become "invisible" by entering the space of Innocence. The space opens up gateways to other dimensions and you can step through these to "pop" out of the dimension where the danger is. You can also freeze time and come back later. Once in a business meeting a partner and I felt/'saw' a dimensional doorway appear in the corner of the room. Later we asked what this was and Spirit explained to us that we could spiritually walk through this doorway and we would have unlimited time available in the 'no-time space' to figure out what to say in the meeting. This way we could have plenty of time to feel through what the appropriate action would be in the meeting.

The Emperors Have No Clothes

Innocence doesn't blindly follow tradition. It automatically breaks old rules, taboos. Its very nature is 'no boundaries'. Innocence speaks up with what it feels and sees and this speaking its' truth changes, trans-forms the situation. It speaks out loud what no one else dares to say, or is even allowing themselves to think. This stirs up, shakes up the stuck realities that we walk around in, that is our Cult-ure. Every culture is a Cult. Every culture has unspoken rules. The vibration of Innocence exists outside of rules, outside of culture. It is the little child pointing at the emperors in our lives and saying 'Look Daddy, they have no clothes' they aren't that important, they aren't really true, they aren't really in control of us. That's one of the reasons we love being around kids, they are still thinking and feeling spontaneously, "out of the mouth of babes" comes simple Truth. I can still remember the day I first realized that I didn't have to answer the telephone, that it was there to serve me and not the other way around. Or the day I realized that I didn't have to take every client that came along. My white Protestant upbringing had programmed into me that I had to be available for everyone that came my way if I wanted to be a "good person". These may seem obvious now but at the time they were huge openings of new vistas of freedom and I know there are other ideas/concepts/beliefs I have that will come undone. We all have the power, the right, the sovereignty to choose where and how to spend our energy and time. And there seems to be layers, new levels of applying this freedom.

39.   **Sex is the Manifester of Intention**
Sex is the Magnifier

"Dark Light" Sex

Sex has been labeled a problem by most spiritual teachers on Earth so far, sometimes **the** problem. Often this is because the spiritual teachers have seen that much of the human sex on the planet is power sex, energy games, devoid of real love or heart, or just simple body sex, lust not connected to the heart charka, disconnected from Love. Let's be clear, lust is a part of God, of Love, lust is created by God. It is lust, or sex *disconnected* from the Source, from Love, from Heart, from God that creates energy that is disconnected from Love, from Heart, from God. The spiritual teachers have seen rightly that much of the sex on earth has been increasing the darkness, the dark light, the disconnected from God-Love energy on the planet. True, much of the sex done currently brings love mixed with "darkness" or disconnected from God energy to the planet. It is the state of the heart that sex is done in that decides what kind of heart or heartlessness energy you are opening a doorway for to enter into this dimension on the earth. And since many people are disconnected from Love, from their hearts and are afraid to be open to their hearts while making love-fucking, then Innocence and Love don't get invited to come into the earth dimension that much. How much innocent sex is there happening on the planet right now? Mostly it's with young lovers and then when we become "adults" i.e. our hearts shut down, we do sex from body lusts or power control games, trying to steal energy from each other, or obligation, or boredom. This is sex without heart. Using sex to gain power-position and energy in the world is **Power Sex**, not **Heart Sex**.

Schizoid Sex, Success & Sex Objects, the Madonna Whore Complex and Power Sex

Notice how deeply many women are programmed to be addicted to power sex. Women view men as "success objects" and actually are programmed to the point where they physically respond, get turned on by men in power, witness Henry Kissinger's comment *"power is the ultimate aphrodisiac".* This is an issue that women need to get real and honest with and heal. And of course many men view women as "sex objects". Many men are so divided between "love" and "sex" that they can't "fuck" their wife, and especially after she's become a mother. This dividing sex and "love" needs to be bridged. The whole Madonna-Whore complex schizoid ness of men needs to be healed by opening their Male Hearts, the heart charka and inviting in real Love.

Practically everyone is objectifying each other for power, status, envy from others games even if very subtly. If we're operating from power sex games and getting others to lust after our "prize", being envious of the man having "bagged" the big titted blond empty shell demon. Or the woman having "snared" the "successful" powerful, rich man - then we are feeding off the envy game from others. Take a moment and feel it, feel those situations. Is there any Innocence in the whole energy manipulation game? When men use their power, their money to control and make "prostitutes" of women, and when women use their sex to turn on the energy in their power source, their man, to get what they want, where is Love, where is Innocence? So when spiritual teachers have seen all this they've labeled Sex itself the problem because there has hardly been any open hearted, innocent, joyful, god-full, and yes powerful, lustful love-making fucking to be found in the adult world of sex on earth. We even call it "adult" this kind of power control energy game sex as if it's assumed that's all it can be. It is time to take back all the energy from those "adult" bookstores, "adult" magazines, "adult" games...and bring them back to Original Innocence. (If we want true healing)

Sex itself is not the problem...The Intention and energy from which we do it is what creates the potential problems.

Sex only magnifies, invites in, and opens a doorway for whatever is in our heart and consciousness. Whatever we hold in our energy field when we make love, fuck, is what we create more of. It is electromagnetic soul physics, the vibrational energy that you are while you come-orgasm is the type of energy that will be filtered through into this world. You are the radio tower, television tower that sends the signal out into the world. The energy that you send out while you orgasm and bask in the afterglow, hums, vibrates like a transmission tower and gets sent out to the whole planet (and universe for that matter). This energy you have orgasmed into exi-stance is your energy, your child, your "creation". So whatever "comes around truly goes around", this new energy that has "come" into being is yours, has your vibrational fingerprint on it, will be with you, you can't outrun it, it is connected to you with a spiritual umbilical cord. This is the law of Karma. Whatever you create is yours. You can also receive it back and "recall" these energies. Thank God for that! We've created some nasty, angry, vicious, revenge, annihilistic energies. There is forgiveness, "grace", Restoration, the "make all things brand new", fresh start that always exists in Love's Created Universe.

This vibrational mixing of intention with sex is the magical power of creation. This is why the pagan cultures would have the Rites of Spring where dancing, circling (female magnetic energy) around the pole (phallus, male energy) would bring in the energy of the God and Goddess, then they would go make love in the fields after being communally charged with this Creative Force. This would bring in "good crops", and it actually works because that was their intention and belief system. There is an energy battle on earth and since sexuality is such a powerful "creator" manifesting mechanism, that's how we all are created; sex is the target of a massive disinformation campaign. The energy controller patriarchal religions had to suppress this sex because it gave freedom of being, freedom of thinking, and the natural sex force automatically wakes up a human. Sex is so strong a direct connection with the Source of All, with God that if one has sex openheartedly it will automatically start reconnecting you to God. So those

153

interested in being "go – betweens" between you and God and controlling souls and their energy on earth had to shut down free sex.

Sexual Rituals-Sadism, Abuse, the Roman Police & Satanic Sex.

There are sexual rituals done all over the planet that shut down God, shut down the open Heart, and kill Innocence. These are often called "satanic" rituals which is what they are in the sense that they shut down an open hearted, open minded, open bodied natural sexuality. These rituals are often done by very powerful people who lead very "respectable", "normal" lives during the day. The best thing we can do to stop this abuse of Innocence, abuse of children, abuse of adult's hearts, is to wisely open back up to our own sexual power, invite God back into our sex, invite Love in, be open with our hearts during sex. Find a partner who wants healing also, who is willing to try to be open. This is a wonderful process. Yes, old fears, old paranoia's, old patterns, old imprints will resurface for healing. There have been horrible things done with sexual torture on this planet. This all needs to "come to light", be healed, rewritten, and resolved. Just as an example of horrible sexual abuse--the secret Roman police during the Roman Empire would sexually torture women with especially made curved knives that would be used on the G-spot of women during sexual excitement mixed with torturous pain situations. Is it any wonder that we are "mixed up" about our sexuality? There are many other instances of horrible sexual torture. Every war unleashes these sadistic spirits to do their damage to the "meek", the gentle hearts of earth. This leaked out into our collective consciousness a bit when pictures of the young programmed automaton U.S. soldiers surfaced after being told to inflict sexual torture on Iraqi prisoners by their superiors. As usual the young brainwashed soldiers took the blame, the woman general was reprimanded and the whole thing hushed up. We have to collectively want to heal this or it will keep happening. Punishing the individual 'perpetrators' won't heal the underlying issue—that we in our gated communities, taking our prescription pills, avoiding our real feelings and impulses around sex at every turn, are feeding the collective sexual dysfunction. If we each do our part, which is to just heal our selves then the whole will automatically take care of itself. These are just examples to get you started. Feel your revulsion, feel your horror, feel your rage, wanting to get back at these torturers. Our suppressed hatred and rage at the spirits that perpetrate these tortures is what feeds these realities on earth. We must feel, and vibrate out these repressed held back, compressed energies in our emotional, sexual, spiritual energy bodies. *"God, Love, Source of All, help me restore myself, reset me, refill me, make me brand new again, and let me retain the wisdom from this experience, thank you God, thank you God"*. Say prayers, invoke Love, real God when you go into these places to heal yourself. The good part is that every time you "recover" a lost piece of yourself through consciously taking it back, having it restored with the power and love of the Creator, your sex will become so much more enjoyable, so much more powerful. Sex will become a "comforter" for you, a nurturer, a wonderful way to refill yourself with the Creative energy of the Universe. So asking Love, real God, to "come" and be with us as we make love, as we fuck, and intending in our hearts to bring Love, openness, Heart to Earth with our lovemaking/fucking will help accelerate the healing of the

154

planet and us. And it will start to bring sex back to what its original role for Earth was meant to be, a gateway for the divine to enter the physical plane, a method for increasing the wattage of divinity, God, Love, into physical Form.

Sex

Ancient Cur(s)e,

Flow Reverse
Yours in Hers
His in Yours

Bursts

A Heaven's Chorus.

That Central Love

When that Great Power
Opens up from Below,
And you're inspired
Your Seed to bestow,

Let thy Heart be there
So that,
The Central Love
You would Know.

Innocence Makes an Appearance

Innocence makes an appearance
In the Halls of Erotic Power.

Every body stops
Every body drops
Their Cocks,

Stillness in the moment of an Eye.

"This is our Domain" isn't it?

He's so frailgentlesoftopen -- wimpy?
Rather ordinary looking,
Yet, there is some strange power, flow,
Something sweeping about Him,
We all look,
Want...

Still,
He scares us,
Because He undresses our souls,
Makes us truly Naked,
Demons that we are
We turn away
Let's get back to the
Business in Hand: Mental Fucking.

Yet,
Lingering,
Turn around, Ear buzz,

"Who was that?"
The specter of another world
Breaches, Cracks the Lock,
Bursts through the Wall,
Crashes the Private Club.

There He stands
In all His Frail Power.

His Heart connected
to his Base,
Calling us out,
Of our Cave,
"Lazarus, Arise"
You are compelled,
The Harvester has Come
For you
Has Love

156

For you
Has You
Will now Take you
For His own
Devices.

There's a Space to play,
A Place to Assume,
A Cornerstone to be,

"*Come with Me*" He says
(if anything)

"*You're mine*
I'm gonna fuck you to Kingdom Come
I'm gonna melt your fears of 'So Long'
Thousands of you shall sing this Song."

Let Me shake your ass,
It'll come to pass,
Let Me come in your heart
I want your Core,

I love you, I love you, I love you,

Come with Me…

40.   Omnisexuality

Life is Sex—Sex is Life

Only those afraid of Life will want to throttle, control, harness, corral, use Sex for their own control purposes. If you enjoy Life, enjoy freedom, enjoy openness, then you will allow others to express however they choose.

There are no "wrong" Bodies

Being to being love doesn't decide it can't love that other being because they have the "wrong" body! This is the "knowledge of good and evil" that I keep talking about, deciding that something, some expression of divine Love is "evil", or "wrong" or "bad". It is this deciding; this judging that places what's being judged outside of Love. It is in our fallen state that we have let the Mind of Judgment take over and decide through *"the knowledge of good and evil"* what we designate as outside of God. And the rest is what has become fallen, divided (into good and evil) history on Earth. We are fighting our selves. We are the divided beings split into good and evil parts and then we continue trying to kill the "other" while all this fighting our selves is doing is bringing the whole thing down into real death, which is the stoppage of energy.

"Categorizing" Minds put us in a Box

The Mind wants us to have definite categories of who we can "love", or how that love "is supposed" to look. Anytime there is a "should", a "supposed to", this means it is expected, ordered, and the Impulse of Life, of Love is not free to express in the moment how it wishes to. This is imprisoned love and feeds energy to the Mind, the Controller, Lucifer. The Mind is not meant to run the Creation, it is meant to carry out as a helper, the directive of the Heart, Divine Will. The Mind has cleverly created control on Earth by getting most people to believe that what they think of as Divine Will is really the Minds' should's, prescribed behaviors, the Mind's preprogrammed formulas for living. Take a look, start seeing in your life where you are living in tyranny of "should's". Practically everything most people do is run by some should, some Mind program of wanting approval or power over others, or running from fear of death. What happened to our freedom to be as we choose?

Sex is the Power Source

Since Sex is the power source of creating physical Life the Mind has developed especially powerful mind control programs around the expression of love in the physical way. The Mind wants contracts, love = ownership, sign on the dotted line, swear to "honor and obey until death do us part" types of controls on expression of sexuality because the Mind can control these expressions and thereby keep the energy imprisoned and feeding the control beliefs/programs in the Mind.
"You're my husband/wife/boyfriend/girlfriend and you're supposed to …..(X)"

There are 1000's of generations of rules pounded in by guilt and should's into our psyches and emotional bodies about how we are "supposed" to act. Yet at the same time we know in our hearts that *"you can't set rules about love"*. So we're caught in the cross-fire of the Impulse of Love-Heart-God and the Fear-Control of the Mind.

New Teachings – New Testaments are Dangerous! (to the hysteric little Mind followers)

It's been a very painful existence for most humans under this yoke of control. It's not painful in the short run (though you're in for a wakeup call when you leave this dimension) if you've shut off your heart and become a blind follower of "the rules". But then you're already dead, a slave to the Mind—Lucifer and likely won't be reading this unless this material starts getting out into the public consciousness and you're finding a need to criticize any new 'truths' because it scares you on a deep level and you have a knee jerk reaction to put down, deride, sneer at, anything outside of your mind programmed belief system. So you have to find fault with any 'new testament' just like the Pharisees and Sadducees at the time of Jesus were threatened by his new teachings. So you'll read this with the purpose of finding fault with it because it has stirred up your suppressed feelings. About those kinds of people, the 'can't think for themselves crowd', the blind followers of 'the rules', the adherents to formula, the addicted to worrying about what others think of them...Jesus said *"Let the dead bury the dead."*
I know that might be a little harsh...but we have to finally speak the truth.

Openhearted Sex dissolves all the "Rules"

Free, openhearted, spontaneous loving sex dissolves all the rules, agreements, contracts on love and sex. But the Mind can still control us if it punishes us with guilt when we break the "rules" about how we "should" be "loving" and how we "should" be having sex. This is so deep at this time in human behavior programming that the individual who breaks the rules is still most of the time branded with a "Scarlet Letter". They're punished and even if they're not actually stoned to death anymore, they are often socially cast out. The woman who has sex with too many men is still called a whore and a slut, the man who feels love for another man is called "queer", or "fag". These "outlaws" are thrown into categories by the Mind. Both gays and heterosexuals are often uncomfortable with bisexuals for example. You're not allowed to feel love for other beings regardless of their body type, you must choose a Mind controlled category to put yourself in. *"C'mon you're either gay or straight, there ain't no in between, c'mon which is it?"* This is one of the Minds favorite ploys, *"You're either one of us, or you're one of them"*. Even the president of the U.S. recently used this Mind-Luciferian ploy when telling other countries of the world, *"You're either with us or you're with the terrorists."* Unbelievable, but it still works because most people are caught in the grip of the Mind. Every teacher, every real spiritual master has tried to point the way to feeling, to being, to the heart beyond the mind categories. That's why you can't make rules about a master's teaching and why the teachings of a true master after they are gone almost always get twisted and taken over by the Mind and degenerate into silly rules of behavior that the Mind loves. *"The hem of yours skirt must be only 6 inches above your ankles, you must cover your whole body except the eyes, you can't eat pork, you can only eat pork on Thursdays, you're not allowed any meat, you must kill the animal this way for it to be "holy", you can't have sex before marriage, you must have sheet between you when you first have sex, you can have sex with men, you can't have sex with men, this is an "abomination" this is holy, you must wear funny hats, you must walk in a procession...you should...you must...etc., etc., etc."*

Love has no rules, except Love. Love is its own law. *"The whole of the law is Love."* God loves, yes physically loves all body types.

God is OmniSexual!

God loves animals, loves "aliens", loves you, loves women, loves men...loves every one and every thing in the creation. God is "Omnisexual". S/He is not "gay" or "straight" or "alien" or "bestial" or anything, **only**. S/he is all those things and **more**. Omni = Everything, Omnisexual, All is Sex, Sex is All, Life is Sex, Sex is Life. No division, no categories, no judgment, no this better than that, S/He loves All of us, all of the creation. And loves us not in a paternalistic, patronizing, looking down from on high "above the lower functions" way, but loves us from inside, inside our cocks and pussies, inside our hearts, loves all of us, just as we are, no judgment, enjoying the physical as much as the spiritual since All is Love, All is God. This is the Advaita consciousness in the Indian traditions that advanced yogis exhibit and share with others. All is One, is God, All That Is.

Beings Outside the Box

One of the most threatening beings on the planet today is the one who refuses to be categorized, and tries instead to live by the Impulse of Life, moment by moment following their intuition. *"No I'm not gay, but yes I've had sex with men." "No I'm not straight but I've had sex with women". "No I'm not an alien but I've had sex with 'aliens'." "No I'm not an Angel but I've had sex with Angels."* This threatens everything, all the categories that the Mind has worked so hard to develop in order to control us all with. In this season of upheaval (up –heaven-ing) the Mind is going to desperately try to put Pandora back in her Box to get everything back under control. But it's too late, She's already out and Loving Freedom is "coming" back to Earth one way or another. We can choose to have this "New Heaven, New Earth" manifest the hard way through plagues, viruses, war, disease, earthquakes, violent weather etc. or we can surrender to the new flow of Life, the new Paradigm and allow our static, stuck mind programming-beliefs-ideas-traditions to gently melt away. It's up to us...but it's coming one way or another.

"The 'monkeys ' (us) are going to the stars. How they are going to get there isn't quite clear – whether it will be a relatively smooth journey or through catastrophic upheavals." Terence McKenna

Get in touch with your Heart, with the Love of God and it will guide you through the coming changes. No rules of behavior will help you anymore. The Earth wants Heart directed beings to live on her and so Chaos is coming to cleanse all those who live by static (dead) formulas and rules. This process is wonderful, energizing and liberating for those who want real freedom and love, and it is terrifying, "doomsday", "chaos" "Armageddon" to those who desperately cling to rules, formulas, Mind programming.

Apocalypse = Full, divine Revelation

The word Apocalypse means- ***Full, divine Revelation.***
The Veil is rendered; we stand again face to face with God, in direct conscious communion with the Creator.

(Look it up in the dictionary)

This is what's coming...

41.   The Serpent, Moses, and the Garden Revisited

"No Fences"

A friend of mine has a desert oasis complete with a waterfall in his backyard. He didn't put up a fence that separates "his" land from the mountain preserve behind his house, but he left it open because he enjoys the animals and the view. The builder couldn't understand this concept of "no fences", *"But it comes with the price of the house!?"* And my friend had a lot of trouble explaining that he didn't want a wall between him and Nature, but that's a different story.

My Brother Serpent Visits Me

I was floating in my friend's spa, looking over at the mountains, the sky, floating, feeling, being, melting, merging with my Core when I looked over at the waterfall in his garden. I saw a serpent's head under the waterfall. The head was maybe a foot long; it was a shape that coalesced from the stones that make up the waterfall. I could see his eye and as I started to feel with my solar plexus it felt like I looked into another vibrational dimension. Then he spoke to me in my heart, not audibly in words as such, but with a telepathic energy transmission from the dimensional place where he lived. He told me of these dimensions he lives in that once were integrated with our current dimension on Earth and that there was a time when beings could move freely between dimensions and that these dimensions will merge again. He told me that he is representative of the vital energy of life, of the Kundalini, of raw, primal, undulating energy flow of Life Force that we rejected in the Garden of Eden story because this powerful energy scared us and we were con-vinced that it was somehow "evil" or "wrong".   This raw, serpentine, primal energy source fed us internally.   In that original creation on Earth, when souls first entered the physical plane we had no need for food, we lived directly off the "manna of heaven" in our Cores, the *"Man shall not live by bread alone but by the very Word of God…"* energy that we all still have inside us but we've been cut off from.   And in the outer world this Love of God manifested as fruits and plants that would feed us willingly and lovingly. We were convinced to reject this source of energy and cut ourselves off from this inner energy concentrated in our heart, brain and spine and ever since we've lived in "sin" (Sin = without, without conscious connection to our inner soul energy), in lack, in having to work for a "living" in "sweat and toil". As he was transmitting this information to me I saw him in his dimension; he was a huge snake, maybe thirty feet long and as thick as my waist around. But I had no fear, just a warm, peaceful, loving feeling of warmth and being nurtured from the inside. As the information was coming to me I was simultaneously feeling this "Comforter-Holy Ghost" as Jesus called it feeding me from the inside. He showed me how his race was just like us, spirits of Love that simply like the reptilian form. He told me that many of the humans today are reptilian spirits that have taken human form because so long ago God had to intervene and give everyone the same human bodies to remain in this dimension on Earth because we were all judging one another

162

based on different body types. Which we still do of course through racism, obsession with plastic surgery etc. He told me that the day is coming when beings will go back to the forms they feel most comfortable in. He showed me that Moses saw all this when he was writing Genesis.

An Age Old Misunderstanding

"And I will put enmity between thee and the woman, and between thy seed and her seed; it shall bruise thy head, and thou shalt bruise his heel." Genesis 3:15

This is how Moses describes how we became set against our selves, against that primal "reptilian" part of our own fundamental nature after we "fell" from Grace and lost direct come-union with God. I understand that many fundamental religionists and followers of man made religions will be scared by this imagery of talking to a "serpent". We have been programmed, brainwashed, deeply imprinted that the reptilian energy is something to be feared. Yet this "reptilian" energy is something deep inside each and every one of us. We could not live at all without it. It regulates the breath, the life force. Snakes kill by stopping the breath. They are *"wise as serpents"* Jesus says. What does he mean by that? Look at a snake sometime, look into its eyes. You cannot fool a snake; you cannot use fancy intellectual knowledge and talk it into being something other than its fundamental nature. It is primal, instinctual, intuitive and watches the world "ruthlessly" in a sense, but it's really strongly connected to the Life Force and can't be fooled. The Snake energy will reflect what's in our subconscious. If we have undealt with issues and subconscious suppressed programming, judgments and beliefs we will see them reflected in the Serpent. Our current civilization has developed a severe age old judgment of this Serpent energy. When we watch a snake move it triggers something deep within us. It starts re-activating our own primal life force, what Hindus call the Kundalini. If you sit and watch a snake move, you will feel your own shivers up and down your spine and it will turn into a comforting energy of life force actually feeding you. This is what Jesus called "The Comforter" and what he promised to send when he left his world. That is the truth of it and until we wake up to this fact we will continue having mind and soul control misguided religions that set us against a part of our fundamental Selves. We will fight our own natures forever if we don't wake up to this.

The Most Fundamental part of Our Selves

The Reptilian is the most fundamental part of the physical form. It is the most basic, it is pure energy moving. No legs or arms have been formed yet, just pure essence rising upward, moving. Did you ever wonder how a snake can move? It has no legs or arms. How does it move so gracefully and fast on the ground? Our "scientism" followers try to explain it by their physics as the *"snake converts lateral energy into forward motion"* but when you watch a snake move there's something more to it. The snake is pure energy. This is why snakes never get fat. They are pure muscle, have you ever seen a fat snake? I don't mean when it has prey it has swallowed but actual loose fat on top of its muscles? Snakes cannot get fat because they are pure energy.

163

All of us out there trying to lose weight would do it easily by contacting this Life Force Kundalini snake energy inside ourselves. It would start a whole new revolution in the weight loss industry! *"The 24 hr Serpentine Energy Fitness Weight Loss Center"! Ok*, I'm joking, but we need to lighten up about this misunderstanding. This misunderstanding and rejection of our own fundamental reptilian energy has caused untold misery and pain on this planet. When we develop as embryos in our mother's wombs, the first stage we go through is the reptilian stage of development. This is when basic autonomic brain functions such as breathing, digesting, eliminating, sensing, seeing, hearing, touch, taste are imprinted into our brains and nervous systems. Rejecting this part of ourselves has cut us off from a deep level of being able to be fed by God-Love. This is the story of "The Fall".

We Will Meet Again

I watched and felt him, my serpent Brother move so deliberately, so powerfully, so fluidly, so peacefully around this 21st century Garden I was in. He showed me one of his other forms, how he can also have a human body with a serpents head, how reality and forms were much more fluid back before the "Fall", before we judged each other. Yes, in a way he looked fierce but that is because his way of being is simply a way of living that does not tolerate hypocrisy or lying to oneself. The reptilian energy is not hateful, "evil" or cruel, it simply is so primal that it reflects what is in our subconscious by its very nature and therefore we've had to make it a scapegoat all this time for the fears and hatreds we have banished to our subconscious. Otherwise we would have to admit our lies to ourselves. When a being is in touch with their primal Life force, their energy of Life in their cores, their spines, they have to stay clear, honest, real with their own energy to remain in touch with this Life Force.

The Caduceus, the medical symbol, has the two serpents swirling around the spinal column. When the serpentine energy of the life force is allowed to flow naturally around the spinal column amazing amounts of energy are released and automatically align and keep healthy the individual. Yogis and spiritual adepts know this "serpentine" primal Life Force energy, it's been called the Kundalini that lies like a serpent coiled at the base of our spines waiting to be let out into it's rightful role in our beings.

The light changed, my new friend left, but he told me that we would meet again in physical reality on earth when the "New Heaven and New Earth" would be a reality.

164

Asclepius

The name, "serpent-bearer," refers to the Rod of Asclepius, which was entwined with a single serpent. This symbol has now become a symbol for physicians across the globe. However, one should be careful not to confuse the Staff of Asclepius, which features a single serpent wrapped around a roughhewn branch, with the Caduceus of Mercury (Roman), or Karykeion of Hermes (Greek). The Caduceus, which features two intertwined serpents (rather than the single serpent in Asclepius' wand), as well as a pair of wings, has long been a symbol of commerce. It is thought that the two were first confused in the seventh century A.D., when alchemists often used the caduceus to symbolize their association with magical or "hermetic" arts. (from Wikipedia)

42

S&M Spirituality-The Game of Submission & Domination

There is a way of being, a way of existing, that lives by dominating other life forms. This way of being gets its energy by controlling other beings and getting these other beings to "produce" energy that the controllers can then harvest and use for their sustenance.

Earth is a Free Will Zone

Earth is not meant to have this modus operandi operating on it. Earth is meant as a Free Will Zone where no one it to control or dominate other life forms but rather the trust and Innocence of opening directly to the Source of all Life feeds every spirit and elemental, Devic, plant, animal life essence in abundance and no one "needs" anything from another but shares and interacts with each other as directed by Love and Free Will.

The Division Bell has Rung

Earth was invaded a long time ago in the land of Pan(gea) by spirits that live by dominating others. These spirits are about to be removed from Earth. The Earth has chosen to Live and not to continue to be dominated by these dominator spirits. These spirits will be removed, forced to leave really, since they do not live by agreement or cooperation but by war, dissension, "*us vs. them*" and "*might is right*". This coming "*judgment day*" is the "*separation of the wheat and the chaff*" that Jesus spoke about. It is also the "*I will set brother against brother*" that he also spoke about. Families will be divided in this process, but for the better, no more unhealthy dysfunctional dominator controller, guilt mongering family relationships. A massive "decloaking" will occur and we will be able to see who is who in this cosmic game of soul control vs. Free Will being played out on planet Earth at this time. Father God, real God, God of Loving Light has acceptance for all spirits and the Dominator Spirits aren't "evil", they simply are what they are and are being true to their nature, often more true to what they really are than the loving or heart or Free Will spirits are being currently on earth. However these controlling spirits that dominate others don't belong on Earth because Earth is a Free Will planet, a Freedom planet. That's why we respond deeply in our cores when real freedom is presented to us. The United States became a beacon to the rest of the world of the hope for real Freedom, being able to live out our personal dreams. The dominator spirits belong in their rightful place where they can experience their "heaven". Hell to dominator spirits might be a free will zone that they are prisoners of! So this separation of the dominator spirits from the heart free will spirits will put spirits back where they belong and free the Earth to go back to her original plan for being.

Animals are Free Beings Also in God's Creation

The Earth's animals aren't meant to be dominated as the dominator god Jehovah claims in the Bible. The animals do look to their "gods" (us) as the conscious, free will incarnations of the Divine but since we've fallen from direct contact with God the animals have come to fear us for we hunt, kill, torture and imprison them. The Earth's animals are meant to live wild and free, and so are we! And it is a long and horrible story of how we've given away our power to the dominator model, a story full of horrors, guilt as weapon, soul torture, deceit, fear, cruelty, godlessness. You will have to heal these spaces in yourself at this time if you'd like to stay with the Earth because She is and will be more and more vibrating out all death and denial from her magnetic field.

'The Very Stones shall cry out' & the Almond Tree will Bloom in Winter

Death and denial will no longer be able to exist in the consciously innocent "Garden of Eden" that the Earth is intending on returning to. So any death and denial caught in your personal magnetic field essence will have to be found, separated from the life essence that it has invaded and gotten control over, this essence will have to be "restored", healed and returned back into your soul magnetic field. This is true "integration", "wholing", "healing". You will notice as you do this you gain power, gain enjoyment, gain play, gain energy. Much of what has been called "letting go" so far on Earth has meant letting go of the essence, that part of your soul that the denial/death is controlling. Literally breaking off a piece of yourself in order to be free from it, like a wolf biting off his paw to escape a trap. This method may look like healing temporarily but you are also losing power and eventually can lose all of yourself. Think of how much power you've given away. You were originally a "god", you could literally fly, dematerialize, change forms. You were consciously aware of many dimensions. You were lovable enough back in the original Garden of Eden that the trees sprang forth with fruit to please you as you walked by. When St. Francis asked an almond tree to reveal God to him in the middle of winter it bloomed and produced fruit! When Jesus came in through the east gate of Jerusalem for Passover riding on a donkey the Pharisees (those anal 'letter of the law' worshipers that always invade spiritual movements) told him to quiet the crowd down because they were being too open and expressive with their love. He turned and told them that if he quieted the crowd down "*the very stones will cry out*". There is a response from Nature, from the Creation towards a loving being. Each and every one of us are also potentially a fully realized, awake, loving being, a "god" that the very stones will cry out to "*Hosanna in the highest*".

The elemental god of stones on Earth is named Arensa. A friend and I have talked to him on several occasions. It's real, it's available to all of us heart free will spirits to open back up to. I know the mind programming, the brainwashing of the dominator spirits on the planet currently through TV, schools, their scientists, etc. is that talking to elementals or spirits is still mostly considered "crazy". So what? Is the dominator system enjoyable? Are you enjoying it? Is there beauty created by the current dominator system? Look around; is there beauty in our cities? Or are cities more like poisonous gas spewing "boils" on the surface of the earth? What do you have to lose? Nothing, you have everything to gain, your soul, your heart , your fun, your unbelievable sex, freedom, abundance without worry, real soul mates, lovers everywhere etc. You only have your pain, your heartache, your disconnect from real Love, from God to lose. Do you really want to live one more lifetime of slow painful death? Do you want to spend the last 20 years of your life worrying about your Social (in)Security, your body falling apart, fearing death? This is the reality for most of us in the current system.

The Dominator Model is Leaving Earth

The Dominator Paradigm is leaving Earth but it will fight "to the death" because that is its nature. I.e. it will keep grabbing as much Life, soul essence as it can and giving it to the "death" it loves and worships. It is very difficult to say these things without it being interpreted as judgmental. We all have such a history with this 'Fall' from direct conscious communion with God-Love-Source that we can't hear about what has happened to us without our filters and judgments immediately kicking in. Try to "feel" and sense and go slow with this information and honestly look around you, be open, be truly what a real scientist should be, open without prejudice (not pre judging until you've truly investigated) to new information and then feel inside yourself, ask your spirit, your soul to lead you towards what's real. If we get honest with ourselves very likely a part of us now wants death also, we think of it as restful, a respite from the "battle of life" perhaps. We've become divided beings, half Life and half Death, to the point that we can't tell anymore who's who, who's a dominator denial of Life spirit and who's a heart free will lover of Life spirit. This is the process of cleansing that is occurring now. The dominator spirits will start doing more and more of their atrocities right out in the open right in front of our eyes. It will look like chaos, pain, destruction as the "waters boil", as the spirit essence boils itself clean on the planet. It can't be avoided. We can however experience it in more or less painful ways, either as a true healing and rebirth of Love and Spirit or as Doomsday, destruction, fearful chaos. The choice is ours.

Why did we "Fall from Grace" to begin with?

Why was the Dominator Paradigm allowed to come to Earth in the first place? You might shake your fist at God and ask. *"Yeah, why the fuck were these controller bastards and death spirits allowed onto the planet? Why have they been allowed to almost bring the planet to the point of annihilation, why are they allowed to poison the water, the air, and all living things? Was it to punish us God? Are you really a vengeful, angry God? If you are I want nothing to do with you, I'll just harden my heart and learn to survive on my own. Fuck you!"*

(By the way, sincere open hearted conscious ranting and expressing your rage at God will really help the planet heal...IF you let it be a two way street and are willing at the same time you scream and rant to let God come in and re-fill you with fresh renewed understanding and energy)

"Rage, Rage against the dying of the Light"—Dylan Thomas

If you can let yourself feel some of your feelings of rage at God, that is a very powerful place to heal yourself and the planet. God is desperate for people who are willing to be real with Him. Most prayer on the planet today is begging. Most of what God gets is people begging for things, for health, for their kids, for money, for favors, for whatever trinket needs. How do you

168

feel when beggars come up to you? Kind of 'icky' wouldn't you say. Well God feels 'icky' with beggar prayers also. God is desperate for those who are willing to be real with him, talk truth, be real with their feelings. Talk to God, open a dialogue about the confusions you may have, this is where the healing needs to happen. Pretending that all is "light" and if I just "think positive", "visualize positive", "think only good thoughts", then God will miraculously descend from the heavens and rescue us all, is Denial. This is denying your pain. And if you don't get real, your "world" will get real for you as a wake up call. Divorce, suicides, school shooting, war, corruption, sexual abuse, drugs and the big equalizer-Cancer are all wake up calls. Wake up! Stop running around as a programmed terrified economic robot! My wake up calls came as a divorce and bankruptcy. Thank you God, I am eternally grateful for snapping me out of my sleepwalking zombie state.

Get Real – with God!
Our suppressed horror that we pretend not to feel is what feeds the death machine on the planet, to the point where God the Father and God the Mother now both need to step in to prevent the whole planet being lost to nuclear/spiritual winter, madness of war and destruction. We need to get real with our pain if we want to remain on our beautiful Earth and help it get rid of the dominator spirits. Do your part, that is all you need to do, and are asked to do. You will do more to give power to the Earth, to the cleansing of the Earth and bringing back Love by healing yourself, getting real, honest about your fears, than by all the legislation you could ever pass in an increasingly impotent government that has little interest in individuals' freedom anymore but is mainly interested in feeding itself, making itself more powerful. And why should this be surprising, any entity tries to grow, preserve itself, and so does the government. The founding fathers of America saw this potential for the virus of the government taking away individuals' power and tried to put in measures to hold the space open for individuals to have freedom and self determination. It hasn't really worked, the fear of (the false) god, the IRS, and the Police is effectively programmed into just about every citizen today and we've turned into good little sheep.
Do you know that there are whole galaxies of 'fallen' dominator spirits? The Milky Way isn't one of them. We are a 'mixed' galaxy and Earth is currently a 'mixed' spirit planet. Domination of false 'gods' will come and go...

But You...are Forever...a Free Soul of God.

169

43

Love is Graduating

Love is graduating on planet Earth at this time. The way we have "done" love in the past is changing. The chaos, pain and confusion that are happening everywhere around love are the bubbling up and out of the chains that have imprisoned love for most of remembered history. All the chains are now coming off, the old dead models are bubbling up, out and away.

Every culture has rules about love: how to date, how to marry, what marriage means, you can't "cheat", you have to do this, you should do that etc. These are the chains on Love. And these 'rules' have caused us 1000's of years of untold pain, because...

Love is Free, it moves with the impulse of Life, of God.

You can't set rules about Love.

Yet we insist on trying to set rules about how love "should" be expressed. This is the right way to feel, that is wrong, this is good, that is bad. This imprisoning of Love with rules is the original Fall, the "knowledge of good and evil." At this time on Earth the energy of Freedom is returning to the planet and all binding rules, imprisoning formulas for behavior are being cast off. These rules are so enmeshed in our emotional bodies, in our psyches that it is very painful to separate them out of us. It feels (sometimes physically) that we are dying, we have "broken hearts", our hearts have been invaded by Mind formulas for living when actually the very essence of Heart is freedom, free expression of Love. So at this time whole cultures, old models, religions, belief systems and individuals are caught in the cross-fire of the old model of love by rules and the new model of love by Divine Impulse. If we are putting our faith, our trust in rules/formulas for Life/Love we are going to be betrayed at this time. We are going to be betrayed by our most trusted "lovers", and "friends". If we don't hear or refuse to listen when our intuition, our heart, is telling us something then there is no other way for us to wake up than by having the outer world "betray" us, cause us "pain". If we don't want the outer world to "betray" us, we can choose to have God "betray" us in Love, to have Love lovingly help us wake up. This probably won't spare us all the pain, but we'll feel more guided and loved as we're waking up and all our old models are being deva-stated (god stated) in our lives.

Your Deity Lies in Love

In Love He will lead you,
a Stray

With infinite kindness
He'll you betray.

There (He says)
will come a day
when you'll be able
To stay.

Highest form of God,
Real-eyes'd in Love.

Yet another leap,
Trans-Forms
into undoer,
Liar, Devil,
Lover, God.

Time to Change the Deep Imprints

Our old models are so ingrained, so pounded into our emotional bodies, woven into our subconscious, that they seem like "truths"—"Of course one should never 'cheat' on ones spouse" "Of course a couple should stay together for life, at least for the children's sake etc." We have a whole subconscious programming by the culture as a whole about what "should" be done. This subconscious programming has taken on the appearance of "laws"-- "that's just how it is", "that's what God wants". Sometimes these "laws" that are really subconscious imprints that have been pounded in by hundreds of lifetimes of programming are so deep that many people won't even approach thinking about them for the fear of what will happen. We have built in automatic shutoffs in our minds. Men will often head for the door when a woman starts crying. Women will head for the door when a man gets angry. We don't know how, no one taught us to deal with our feelings, never mind the deep subconscious guilt and "should" imprints that run most people. Did you have a course in school on "How to effectively feel and deal with emotions 101?" or "How to locate and defuse subconscious imprints that imprison you 202?" Of course not because the current paradigm of control, domination and mind programming doesn't want the "cattle" (us) to wake up.

When something is set in concrete it becomes static i.e. it stops moving and IT DIES! Setting rules about how love should be expressed eventually kills Love. Actually Love leaves, it moves on and we're left holding the empty bag (the dead body), the booby prize. The Life Force, God, Love, the Divine Impulse of Creation is you, is your very center, is in your sex. Your sex and Love are the same force, the rest is "knowledge of good and evil", formulas, rules, judgments, "shoulds", "imprints" for how to behave. But just reading this and understanding it intellectually does not heal it. We must go back into the emotional body which has been imprisoned by all these rules/formulas for behavior and let the emotional body vibrate these chains out of it (i.e. scream cry, hate, love, joy, fear, anger etc.) E-motion = energy in motion. If we don't move our emotions our energy gets stuck, static, starts to die. Look around you...we are for the most part terrified half alive economic zombie slaves walking around today on the planet. This is the

"Glory of God"? This is "all that we can be"?...c'mon someone has to say "The Emperors have no Clue!" We can't intellectualize our way to healing at this point. Just the same way you can't drug your way to health no matter how many TV commercials of people running through meadows ecstatically happy the pharmaceutical companies pump at us during the evening news. This is why all scientific schools, approaches to healing will ultimately fail. We must include the emotional body in our healing. It is half of us! Just like you can't walk on one leg very well, or function if half of your brain is removed, so we can't function wholistically, as integrated fully functional human spiritual beings without healing our emotional bodies.

The End of All Schools

A school of "healing" that replaces old formulas with new "refined" formulas, a better "truth", gives you a new model, a new framework to view the world through, won't work in the long run at this time on earth because the Earth is returning to rulelessness, to Freedom of Love, Freedom of Will, Freedom of Individuals, Freedom of the Divine Impulse. Many people will view this as chaos, Doomsday. Others will experience it as liberation. These "finer" models of living, therapists, schools of healing, all the Human Potential movement is necessary and helpful because it makes us feel safe. We think we "understand" what is happening to us so we are willing to let go a little of the old us. This is a necessary "trick" by real Love to have us move our energy, change our ways at all. God guides us perfectly from where we're at, He doesn't give us the billion watt vision right away when our circuits can only handle 150 watts because we would overload and blow our circuits. But eventually our Love will have to graduate to live directly from our own Hearts, from our own knowing, from the place where we and God meet in the core of our being. And the Earth is also graduating at this time and any spirit that wishes to stay with the Earth will also have to graduate to being in flow with the Divine Impulse of Love. When it asks you to move, when Love moves, you will have to move with it or you'll soon notice that "The thrill is gone" in your relationship, your work, your life.

No More Good-Bye's

We can't imprison love in one body; we can't insist that the Divine Love Impulse stays in the one body, the one being we happen to be with for the moment. We must hear the truth about how we feel and when it's over move along with Love knowing that we are doing our own hearts deepest, most joyous plan for us that we could imagine that is best for all involved. In the awake enlightened state "good byes" make no sense; "losing someone" makes no sense because when you are in touch with your essence, your heart, you are in touch with all Life. But you can't fake this, just because we understand the concept with our minds and it rings true deep inside us, we still have to walk into the feelings, into the humanness and allow it to be transformed from inside the experience. We must "walk the walk" as well as being able to "talk the talk." We can have this awareness, this state of being, we can be this for real, now, at this time on Earth, if we're willing to listen and follow our Hearts, the "still small voice" of God. We don't need to retire to the mountains, spend years in a cave, we can have it now. Yes, there's willingness to follow our intuition required from us. God is so ready to Love and help us at this time, there are legions of angels and spirit guides waiting for us! To simply say "Yes, I'm ready, my old ways don't work, please help me and show me."

When you follow Love you gain Energy, Freedom, more Love
Remember, you will not ever lose love when you follow Love. You will gain in your deepest dreams. Your mind, the old "rules" will however try to point out how you made a mistake. Others still living by the "rules" won't understand, will think you're "wrong", "immoral", "evil", etc. but remember they're the ones that are insane, trying to force Love into their little boxes and reacting with fear if someone does something different than the programmed in rules for how to behave.

It's only because we are divided beings not in touch with our God-Nature that this is even an issue. If we all were fully in touch with our very Beings, we would automatically follow the Divine Impulse and the question of "right and wrong" simply wouldn't exist. But at this point we've spent thousands of lifetimes building up "truths" and rules about living and loving that are deeply pounded into our emotional bodies.. We've lived in the Mind for so long that when the Heart stirs it seems very painful, i.e. *"Love Kills"* (the Sex Pistols), "love hurts", Romeo and Juliet the true lovers die painfully and can't survive in this world and thousands of movies, books and poems are written about love gone wrong. Yes, Love does hurt when we are a fallen, divided, out of touch with Love being, because when Love enters you it starts to automatically push out the lies, our dead old energies and static belief systems. But we have no place else to go if we want healing. Otherwise it's just another lifetime of staving off an inevitable death. And remember we cannot be hurt, we are invincible, our vulnerability is our strength. The safest thing in the world is to be a new born baby even though it may seem the most vulnerable. The most dangerous thing in the world to be is an emotionally suppressed, "successful" adult, surrounded by body guards, even though it might seem to be the safest thing.

Time to Graduate
Love is graduating on Earth. It is freeing itself from the chains of the Mind rules we've tried to imprison it with. We can also free ourselves from all the mind rules that imprison us right now. Get honest, get real, start feeling how you really feel, intend with your heart to wake up, ask for help, trust in Love.

To permanently change the Earth back to its Original Paradise all we need are 100 fully awake humans. The energy from these 100 awake god-humans would reverberate-vibrate so strongly inside the collective consciousness of earth that it would set off a energy activation in everyone's consciousness.

44.   I Am a Piece of God

Every Technique, Every Formula will stop working

No formula will ever work for long. Techniques are invented to take you beyond techniques. It doesn't matter how refined the technique of meditation is eventually it won't work. Why? Because we are gods. And gods have free will and are free to create however they choose, beyond rules, beyond anything...free to create whole new universes. Techniques are helpers, tools, like a ladder that you use to get to the window, but when you reach the window into the new world you need to leave the ladder behind.

Your Intuition is your direct connect with Source, God, The Creator, Awareness, Consciousness, the energy that is you in its core. This is You. And the magic is that this intuition if listened to and followed by everyone works in concert, synchronicity for everyone and the whole.

The Kingdom of Heaven *is* Within.... You cannot exist, you cannot be here if you aren't a piece of the Source, a piece of God. The energy that keeps your heart beating is Source, is God. The energy that keeps electrons and protons/neutrons in an atom from flying apart is God's thought. You are a piece of this larger consciousness.

Try saying:

I am a piece of God or

I am a piece of Awareness, Consciousness, Source, Love, whatever feels good to you.

I am a Christ of God

(Christ means cross-ing of worlds, where the Eternal cracks through the crossing of dimensions-worlds into this world. Going back through your own Christ, crossing, gateway is the only way back to God.

There is no 'Cookie Cutter' Enlightenment

There is no cookie cutter enlightenment. Everyone will have their own way home. Your intuition will take you home. And your journey will be enjoyable for you. What a miracle! The way home is enjoyable! Comfort and Joy! Fully enjoying your self is God. God-Source is ecstasy, fun, laughing, orgasm, enjoying, feeling filled with peace, love, everything. Do you think God would set it up that it would be difficult, painful, sacrificing, to reach Him? Would you as a parent do that to your kids? Give birth to them, send them out on their own, then go hide somewhere on a mountain top that is impossible to get to for a normal person and then say come find me and I will give you all the things you are looking for? That's crazy. That's the invention of priests who are interested in being between you and God for their own purposes of power, ego, control, etc. We're addicted to priests, religions, churches, difficulty, pain, struggle. You can choose to go home by loving God, by having a love affair with God, seeing God in everything. You can do it by

174

simply becoming Awareness, by becoming the witness watching All passing by. You can choose your own way home.

You don't have to give up anything to find God!

It's never either/or, it's Both & More!

You don't have to give up anything to find God! In fact everything you do will be more enjoyable if you invite God, Consciousness, Awareness into whatever you're doing. The more awareness, the more energy you have while you're eating, watching the birds, smelling the flower, having sex, making money, dancing, swimming, walking, driving, the more fun it will be! Invite God into everything you do. Invite your higher more aware Self into everything you do! It will be a lot more satisfying.

For example, have you ever had a meal that was just so intensely satisfying, almost orgasmic they way the food tasted? And then when you try to recreate it, you bring your friends to the same restaurant, or try to cook it again it doesn't work? Why? Because it is you, you are bringing the en-joy-nment of love-God to the table. You are the source of the enjoying, not the food itself.

In fact whatever is enjoyable, en-joy-ning, joins you with God! Whatever is bringing Joy into you, into your being, into your body, into your mind, your heart, your mouth, your ears, will bring you home. When you are doing what you enjoy you are centered in your self, and you are a piece of God.

"The first sign of spirituality is Joy!" (Swami Vivekananda)

"I have come to bring you Life and bring it more abundantly!" (Jesus Christ)

Enjoy the World! With God!

Enjoy your Body!
Enjoy your kids!
Enjoy your parents!
Enjoy your friends!
Enjoy eating!
Enjoy making money!
Enjoy sex!
Enjoy your dog!
Enjoy your cat!
Enjoy watching TV!
Enjoy your car!
Enjoy being aware!

And be aware when it's not enjoyable anymore. Whatever you're doing, if it's not enjoyable anymore, stop. Do something else that you enjoy. When the joy is gone so is God.

God is the nearest of the near, the dearest of the dear. He is inside your heart beat. We spend our lives, literally ex-pend our lives, and drain our life force in searching outside ourselves. It's crazy how easily we've been duped.

175

Do you know that you have the right to become completely awake in God?

You by simply Being, being here, having been created, have the right and the ability, to become a self realized piece of God.

No one, nothing can stop you if you want to become completely awake in your self, in God.

You can become enlightened by anything. You can become enlightened by running, by completely running and letting yourself become one with running, feeling the breeze, the sun, your body, and you melt into oneness. You can become enlightened by simply sitting in your garden and becoming one with the yellow rose, the gecko, the leaf falling from the tree. You can become enlightened by working to assist others, by cooking food for other people, by pouring your love into your cooking and serving it with love to those who'll receive it. You can become enlightened by completely appreciating nature, traveling to wilderness and experiencing the grandeur of Nature. You can become enlightened by competing/fighting/contesting with another. If you let yourself completely go in the battle you will find yourself on both sides and then the two will merge. You can become enlightened by completely saying yes to the total craziness, uptightness, maniacal search for money, controlling each other, sexual fixations, hatred, war etc., in short all the "wrongs" that mankind perpetrates on each other, If you can say Yes to them, allow them to be, paradoxically they will stop, and you will become enlightened.

No need to push the saying, no efforting, no affirming, just say it. Say it through out your day, in the car, quietly in the grocery store, while you're at work, on the phone.

I am a piece of God

45.

An Open Healthy Enjoyable Sexuality
or
War, Disease, Soul Death & Destruction

Which Would You Prefer?

There is no way to really suppress who we are. There is no way to effectively push down the natural energies that we are made of. You cannot cut off one of your legs and still be able to run easily, naturally the way God intended. Just the same way you cannot cut off big parts of your Emotional Body and still be able to function like a healthy, loving, open-hearted, fun, strong, wise human being as God intended. But that is exactly what we're trying to do in our current misguided attempt at "civilization".

We can play "whack a mole" with our natural energies, that game at the local county fair where moles pop their heads up out of holes and you try to whack them with a hammer to score points. They always pop up in another hole no matter how many times you whack them on the head. When we try to suppress natural parts of ourselves this is what we're doing, we're whacking (apropos) the part we've decided is "wrong", "base", "evil" on the head...and then it pops up somewhere else always, inevitably.

Sexuality in particular is a huge amount of energy that we have tried to suppress in almost every 'conceivable' way. Religions that blaspheme and misinterpret real God have been used to 'push down' the natural sexual urge. How can you suppress, make wrong, call 'evil', 'base', 'animalistic', the Creative Force of God in the universe and not expect to get very weird, twisted, damaged, unhealthy acting out of this energy? Are we that blind? Are we that stupid? Are we that naïve? No of course not. The people at the top of these religions, these social rules, this mind control programming on the masses of people know exactly what they are doing. They are stealing this creative energy that is in Sex for their own purposes of control and energy feeding. The amazing thing is that we are still going along with it. It's a very clever plan where the cattle, the sheep, the 'chickens' (us) in their coops (our houses) actually check up on each other and keep each other under control. Of course the 'owner' of the chickens comes and takes the young male roosters off to fight each other and get killed (our wars), steals the eggs (our children), and eventually kills and eats all the chickens (us). It's a neat trick to get the slaves to keep each other enslaved and make sure everyone stays in their box and no one gets free.

The "Twisted Garden".

The problem is that when you damn a river, when you block the natural flow of Life Force, of God, you get twisted unnatural and ugly creations. Have you ever noticed that a manmade 'damn' is never as nice as a God-Nature created lake? Our 'damns' are incredibly ugly, large blockish gray and drab cement structures. Or even if we try to 'design' a town lake it still is never even close to having the same natural beauty that Mother Nature –Father

177

God-Love creates easily and naturally. In blocking-'damning' the natural creative force of sex inside us humans we've gotten a 'twisted garden'. The things that grow inside this twisted garden-civilization are, grotesque, ugly, thorny, painful, indigestible, and give no nourishment. By suppressing our healthy, normal, sexuality we've created lying, 'cheating', 'suspicious minds', a massive pornography industry (just look at the internet), a literal global sex slave trade today with 10's of thousands of women and young girls being trafficked as sex slaves. Yes today, right now it's still going on. By suppressing our normal creative urge we've created so much psychological pain it's almost incalculable. Twisted domination sex, priests secretly butt-fucking altar boys thereby damaging them psychologically for life, men dominating women in loveless marriages being the norm, the Madonna vs. Whore complex for women, the Good Provider/Nice Guy vs. "Bad Boy" schizoid ness for men, hiding, scheming, guilt ridden obsessive compulsive addiction to unhealthy sex, and these are all symptoms of our Original Sin. It bears repeating over and over again until we change this false imprint we're living under;

If we really understood the following statement and healed our selves regarding SEX, the Garden of Eden-Paradise, Shamballa- Nirvana- Heaven would truly return to Earth:

~Original sin is placing sex outside of God, outside of Love, outside of being acceptable in God's eyes.~ That's it. That's all there's to it.

God enjoys sex. He created it! What kind of God would create something that was not 'God' or that He didn't enjoy? Only a sadistic God would create something not 'good'.

That the above statement is shocking is a symptom of how amazingly disconnected we have become from healthy original creative God-Sex.

If Men have enough fulfilling Sex they will not go to War!

If the young men in a country have enough love mixed with enough sexual fulfillment they will not have enough pent up psychological rage that the leaders can use to manipulate them into going to war and being willing to die for some made up '(un)-holy mission.'

This next illustration may shock many of you, will likely seem unbelievable but nevertheless it's true. There is a tribe of people in Asia where when the children reach puberty they are all allowed to live together in a special house in the village. They are allowed to have sex with each other in any way they want and with whoever they want. Boys-boys, girls-girls, boys-girls. Amazingly very few pregnancies occur and when they do it is right that the baby should come into this world. 'Cheating' among the adults in this tribe is practically non existent. There are never any murders because of love triangles. By the time the children are adults they have found who they want to be with and have no roving eye, no 'coveting the neighbor's wife'. Examples like this are carefully kept out of our school systems or our media. Why? Because the people would begin to wake up if the truth came out.

178

Knowing the truth will set you free—but first it will piss you off!

There are tribes in the Amazon where they have an accepted custom where twice a year the young men of the village go off into the jungle and when they return to the village they take women of their choice out into the jungle and have sex with them. This is an accepted, natural release for the young men. And the women! This prevents anger and pent up sexual frustration from spilling over into wanting to go to war with other tribes. And believe it or not the other men understand and accept the practice.

'Now if you or any other really intelligent person were arranging the fairnesses and justices between man and woman, you would give the man a one-fiftieth interest in one woman, and the woman a harem.'- Mark Twain from *Letters from the Earth*

Hieros Gamos-- the Sacred Sexual Union

In western culture we used to have the Rites of Spring and the Beltane Fires where it was accepted to have the Sacred Marriage, the Hieros Gamos, with someone other than your wife or husband. This gave a safer outlet of the natural sexual creative urges instead of them turning into violence, 'cheating', secrecy, 'adultery', burning at the stake, stonings, having to wear a 'scarlet letter', soul eating guilt etc. These 'Rites of Spring' that honored the re-birth of God-Life into the world have degenerated today into 'spring break' where massive amounts of alcohol are used to suppress the guilt and engage in mostly debauchery and altered state guilt filled sex instead of a Sacred Union between the God and Goddess. It's so obvious by now—every human is both an emitter and receiver of electromagnetic energies and finer consciousness-soul energies. Which do you think emits-emanates healthier soul energy vibrations into the collective consciousness-- The Sacred Rites of Hieros Gamos where the God and Goddess have sex to energize the land, the crops and the people... or alcohol fueled, impersonal, unconscious sex in Cancun or Daytona Beach?

Time to Mature-Grow Up- and become 'Adult' Spirits

It's time to grow up and get healthy with our sexuality. How many wake up calls in the form of rapes, military sadistic sexual torture, sexual predators, sexual diseases, AIDS, 'affairs', 'cheating', pornography, sex clubs without love, strip clubs, prostitution, sex slavery, etc. do we need before we realize we need to accept our sexuality and find healthy ways to allow it to create (in) our world?

Real Love, God is in our Sexuality is the Source of our sexuality, created sexuality and loves and enjoys it. We need to accept this or we will continue to reap what we sow and have unhealthy, unloving, un-Godly, sex.

46. The Divine Spout

Imagine a spout--one like we see water running into a fountain in Rome. The water is always keeping the fountain filled-- for the birds, for the people, or just for beauty's sake. Why do we love fountains? The whole world over we've created beautiful artistic fountains of beauty bringing us our water. Why, what do they represent to our heart, souls and spirits?

The Living Waters

Our Fountains represent the Living Waters, El Dorado, the Fountain of Youth, the Life Force, the Source of All That Is. You have a personal Divine Spout of an endless supply of Love, the basic building block of the Universe. It can't run out, it is the magic, the miracle of Love, of Creation, it comes from seemingly nowhere and fills you, fills the creation, makes it glow from within, makes it effuse love and light. This Spout of Love is your divine birthright. Love is the basic building block behind the "Big Bang" that exploded the material universe into being. It is the Creation arising out of the Nothing. Making love, orgasm, is the same "bang" as the original Big Bang, the holy orgasm of Love. We were created in this same way, by God the Father and God the Mother "banging"-merging-intercoursing. We are made in their Image, we are the stuff of the Universe. We can receive anything in the Creation, it's all there for our asking, *"ask and ye shall receive"*, and if we believe-have "faith" so it will be-come. We are the Divine Children and we deserve all the gifts the Wise Men bring to us. God the Father and God the Mother want to help us heal now so we can consciously return to our inherent birth right as the Divine Child.

Image-In whatever you want

Imagine yourself as a child, a divine innocent child, with your personal Spout. You simply wish for whatever you want to have, to play with, to come pouring through that spout-- colored water, liquid light, molten gold, playmates, lovers, other worlds, safety, support, material comforts, money, credit cards, cars, houses, hot tubs, sexual fantasies, magical forests, animal friends, spaceships, whatever you can Image-In and that is aligned with your real Will, the will of your Soul, which is "God's Will", will come down that Holy Spout. This Divine Spout will start working for you when you become innocent again, when you go back to the moment before Adam and Eve *"knew they were naked",* before we allowed ourselves to be talked into by the Mind into believing that we were are somehow bad, shameful, sinful (not innocent). For Innocence is the key to activating the Divine Spout of Plenty, *"become ye as little children".* When we remember that it is the Love, the basic building substance of the universe that comes first, that feeds us, that takes care of us, then that Love will take whatever form you wish it to. *"...No other gods before Me."* God tries to help us not to place our trust, our hope, our security in the things, the images we image-in to the Creation, but in the Love-God-Energy-Source which creates all the forms. Some of us can still see God in a flower, a sunset, but can we still let God into our bodies? Into our Sex? Into our TV's? Into our businesses? Can we, or have we banished God-Love from certain areas of our 'creation'? Well, S/He is there too. God is in every thing, we are the ones that through our *"knowledge of good and evil"* have decided God out of existence in certain forms we've labeled "base", "wrong" or "evil".

There's nothing inherently evil about technology or materiality in and of itself but anything cut off from God-Love-Heart becomes lost and destroys itself eventually. Which is as it should be, 'mortal creations' should die, they are 'mortal'. Technology without God-Love will put itself out of its own misery. There is a choice happening on Earth right now between the collective death wish and the collective Life wish. Technology used in Innocence with Heart will simply be another exploration of Love, another thing coming down the Divine Spout to play with that will automatically vanish back into the formless ethers when our attention goes on to something new.

When we're in contact our own fountain of Love in our own heart, then our Divine Spout in the "outer" world will also appear. It will love giving to us our hearts desires, the filling of our inner heart will be reflected in the outer world filling us with our material desires.

47.   Nowhere to Run

So Now that I Know Everything—Now What?

So, you've done all kinds of spiritual practices. Perhaps you are a healer or practitioner yourself. Maybe you help others start on the path of self-discovery. You've seen how they project their own awakening on you, how they wake up a little and go back to their old ways, how when we encounter the real gateways when trying to become "living souls" again most of us run the other way. You've seen how interaction with the other dimensions scares people. You've seen 'spiritual amnesia' at work, where people forget and deny the magic they've experienced with you because it's too threatening to their reality. You've had magic happen, perhaps you've traveled through time, perhaps you've seen physical healings, 'coincidences' happen all the time now for you, whatever you start thinking about starts manifesting, you 'know' everything. You've had enough information. You've experienced beyond a shadow of a doubt how your reality gets created by you. It's been years of very magical and beautiful experiences for you...

...but you still haven't reached the level of spontaneous contact with the Love at the Source of the universe that your cat has.

NowHere to Run.

You have nowhere left to run...you've run out of "causes" to get excited about...you have now-here left to run...you have **now here** left to run...you can't run...and Now Here is All There Is.

Every technique, no matter how refined and clean is missing something, methods for "releasing", for "creating", for "being in control" leave your heart cold. Visualizing, repatterning, breathwork, energy releasing, discreating, yoga asanas, body work, past life journeys, astral travel, dynamic meditation, etc. They're all beautiful and helpful and timely miracles...and after a while... still missing something. What's left...?

What's left is the place we've run from since our emergence... our selves, our inner worlds, our feelings, exploring the real final frontier inside our own beings.

And Now & Here it's the only place you'll find your healing and you have nowhere to run.

"...I'll meet you there" - God says.

48.   *"Yes, the River Knows"* (J.D. Morrison)

&

Owl, with His Silken Glide, Shows the Way

I'm walking on a path through a pristine, untouched portion of Oak Creek canyon in Sedona Arizona. I've just crossed the river. *"Yes the River Knows",* the River that just talked to me about unlimited flow of Life energy. It told me to look up, to the top of the canyon.

And then it said:

"I have been flowing since I was at the top of that canyon wall. That's millions of years in your time. I have been flowing steadily from the springs at the head of this canyon. The River of Life, of God, of Energy inside you is like this. It is in fact more Eternal than me. That which you really are flows outside of Time. It IS forever. If you contact this Spring, this Source, you will remember who you are. You will again be able to express and flow inside this dimension the way you did originally and are meant to. And when you humans reawaken to this eternal part of you then the Original plan for this earth will be again. And then we can again play openly together. I will pass away someday but I want to give this to you: this remembering of who you really are. And maybe you will remember me and this day sometime when you are in a new place, a new Creation."

I walked up to a path along the side of the canyon walls. A path that reminded me of lifetimes as a Taoist monk and Yogi, walking the serpentine craggy paths of the mountains in China and the Himalayas. I felt fondness, warmth for those lifetimes but now it's another time, and there is something to do 'in the world'.

I had heard from down in the meadow before I crossed the river, an owl hooting. *'How wonderful if I could see him'* I had as a fleeting wish-thought. Ever since I had an owl in the redwoods of California try to land on my arm I had a deeper understanding of owls and them being a gateway between the physical and spiritual worlds. As I reach a certain point on the path I feel a 'quiet' settle on me and I stop. I go 'still', I become alert, feeling-sensing-listening with more than just my senses. I slowly turn to a certain point up the hill and there on a lower branch of a pine tree sits a large owl. We look at each other for a few minutes. I am amazed at how close he is and how clearly I can see him. *'Thank You'* I say to the spirit behind him and I ask what he wants to share with me.

"*Smooth, easy, gentle, soft, quiet, calm, serene, confident, watcher, 'in the world yet not of it'*" he says. And with that he gently launches himself from the branch and glides soundlessly off.

I can feel his soft-gentle, yet strong confident presence, 'unruffled' by any 'doings' of a fearful world.

'*Thank You*' I say again and know I will see him again.

49.   The Ultimate "Warfare"

Earth is a Free Will Planet

The Earth is a Life planet, a Free Will planet, a "no one controls another" planet, a conscious communion with the Creator planet. Earth wants to give to us, to give openly of her cornucopia of bountiful harvest. We aren't meant to have to "work for a living". We are meant to live in direct conscious communion with the Life Force inside us. Earth responds to this Life Force and we elicit a loving response from the very earth when we co-operate with the Life Force, God. There is an Avatar (a descent of the Divine into human form) in India today that the trees manifest fruit for when he walks by, the ocean wraps around his ankles and leaves a strand of pearls out of love. *"The rocks themselves shall cry out."* Jesus elicited the response of loving praise from the Natural Creation around him by simply being his divinity. When St. Francis asked an almond tree in the middle of winter to reveal God to him, it bloomed! The avatar Krishna manifested all kinds of "leelas", playful miracles when he was on earth. These are historical facts and just because a large portion of our current level of mass consciousness may not be able to understand or accept it, doesn't make them not true. We are also sons and daughters of the Life Force and the Earth longs to for us to return to the place where we are able to receive her loving response, her abundance that she longs to give us. She doesn't enjoy us forcing her, raping her into submission and using her without gratitude. And this using the earth by force can only go on for a limited amount of time. It is a "mortal" i.e. will die method of doing things. Just look around you, this is the ugliest "civilization" that has ever been created on earth...and its days are numbered unless we bring the Heart, Love, God back into it. Go to any large city, any mall, any industrial section, any suburb, any downtown and feel the cement, the steel, the hardness, the coldness of heart and compare it to wild free nature. Which is more loving? It's so obvious. The mental programming-brainwashing that Nature is dangerous is a blatant lie to keep the sheeple (us) in line and not re-awaken to a loving connection with Nature because when we realize that there is a loving Creator and a loving Earth that will support, nurture, provide for us, then we can't be controlled by fear and the lie of scarcity. We won't have to buy oil, gasoline, insurance, pesticide riddled foods, have our kids brainwashed by ineffective inaccurate education, have mortgages, be fooled by false religions etc. We will be free, sovereign souls created by God again and we won't be controllable through fear anymore. A few years ago outside of Phoenix a little three year old girl was "lost" in the desert. All she had on was a thin dress and no shoes. When found 3 days later having been through 110 degree heat, having to sleep outside, she was FINE! She said her "friend" had come and taken her by the hand and helped her find water and had led her in the right direction. When asked what her "friend" looked like, she said she was dressed in white, tall and had wings.

Original Paradise was a real Place

Currently practically all of the Earth's originally innocent spirits are infected with guilt, with "original sin", with not feeling worthy of receiving directly the love of Father God and Mother God. There was a time on Earth of what's called "The Garden of Eden", in the Land of Pan, Pangaea, the original land mass on earth, before this one land mass broke up into continents. In Pan the very reality, the fabric of physicality, the water, the rocks, the plants, the mosses, the wind, the trees, the springs, the mountains, the sky were of a somewhat different physical consistency. Our level of consciousness directly affects the physical world around us on an atomic level. We are the "gods" of creation. *"Is it not written in your law Ye are gods?"* Jesus spoke directly to his disciples. Was he lying? Back in Pangaea we were still consciously "gods" and the physical creation around us, nature, responded with more life force, energy. There was light shining from within all things that we all were aware of. It is still there but the level of collective consciousness reality today for the most part can't perceive it. That time on Pangaea was a time when the *"lion lay down with the lamb"*, when no creature had a need to kill or eat each other. Our current reality of being cut off from the "manna", from Love, from God creates limited amounts of life force energy so we need to consume things to extract energy from them. This is not a natural state for this planet, no matter what those who believe in the "kill or be killed", "survival of the fittest" "dog eat dog" Darwinian law say. We are meant to receive the manna from "heaven" (the life force within us, "the Kingdom of Heaven is within") directly. But again, we've been con-vinced that we are not "good" (the *"knowledge of good and evil"*) enough to be able to receive God, the unlimited Source of All inside us anymore. So then it degenerates into a game of stealing energy from one another. This takes many forms, psychic energy games of control, denial of real feelings, psychological dysfunctions, sexual energy stealing, actual killing each other, taking energy out of the Earth without love and the millions of variations we've come up with.

Vampire & Denial Spirits – Time to go!

This stealing energy reality that now pervades the planet was brought here by beings that don't belong on Earth. Earth is not their home planet and they need to leave now. The coming upheavals of consciousness and physical earth will "cast out" these vampirous spirits that feed on others from the earth. It will be a time of "tribulation" as Christians call it since they aren't going to go quietly. These energy vampires aren't "evil" per se but they don't belong on Earth anymore. There are whole planets that have been "killed"; their electromagnetic life force fields have been stripped, their atmospheres ripped away, and some planets have actually been blown apart. The asteroid belt is the remnants of a planet that was destroyed by the collective consciousness of warfare, hatred, control etc. of the beings that lived upon it. Many of those spirits then came to earth and have now "infected" Earth with their ways. It is not Earth's fate to be destroyed. Father God and Mother Earth have agreed and together have planned the "clean up" of the Earth. We as individual spirits have the choice of going along with the Free Will, open hearted, direct connection to God plan for earth or not. If we choose to stay closed and not open our hearts we will be "relocated" to other planets in the universe that are still going through that level of evolution of consciousness. The Creator has acceptance for all spirits including the energy vampire, but not all spirits belong together. There are places for all manner of being, but the Earth is a free will planet so those that override others free will will now be removed and put in their right place. Their right place will be right for them, in fact for some of them it will be their "heaven". It may not be your heaven if you enjoy openness, direct communion with love, innocence, but for spirits that don't want openness, direct communion with the Source it will be painful for them to have to stay in too rapid energy vibrations and your heaven could be their hell. Earth is a life planet, it does not want to be imprisoned, raped, mined, polluted, teased, prodded, genetically engineered, drugged and poisoned. None of these ways of obtaining energy/food are part of the Earth's destiny and aren't needed by spirits who are willing to open directly to the Source of Life in the core of their beings. This model of enslaving and forcing someone/something to give up its energy to someone else is leaving Earth. Death, slowing down of vibration, is leaving Earth.

These energy stealing spirits refuse to go directly inside themselves to the Source of All to obtain their sustenance. They gain it from others. There are many ways they feed off the Earth and its spirits. Current history has been written mostly by these spirits. You've heard it said that "*history is the history of war*". The true earlier history of Earth is called "myths" mostly because the vampire-war-killing-feeding spirits have ruled the Earth for the last 300,000 years or so and have written history according to how they believe it to be. There is an earlier history but as they even tell us, "*History is written by the victors.*"

Science is used to force the Earth to do things against its will. Most "spiritual" schools and religions are mostly ways of feeding off the masses of people. Any go between between you and God-the Source inside your own self is often there to steal your energy that your open heart has access to.

How can we cleanse ourselves and the earth of this virus that is sucking the life out of the planet (and us)? Warfare and killing the "other" is their invention, their game and they win energy no matter who wins the war. The Earth and our souls never "win" when warfare occurs. There is always pain, emotional scarring, fears and hatreds solidified, and these are the things that the control spirits use to control us and pit us against each other so they can feed off the energy of fear that they propagate in us. Jesus tried to point this out when he said "*Turn the other cheek.*" Don't fight back, it only feeds them, encourages them and drains us. But we cannot just tell them politely to "get off our planet please", because they won't. We can't kill them off the planet and we can't just go on hoping that God will cleanse it all miraculously either. Because when we've given our divine energy away to these energy stealing spirits we've lost our direct communion with God. So what can be done?
We can heal ourselves.

The Most Powerful thing you can do to Heal the Earth is to Heal Yourself

The only reason these energy feeding spirits gained a foot hold on Earth to begin with is that we had the seed of guilt, of fear of God in us. If we had listened to our hearts to begin with this whole painful, long process of "fallen" beings that we've become would not have had to be gone through. But we went ahead into places we weren't ready to handle even though our intuition warned us we weren't ready. There is a lot more to the long and terrible story of our Fall from being in conscious, open contact with our divinity of course. Just like most beings on the earth right now can't consciously speed up their physical bodies, turn into energy and go visit the cauldron of Loving Light, the Source of All, just so are there automatic laws of attraction operating in the Creation. There are "*many mansions*" in the Creation, many different vibrational levels. These vibrational levels are like TV stations, you can choose which ones to tune in to. There are many different dimensions of existence in the Universe and they are separate existences, separate ways of being.

If originally the Earth Spirits had been clean energetically and able to follow their intuition, and willing to see all they needed to see about themselves and what they were ready or not ready to do, then the energy stealing spirits would not have had any denial, any unawake areas in the Earth Spirits consciousness to attach to. These "denial" spirits, these vampires of soul essence cannot attach to a healthy spirit. Just as disease cannot gain a foothold when our immune systems are powerful and operating in the same way there is no place that the vampire spirits' disease can find a place to enter in a spiritually healthy spirit. Just like a being filled with the light of Love can walk through a leper colony with no fear. Once it's got a foot hold a parasitic spirit will try to increase its energy by stealing yours, because you are its life source now. Yet these "denial" spirits really seek death but will never tell you so. It gets complicated because practically everyone of us are mixed together now, we've mated, created mixed children with each other and in this coming time of "*separation of the wheat from the chaff*" long standing family affiliations will be split up.

Your healing yourself, resuscitating these dead areas in your being and reclaiming your power where you've relinquished it is the way to regain the power you had originally on earth. It is the ultimate "warfare" if you will, by not warring, but inwardly healing yourself and these old patterns, spirits, that have tortured you, controlled you will not be able to find a dead/weak spot in you anymore to us to control or feed off you. It will not be easy but God, the Earth itself want this healing and will help you every step of the way.

If you radiate fullness of energy and freedom then the energy stealing spirits will automatically leave the matrix of the planet, there will be nothing here that attracts them, and the earth will literally cease to exist in the reality of the energy vampires. We will disappear off their radar screen. Just the same way that many realities exist around us right now that we are mostly unaware of, other dimensions, the devic kingdoms, the spirit worlds. Just being, just being You, the real you, being willing to see your places of not knowing, to heal yourself, to follow the path of Heart will automatically remove you from or push away those beings that cause you pain and suffering. With enough of the Earth spirits doing this personal healing we can rid the planet of these poisonous, vampirous, life draining patterns that are currently dragging earth down and off her destiny path.

All you need to do is to focus on your own becoming whole again and it will be the ultimate "spiritual warfare" to heal the earth. Call on Father and Mother God to cleanse the Earth, to assist you in your own awakening and healing. You won't need to do anything you really don't want to do. All that you will ask of your self is to just become more and more the real you.

~Epilogues~

To wake up from the Karmic Veil, to undo the "fall" from Grace, to become free again instead of fear ruled robots, there is only one thing that needs to happen. It is what Jesus came to show us, what every master comes to share...it is to kick start the Human Heart, to put us back in touch with the Heart of Love, the Heart of God, our Heart. Jesus was/is an embodiment of the Cosmic Heart., the Heart that is intended to lead us by Love into areas for exploration in the Creation. When the Heart leads we can't fail, we can't get hurt, and we can't "fall" from Grace, from Oneness. For in the very act of feeling Heart we are already in direct communion with God, with Source. It is only when we either can't hear or choose to not follow the Heart's voice that we can "die", die a slow spiritual death in the wasteland, on the Plane of Reversal.

Can you "Imagine" no Laws?

Laws, rules, regulations, policies for living, for behavior, like the Ten Commandments and other God-given laws are only necessary when beings have stopped hearing-listening to the Law of Love in their hearts. Manmade or God given laws are only necessary in the fallen state. Can you imagine a day when all the laws are repealed, wiped off the books and the Law of Love has returned to the human heart instead of men in uniform or priestly robes? It's what John Lennon sang about in his song "Imagine". It's what Jesus meant when he said, *"I've come to fulfill (fully fill = to complete) the Law."* Fully fill our hearts, *"My cup runneth over"* with Love and we have no sense of lack. No need to steal from others in order to "get our share". We will have more than our share; there will be no "need" to share. We will not feel attacked, wronged by others; no need to fear loss, for all we could ever wish for is already in us! We are instantly given anything we wish for.

An Awake Heart or Dying of Cancer?

The Heart is innocence. Heart and Innocence on earth today are mostly preyed upon, laughed at as "naïve", considered impractical, and seen as "weak", "childish". Still, Jesus came right out and said it. *"Become ye as little children."* This is directly opposite of what is supposed to work to give us power in the world of adults today. Yes, we can gain power and envy of others while suppressing our hearts but most likely we'll end up dying of cancer. Which is the better choice? Which do you prefer, your awake and feeling heart guiding you or dying of cancer? We really have taken the gifts of God, of the Creator, of Love, of Mother and created a hell out of our heaven that we were given.

So how do we wake back up again to feel the Heart again? Just that, allow yourself to FEEL AGAIN! Ask God to help; *"God help me reawaken my heart, let me safely feel again."* We already feel all the time; we just ignore, suppress, hide, or make fun of our feelings. I'm not saying to go wide open with your feelings all at once, they'll lock you up! But start noticing your feelings, express them where it feels safe, make a start. The Heart feels, the heart loves, the heart hurts, and therefore the Heart has a difficult time existing in this mechanized world but it's our only real chance of waking up and stopping the soul destruction happening on earth right now.

Feeling

Feeling is for(e)most
A terrifying thing,

Yet it's the only place,
where both God and Human
can Sing.

Leading with our Minds = Twisted Creations

Right now on Earth almost all of us are leading with our minds "thinking" (there's the problem) that it will protect us. We're trying to "figure out" Life, to understand it (under- stand, stand under). When we are observing, trying to understand Life, we aren't feeling it, merging with it and the paradox is therefore we can never understand it! It's like standing on the side of a river and trying to imagine what it would feel like to swim in it. We can never understand Life with the Mind. The Heart is Life. It's where your Life Force lives. The physical reflection of this truth is that your heart, your physical beating pumping blood heart is at the center of your body, you need it above all else to live. Your brain can go "brain dead" and your body still lives but if the heart stops beating everything dies. It is the same with your spiritual life. The signs are all around us if we only look. It is true that the Mind is also part of God, part of Life of course; but the Mind is not meant to lead in the Creation. The Heart is meant to lead, to initiate, and the Mind helps to carry out the Hearts ideas. The "fall" is when the Mind took over and started evaluating (good/bad, good/evil, yes/no, yin/yang, positive/negative) everything. And as I said, most people today are living in their Minds trying to calculate, to mind-game, to best each other with trickery, to beat the "other". *"Oh, what a tangled web we weave when at first we practice to deceive."* Shakespeare said seeing this hall of mirrors that the Mind creates when it has no heart to lead it.

Psychic Warfare- *"My Lawyer is bigger than yours!"*

So it's become basically psychic warfare in trying to "win" over others on earth today. Win what? We can't win anything by putting others down because they are literally another part of our own Self. It is impossible by the laws of electromagnetic soul physics to want to diminish someone else and not also do it to our selves. It is the law of Karma, it is *"He who lives by the (lawyer) will die by the (lawyer)."* We've created psychic war everywhere; the "battle of the sexes", "business is war" "The war on drugs" "The war on cancer", "The war on terrorism" etc. The Mind is in charge of humanity on earth for the most part, not the Heart. We've given up on

192

"childish" things like love and now as adults we practice the art of deception to win fleeting temporal power. We've decided if we can't have love we'll at least have power. We form relationships based on power gain. We have sayings such as *"Success is the best revenge."* We got hurt and betrayed in love and decided to get revenge by being "successful" which implies hurting others back. I'd say that is really the childish, reactive, ignorant thing to do. We're not grown enough as Spirits to be able to face our feelings but need to blame others for our pain and "get revenge" on "them" for hurting us. It is time to grow up on Earth. Unless we consciously choose to wake up then this Season of Chaos, this Cleansing, this Apocalypse (full Divine Revelation) coming to earth will force us to find our Hearts again or we won't be able to survive.

The First Step

The first step in the Soul Recovery Program is to find your lost Heart. Once we've re- contacted our Intuition, our Heart, the Voice of God, then we'll be able to hear God's direction and we can start healing ourselves, reclaiming our power. Listening to someone else's formula for finding Love-God is not going to fulfill us. It can help us along the way but we have to follow our own unique way of experiencing Love-God and our heart is the perfect guide. And we can do it! Re-contacting the Heart is plugging in, it's the wake up, the "born again", and then we'll still walk our Destiny Walk and there will likely still be times that we'll ask "if this cup can be taken from us". The second step is walking our Destiny Path. But for now hearing the Heart is the first step needed on Earth.

51.   Waking From a Thousand Year Sleep

When we first start to try to move our emotions openly, honestly, spontaneously and to let ourselves feel how we really feel about things, it will be a little scary, uneasy, something we aren't used to. We have learned to survive by hiding how we really feel, by pretending that we have it all together, by telling ourselves everything's OK, by putting on our "brave face", by shutting off our emotions. On the other hand if we are used to expressing and blurting out all the time exactly how we feel in a knee jerk reflexive way and letting our emotions run us constantly, then stopping to think and trying to let in awareness and consciousness into our emotions before we blurt them out will be something new for us. We had a terrible "fall" here on earth and we really hurt ourselves and we didn't know how to operate our Hearts and Minds together co-operatively, we didn't know how to express as souls in a denser, physicalized creation and so we shut down. Now it's time to go back and "undo the Fall".

We've been asleep for 5 million years! Let's be patient with ourselves

Imagine waking up after sleeping for a thousand years. Your bones would be very stiff, it would be hard to walk, you would feel disoriented, you'd need to be careful and slow in first moving about, you'd need to be patient with yourself. Well, we have been living under a "state of emergency" on earth ever since our disconnect from our Souls, from God, from our Hearts. We've been in survival mode, we've had to close our hearts down, to protect ourselves. So when we are trying to reconnect to our Source/our Souls, we are going to feel like we are being born again, because we are! We are going to feel like babies, very vulnerable, very tender. It is important that we give ourselves space and time to do nothing, to just feel, to just be, to just sit in the garden, the park, in the bathtub, in bed, whatever we need to do to feed our new births. Give yourself a bath, give flowers to yourself, curl up and hold yourself while traveling to the sea of warm golden energy, do whatever feeds you, do it just for you.

If you really want to contribute to healing the world, heal yourself first

This re-birth, or birth into a fuller you, is necessary to reconnect with your own Soul. By the way this will also do the most you can do to heal our planet as well. Each time a soul reconnects with itself, explosions of harmonious symphonic electromagnetic energy go off. Vibrations of love reverberate across time and space, a thousand (Berlin) walls come tumbling down, energy is created in massive amounts all across the Universe. So you giving yourself a bath and nurturing yourself is sometimes the most holy thing in the whole Universe! Really...So is making love with someone you really love...so is really enjoying, being really present while you are eating a great meal...so is letting water flow over your body in a stream...so is hearing the breeze through the trees...so is letting someone in in traffic...so is speaking up for yourself when you aren't being honored...so is sobbing with sadness at the loss of your heart...so is simply telling your truth about how you feel vulnerable and like an innocent child...so is expressing your anger and yelling at God for having created this mess...so is asking God for

Let's Give ourselves the Space to heal, to learn again to live from our Souls, to be patient with our selves as we're waking up from our five million year long sleep. This is about reconnecting with the most holy of holies, our own souls, our direct linkup with the Creator of all the Universes. And if this doesn't happen instantly after taking the latest super duper enlightenment seminar let's be patient with ourselves. Most of us give ourselves more information on how to learn to drive a car than we do on how to learn to drive our souls, emotional, spiritual and mental bodies. Is it any wonder we are "crashing" into each other out there?

This is the ultimate project, the only journey left, the inner journey, the final frontier, finding our selves again. The ultimate adventure travelogue. help in your confusion for what to do next.

52.   Stepping off the Merry Go Round

The Merry Go Round is keeping everyone in a constant state of giddy excitement mixed with terror while the real world is turning into a blur spinning by outside on the periphery. The "vehicles" we ride, the gaudy painted horses with frozen grotesque smiles enchant us. We cling to them for safety. Sometimes we want a different horse and will jostle and compete for the prettiest-strongest-biggest horse, and then again we're whirled around into a trance of distorted reality.

After some time it's not so merry a go round anymore. We realize (real eyes) that the horses are dead, their eyes are empty, their smiles loveless and the operator is cynical, hateful, secretly hoping that we'll fall off and hurt our selves.

You can get off the merry go round if you wish. But it will take some willpower and most of all Intention. You will have to get off your "safe" horse in direct violation of the posted rules—

"For your safety, under no circumstances get off your horse while the merry go round is operating."

---The Management

You will risk being yelled at by the other riders, being punished by the ride operator, being banished from Crazy Play Land. You will have to stand up while centrifugal forces will try to throw you off balance. You will risk falling and banging into poles and horses. Your senses will be distorted on your way to the edge. Only your internal sense of direction will guide you. Yet you will have to make your way to the edge of the merry go round where it spins the fastest and there you will have the final test, to summon your courage to jump into that spinning blurring world of distorted images whirling by and trust that when you land you will survive.

You will survive. Everything will stop. For a while you may feel like some of you is still moving to the old crazed carnival song. You may be bruised, you will probably be disoriented. You might need some time to recover, to just lie there quietly to regain your senses and allow everything spinning in your being to stop. And as you come to a stop and become still you will feel the grass again, the security of the Earth holding you, the warmth of the Sun loving you, the caress of the Wind guiding you. And you will have a new world waiting for you.

If you wish you can return and stand by the merry go round and call out to your friends that it's safe to jump, that there is another world waiting outside the perimeter. Most will not hear you since for them nothing exists outside the Carni-Val. Some will see you and it won't be their time, you'll see them on the next go around. Others will hear you and move towards the edge and look but then go back to their spinning worlds. And some will come to the edge and with hearts in their throats will jump towards you and will join you in the new world to explore.

You can also get down off your horse, walk to the center of the merry go round, tell the operator to get the hell out of there and shut the whole thing down and simply walk away.

In the end it doesn't matter that much what you choose. You can always redo your choices.

~Selah~

~Amen~

~Amin~

~Om~

For more information on 'Sanctuary for Souls' workshops, personal Soul Script readings, Counseling sessions, our online video Course of Awakening or ordering Books, CD's or tapes by the author please visit us on the web at:

www.CourseOfAwakening.com

www.SoulCounseling.com

www.SedonaSoulCounseling.com

www.SpiriTravel.com

for our 'Spiritual Adventure Travels' - where we play with Wolves, walk with Wild Horses, swim with Manatees & Dolphins.

~~~~~~

Tobias Lars-- B.S., MBA, Mensa, is a resident of Sedona Arizona and a Spiritual Teacher and Business Consultant with over 25 years experience in physical and spiritual healing. In his varied career he has also been the founder of two international trading companies, a national seminar leader in cutting edge consciousness development, owner of a video production company and a Yoga teacher. He currently works as a spiritual counselor focusing on Soul Activations and Soul Counseling.

Thank you for ordering this book. Please feel free to send your comments, thoughts or experiences to:

TobiasLars@soulcounseling.com

Made in the USA
Middletown, DE
16 July 2018